Stratford Gold

Stratford Gold

50 Years, 50 Stars, 50 Conversations

with
RICHARD OUZOUNIAN

McArthur & Company
Toronto

First Canadian edition published by McArthur & Company 2002

McArthur & Company
322 King St. West, Suite 402
Toronto, Ontario
M5V 1J2

National Library of Canada Cataloguing in Publication Data

Ouzounian, Richard, 1950-
Stratford gold: 50 years, 50 stars, 50 conversations

Accompanies a 13 part TV series on CBC, starting in June 2002.
ISBN 1-55278-271-9

Stratford Festival (On.) –History. I. Title.

PN2306.S7099 2002 792'.09713'13 C2002-900598-1

Design & Composition: *Mad Dog Design*
Cover & f/x: *Mad Dog Design*
Cover Image: *William Hutt as Prospero in "The Tempest" 1976. Photograph by Robert C. Ragsdale*, F.R.P.S.
Printed in Canada by *Transcontinental Printing Inc.*

The publisher wishes to acknowledge the financial support of the Government of Canada through the Book Publishing Industry Development Program (BPIDP) and the Canada Council for our publishing activities. The publisher further wishes to acknowledge the financial support of the Ontario Arts Council for our publishing program.

10 9 8 7 6 5 4 3 2 1

This is dedicated to the memory of
Susan Wright – great actress, great friend.

Contents

Introduction

It all started with Timothy Findley.

We ran into each other in Stratford one day in the summer of 1999. As tends to happen with Mr. Findley, one fascinating anecdote led to another, and before too long, I was hearing stories about the Stratford Festival's opening season which had never found their way into any book. (Yes, they are all here.)

That conversation lodged in my mind, and—stimulated by the knowledge that 2002 would be the Festival's Fiftieth Anniversary Season—it turned into an idea. Why not put together the story of the Stratford Festival as told by the people who were there? No historians need apply, please, no critics or commentators. Just actors, directors, designers, and musicians, reminiscing in conversation. It seemed like a good idea to me, and so, in the spring of 2000, I proposed it as a series to CBC Television. They eagerly accepted it, and before I knew it, I was conducting fifty interviews. The first was with Christopher Plummer on the stage of the Festival Theatre.

The next sixteen months would take me from the set of *Will and Grace* in Los Angeles (Eric McCormack, of course) to a mountaintop in upstate New York (that would be Zoe Caldwell). Along the way, there were numerous jaunts to Stratford, shoots in Toronto, and flights to Manhattan, before the whole process concluded with Maggie Smith in London last October. The editing process then began, with over seventy hours of interview footage to be turned into eight hours of television. And after that came the chance to preserve still more of it for posterity in this book.

There are several things to make clear about *Stratford Gold*. It is not a definitive history of the Stratford Festival, nor does it pretend to be. I selected fifty people from various times in the Festival's past, and hoped to use their remembrances to present an impressionistic portrait rather than a photographic likeness. Yes, there are people who aren't mentioned, productions that are bypassed, and events that have gone unchronicled. If some of your favourites are missing, you have my apology. There will be other books to give a complete picture of *what* happened during Stratford's first fifty years. This one is aimed at telling you *how* it happened.

I had three questions I asked everyone. I began by finding out how they first became aware (or involved) with Stratford. After that, each interview's journey is different, until two final questions, when I ask them what they wish for Stratford's future, and what words come to mind when I mention the Festival.

The Stratford Festival has been enormously cooperative in helping this all to happen, but they had no input as to who was interviewed and made no attempt to influence what was included in the final project. I thank them for their support and their tact. From the CBC, I have to express my indebtedness to Kim Murton, Fred Nicolaidis, Tracy Donaldson, George Anthony, and Deborah Bernstein, who all helped this to happen. Within the Stratford Festival, enormous debts are owed to Jane Edmonds, Ellen Charendoff, Kelley Teahen, and Ivan Habel. At McArthur & Company, a deep genuflection to Kim McArthur, Janet Harron, Ruth Shanahan, and Pamela Erlichman. And to my editor at the

Toronto Star, John Ferri, my appreciation for letting me fly off around the world at a moment's notice. To everyone I interviewed, my thanks for your generosity and cooperation.

And to all the rest of the people who have made the Stratford Festival a reality for the past fifty seasons, you have my everlasting gratitude. While it's true that Shakespeare once wrote "All that's spoke is marr'd," I hope in this case, he'd be willing to make an exception.

Tom Patterson. Photographer unknown.

Tom Patterson

Tom Patterson was the visionary who first thought up the concept of the Stratford Festival, and through sheer tenacity, saw it through to its successful opening. The Festival's Third Stage was re-named in his honour in 1991. I spoke to him in Toronto in the spring of 2000.

OUZOUNIAN:

Where did the idea of having a Shakespearean Festival in Stratford first come to you?

PATTERSON:

I remember the exact spot: it was behind the Collegiate Institute and let me tell you what led up to it. Not many people know it, but Stratford had one of the first major strikes of the Depression. And all of the major factories were out and the town was split right down the middle. The reputation of the town as a home for industry was destroyed. Families were broken up over it. And eventually, the government sent troops in with tanks, and it was like a war. People were hiding behind buildings and had rocks that they were throwing at the tanks. And we knew the town was dead or dying and we had to do something.

I was part of a group that was in our last year in high school. Our teacher was wonderful, Rose Guinn—she didn't really care whether we were in class or not, because you know, we were relatively good students and we'd already passed anyway.

So we'd sit around and get into conversation, and we used to talk about what the hell was going to happen to Stratford. Well, because of the name Stratford, I suddenly suggested a Shakespearean Festival, and everybody said, "Yeah, Tom, that's a great idea." So I just held on to it and bided my time.

Several years later, after the War, I was working with Maclean-Hunter and I was covering the convention of the Canadian section of the American Water Works Association and there was a hell of a lot of liquid being consumed, but none of it water. The mayor of Stratford was there, and he was a drunkard. I can say that now 'cause he's gone, but everybody in Stratford knew it anyway. And he had a party where he was entertaining guys and he was bragging about Stratford. So I said, "What do you think about a Shakespearean Festival?" And he said, "Sounds great to me. That's fine. Go ahead. See what you can do." That was it.

Well, now I had the blessing of the mayor. So I came back and talked to some people in Toronto and in Stratford and said the mayor was all for it, and it just grew from there.

OUZOUNIAN:
How did you get to Tyrone Guthrie?

PATTERSON:
Well, first I went down to New York, chasing after Laurence Olivier. And as a matter of fact, the city council gave me a hundred and twenty-five bucks to go to New York to get him. But he had plans for the next two years and he wasn't going to change those plans for some kid from Stratford.

So I came back to Toronto, and Dora Mavor Moore said, "Well, as far I'm concerned, the greatest Shakespearean director in the world is Tyrone Guthrie." And I said, "Okay, I'll get him."

First, I phoned the Old Vic where he was working then. And they said, "Well, he's not here. He's up at the Edinburgh Festival." So then I phoned Edinburgh and they said, "Well, he's not here. He was a couple of days ago, but he's gone back to Ireland." And they gave me his number in Ireland. So I phoned Ireland, and I had great difficulty getting through because there were only thirteen phones in the village. And Guthrie's number was thirteen. The woman on the switchboard thought I was a mad Irishman who was joking because nobody ever called from Canada, and she hung up on me. But I kept phoning back. And finally, according to Guthrie, she got so excited when she finally realized that it really was Canada calling, she ran out the door calling, "Mr. Guthrie, Mr. Guthrie, Canada wants you."

He got on the phone and I outlined the idea and said we'd like you to come out here, and say what you think about it? And he said, to my surprise, "When do you want me?" And I said, "As soon as you can get here." And he said, "Well, I'm busy with so and so, but I could come out in July." This was July of fifty-two. I said great. Then he asked, "How much are they going to pay me?" I said, "It's not much, but would five hundred bucks be okay?" There was a long pause at the end of the line and he finally said, "Yes."

Well, he finally came, and when he'd been out in Stratford for a week, on a Sunday afternoon in my garden, we were going over the week's activity and he said, "Incidentally, Tom, there's a rather embarrassing question I have to ask. Do you know when you mentioned my fee that the line broke down? I didn't hear the amount—how much am I getting?" This is the greatest Shakespearean director in the world. And I said, "Well, I know it's not much but five hundred bucks, how does that sound?" He said, "That's fine. Okay."

OUZOUNIAN:

How did you decide on Alec Guinness to lead the company?

PATTERSON:

Guthrie insisted that we had to have a star, someone known in

North America, to launch the event with stature, but he had to be a good actor as well. Guinness's name came up. I provided the information that he was a star enough. And Guthrie provided the information that he was actor enough.

OUZOUNIAN:
What kind of a man was Tony Guthrie?

PATTERSON:
The thing that amazed me more than anything, I think, was that he was so unassuming. For instance, the first night he was here was in the old Windsor Hotel, the one they now call 23 Albert Place. Well, I got him in the room and got him settled, and the next day when I went to pick him up I asked, "How did you sleep?" And he said, "Oh, I had a great night." I looked at him and wondered what kind of a great night he could have had in Stratford in 1952! *(laughs)* Well, what he did after we left him was to go and talk until four in the morning with the night watchman in the hotel, who was a retired guy from the railway shops. Guthrie wanted to find out about Stratford from the ground up, you know, not just listening to the board people.

I think in the next two weeks, he met almost every shopkeeper in Stratford. Went and introduced himself and said, "How are you?" And by the time he left, people were meeting him on the street and saying, "Hi Tony, how're you doing?" He was that kind of guy.

OUZOUNIAN:
When the actual opening night came, what did you feel?

PATTERSON:
Sleepy. *(laughs)* I'd been running all over town, looking after all these guys who were coming in, making sure they were comfortable and so on, and then you know, all the business that goes on. So, on opening night, I finally sat down in the front row and I fell asleep with relief.

OUZOUNIAN:
When did you know it was going to be a success?

PATTERSON:
About three months before we opened up, because the ticket sales—from all over North America—were just incredible.

OUZOUNIAN:
What went through your mind at the opening night party?

PATTERSON:
I thought, "Here's this kid from Stratford, thirty-three years old, no experience in the theatre, only been to a couple of live shows before in his life, and here he is talking to all these big shots and they're treating him more or less as an equal." I couldn't understand it. I mean, what's wrong with them? If they treat me this way, they can't be that important. *(laughs)*

OUZOUNIAN:
Did you always think there was going to be more than one season?

PATTERSON:
Absolutely. When we got the advertising going, I insisted that it be called the First Annual Shakespearean Festival and somebody said, "Are you sure it's gonna be annual?" And I said, "You're damn right."

OUZOUNIAN:
What do you wish Stratford for its fiftieth anniversary?

PATTERSON:
A hell of a successful season.

OUZOUNIAN:
And when I say "The Stratford Festival" what words pop into your head?

PATTERSON:
People. The people who built this place. The people who came here. All of them. Guthrie. Guinness. Was it really fifty years ago?

Tanya Moiseiwitsch 1974. Photographer unknown.

Tanya Moiseiwitsch

Internationally renowned designer Tanya Moiseiwitsch was a long-time collaborator of Tyrone Guthrie's when he brought her in to design the Festival stage and the first two productions at the theatre: *Richard III* and *All's Well That Ends Well.* Her influence on the visual element of the Festival's history has been profound and she has returned on numerous occasions, most recently for the 2000 production of *Tartuffe.* I spoke to her in the Festival Theatre in the summer of 2000.

OUZOUNIAN:

How did Tony Guthrie first get you involved with the Stratford Festival?

MOISEIWITSCH:

We were working together at the time, at the Old Vic, putting on a show for the coronation, *Henry VIII*, I think it was. And we were working on that when this idea was maturing. But before that I had met with Tom Patterson in London, and in the course of the conversation, I learned that he had this idea about a Stratford Festival, and by the time he finished talking, I was bowled over. It sounded so marvellous. But not quite ready. Like it hadn't even begun. And I don't think any concrete had been poured. And the idea of a tent, of course, was marvellous but a little bit shaky on the speed, if it was going to be ready in time. Everything was a deadline, I gathered. But all I was supposed to do was design—ha ha ha—the stage. And it's now known as my stage, but not strictly true. Guthrie knew exactly what he wanted, drew it on the back of an envelope. He drew very well. And I had to turn it into a half inch to the foot scale model.

He was my favourite and wonderful director. If he said, "Go to Canada," I'd say, "Yes, lovely, what a good idea." And we—he and his wife Judy and I—didn't come the ordinary way. Oh no. They had to have a cargo boat from England, and all the way up the St. Lawrence at this end, until it went no farther. I think it took about ten days but so long ago, I wouldn't swear to that.

OUZOUNIAN:

You said that Tyrone Guthrie was your favourite director. What was so wonderful about him?

MOISEIWITSCH:

He had a marvellous mind and his whole attitude to theatre was, I can't say it was charismatic 'cause that's a really silly word, but he painted pictures in your mind. He didn't paint on paper but he could draw. He drew very well, which threw me a bit, put me to shame. And he said in due course, we've got a Canadian architect lined up and when we get there, you'd better meet him and make sure you understand. He was very good at putting people together whom he knew would get on, and Robert Fairfield was a saint. He took one look at the model and said, "Okay."

Everything that Guthrie had asked for, Robert Fairfield interpreted that into real life. But I got to know the builders here and they were hardworking people. And they all put their backs into this. One or two crises arose, I'm told, about money, which I never got to know about fortunately, because I had two shows running one night after the other to prepare. Well, of course, the designs were done way back, but by the time we got here, everything was humming.

And then, of course, the tent, which was the biggest, I

think, of its kind, was being made in Chicago. And with it came a tent master who we all thought was a very charismatic character, called Skip Manley, who shinned up and down heights like he was going up Everest.

We all finally got the theatre put together and opened on time. I don't know how. Somebody called it a miracle and I think they were right.

Now there were certain little hiccups. One of them was the train going past. In those days it made the "whoo whoo" sound, which happened just as the plays were opening. It wasn't very conducive to Shakespeare. But Tom Patterson asked, and they very kindly changed the timetable so it didn't go "whoo whoo" just as Alec Guinness was trying to speak.

OUZOUNIAN:

Had you always intended that the stage should be bare except for a little bit of furniture or emblematic devices or things like that?

MOISEIWITSCH:

It started in a rather austere manner, but if actors rushed on with a lot of banners, they looked like a lot of soldiers, many more soldiers than they in fact were. And crowd scenes were Guthrie's really happiest time, the high spots of every production he did. And there were sword fights. Very dangerous. People in the front row were quite nervous. I'm not surprised. And the room offstage, I think, was so sweltering hot—it was July. But the actors didn't complain. They just got on with it. Everything was pioneer time and everybody worked twenty-four hours a day.

I think I was one of the luckiest people in the world to be here, because the whole attitude towards theatre was so enthusiastic. Oh, there were one or two people who said, "It won't work. No, no. It won't work." But all the others just said, "Wait and see." They had faith.

OUZOUNIAN:

In addition to Tony Guthrie, you collaborated with some of the other artistic directors, such as Michael Langham. What was Langham like to work with after Guthrie?

MOISEIWITSCH:

He had some of the same attributes, like his enthusiasm and his knowledge, his point of view. And like Guthrie, he had the most marvellous visual sense. He knew in his mind what scenes were going to look like. And he was marvellous to work with.

OUZOUNIAN:

The Cyrano de Bergerac *you created together is legendary. What do you remember most from that?*

MOISEIWITSCH:

All the problems we had with the final scene. There isn't a ceiling on the Festival stage, you know, it just goes up to infinity. And in the last scene, Michael wanted maple leaves, dead leaves to keep falling down throughout the scene. Well, how? There's nowhere to put them up there, and release them, like you normally would: open a bag and down they'd fall. But Jack Hutt, who was Bill Hutt's cousin and the stage manager, he invented a sort of elongated tube and you could push the leaves down the tube and eventually they reached the stage: plop, plop, plop. Down they came. It worked. And it was wonderful because Chris Plummer was at his most romantic and everything about it seemed just perfect. I loved working on that show.

OUZOUNIAN:

What about a show you designed that keeps coming back over the years, like Tartuffe. *First in 1968, then revived in 1984 and 2000. Did you think that was going to keep popping up?*

MOISEIWITSCH:

I just thought it was a very good production and I loved working on it. I never thought I'd be asked to put a realistic room on that stage, but just add pieces bit by bit, one at a time, until you have everything you need but no more. No clutter.

It's amazing to see a show you first worked on over thirty years ago being revived with new actors and a new director. And it's wonderful to see the theatre absolutely packed, because that wasn't so on some occasions during its history. This year, my goodness, I haven't seen an empty seat anywhere. Isn't that lovely?

OUZOUNIAN:

Is there anything you want to say to people about the next fifty years in Stratford?

MOISEIWITSCH:

I'm no good at prognostication. I can't envisage what's going to happen next. I know it's grown and grown. They've got an academy now up with young people studying how to be actors and everything is on the up and up. I think Tony Guthrie would have enjoyed seeing how well it's prospered. I know I have.

Don Harron as Tranio in the 1954 production of The Taming of the Shrew.
Photograph by Peter Smith and Co.

Don Harron

Don Harron is one of Canada's most beloved celebrities, best known for his comic creations, such as Charlie Farquharson. But back in 1953, he was a part of the first season of the Stratford Festival, playing Bertram in *All's Well That Ends Well.* He stayed two more years, appearing as Tranio in *The Taming of the Shrew* and Octavius Caesar in *Julius Caesar.*
I spoke to him in Toronto in the winter of 2001.

OUZOUNIAN:
What made you want to be part of that first season at the Stratford Festival?

HARRON:
Tony Guthrie. I've had two mentors in my life. One was Northrop Frye and the other was Tony Guthrie. Those two people I would have followed anywhere.

Guthrie was an enormous man. Like Charles de Gaulle in shorts, you know? And I'd seen a lot of his work in England, which I loved, and I was prepared to do anything for such a great director of comedy. Now, you never auditioned for Guthrie, he just interviewed you—and when it was my turn, he said to me, "What would you like to do?" And I don't know what made me say this, but I said, "I don't care. I'll sweep the stage. I just want to be part of this." "Very good. We'll be in touch." And of course I got one of the lead roles in *All's Well That Ends Well.*

Let me jump ahead a bit to the day of the opening. I was very nervous and so I got to the theatre early on opening night. About an hour before the curtain went up, there on the stage were Tony Guthrie and his wife Judy, both of them as tall as basketball players, sweeping the stage. So he did it instead of me.

OUZOUNIAN:

Go back to the start of rehearsals. What do you remember from then?

HARRON:

Actually, my first memory was from the night before rehearsals started. Tom Patterson was there welcoming us all and Guthrie had assigned every actor to a family in Stratford to have dinner with. Which was a marvellous idea. Guthrie had explained to us that national theatres don't really mean anything. A theatre has to have its roots in a local community and must sink them deep and continue to do so. Which they've done in Stratford. And that first night was wonderful. Then I presume Tony went home with Judy and had an English high tea while he memorized the names and nicknames of every single actor in the company, because that's how he addressed us the next morning for the first rehearsal. It just stunned us all.

OUZOUNIAN:

How did Guthrie direct? Did he talk to you much about the meaning of things?

HARRON:

He did at the beginning. That first day, he took every actor, no matter what they played, and gave a kind of little biography of the kind of person their character would be. I don't know where he got it from, but we all went home just aflame with excitement. And he said, "Now go to your bedroom and that's where the great creative work is done." So we'd come back the next day, but we were never as good as he described.

OUZOUNIAN:

Any pictures in your mind from the rehearsal period?

HARRON:

When I wasn't onstage, I used to watch the Stratford farmers, who'd sit in the open air before we got the tent up, and look at our rehearsals. One would ask, "Would that be him?" and another would say, "Oh yeah, that's Alec Guinness, the movie man." Now, Guinness was playing Richard the Third with a lot of gruesome physical contortions, so the first farmer said, "He's got his words down. Now he's practising his gestures. And he's done pretty good for a fellow with the arthritis awful bad." *(laughing)* I've never forgotten that.

OUZOUNIAN:
What do you recall from the opening night?

HARRON:
It was eighty-seven degrees and humid. We were all wretched and soaked through. And at one point, I looked out in the audience and it was so hot and humid that bodies were fainting. And they were being passed along the row to the St. John's Ambulance person at the end of the row. Rather like hotdogs at a football game. But the thing that struck me as I looked out, was that the people passing them along were not looking at the bodies. They were looking straight at the stage and I knew we were there.

OUZOUNIAN:
What was it like playing the romantic male lead, Bertram, in All's Well That Ends Well*?*

HARRON:
It wasn't exactly a picnic, because he's a very unsympathetic character. He's a snob and he rejects this wonderful wise girl, Helena, played by Irene Worth. I told Guthrie I was worried about my character and said, "Do you think that I should play him younger than my twenty-eight years?" Guthrie just gave me a withering glance and said, "Don't think so. Think that would be rather mutton dressed as lamb." *(laughing)* And I thought, okay.

OUZOUNIAN:
Did Guthrie's legendary salty language ever get him into trouble?

HARRON:
It came close one day. *(laughing)* He was staging the party scene in *All's Well*, and trying to get us to work up to the appropriate level of revelry, and he had all these people from the United Church choir in Stratford standing onstage. Suddenly, he came down like a whirlwind from the back of the theatre, saying, "No, no, no! Don't you understand me? You're supposed to be joyful! Why are you people all so fucking Ontario?" I looked at the members of the choir and they looked sort of stricken. Except for two women who never stopped smiling. They were married women. I think they'd never heard that word before.

OUZOUNIAN:
What was it like going back for the second year?

HARRON:
We were nervous about doing *Measure For Measure*, which is a wonderful play, very subtle, but it was not going to be directed by Guthrie. He had turned it over to his right-hand man, Cecil Clarke, who was the greatest second-in-command for a theatre company, but wasn't really a director. We could see it going down the tubes and finally Guthrie had to come in for the last three-and-a-half, four days and restage the final scene. That's all he had time to do.

OUZOUNIAN:
What kind of a critical reaction did Measure For Measure *get?*

HARRON:
After the first season, the critics were expecting a lot and they were very unkind to James Mason, who was playing the lead. I think they took it out on him, rather than on Cecil Clarke. The rest of us got fairly good reviews, but we all felt for James, who everybody adored. He really was loved by the whole company. He was such a sweet, gentle modest man, unlike the

roles he often played. You know? Lowering villains.

We also felt bad because on opening night, in the middle of the intermission, his wife, Pamela, came backstage and said to him, "This is all stupid and you're dreadful and I'm leaving." And she stormed out, leaving him to do the second half. So we really pulled together because we loved him so much.

OUZOUNIAN:

In The Taming of the Shrew, *you played Tranio. What did you look like?*

HARRON:

A goof. Guthrie wanted me to play it in buckteeth. And he sent me to my dentist in Stratford and got me a wonderful pair of choppers. I got lots of laughs from spraying all over the stage with the teeth in. Then I went to the barber and got a Guthrie haircut. Guthrie always had military haircuts, so I had my head shaved with my ears sticking out. I was making fun of him and he loved it.

The third season, I was in *Julius Caesar.* I played Octavius Caesar and I remember putting on a Roman nose and looking like a cosmetics advertisement—very pink. Michael Langham sort of let me do what I wanted in the part, which was great. And then he took me out to dinner at the end of the season and said, "What do you want to play next year?" And I said, "I want to play the Chorus in *Henry V*, because I see him as an ordinary guy in a workshirt and pants against all those fancy costumes." Michael said, "Wonderful, wonderful!"

But a few months later they called me up and I was not offered the Chorus in *Henry V*. They said, "You will be Lord Scroop." And I sent a telegram to Michael saying, "Scroop you." So I left and I went down to work in New York for the next few years.

OUZOUNIAN:

What comes to your mind when you think about Stratford?

HARRON:

That I was so lucky to be there for that first season. I've had many openings in New York and in London, but never one like that. Never one that felt that the entire country was on the block.

I also think about how the town of Stratford was well cast for their part in all of this. They have never let the Festival down. I'm so proud of the people in that town. It's such a pleasure to go there.

OUZOUNIAN:

Do you have one particular memory of the first season?

HARRON:

Yes. Guthrie and his wife sweeping the stage. Instead of me.

William Hutt as King Lear in the 1996 production of King Lear.
Photograph by Cylla von Tiedemann.

William Hutt

William Hutt joined the Festival in its very first season, and has been a part of it for many of its fifty years, working with every one of its artistic directors. His performances as King Lear, Prospero, Tartuffe, and James Tyrone are among the greatest in the Festival's history. He returns this season to play the King of France in *All's Well That Ends Well*. I spoke to him at the Festival Theatre in the fall of 2001.

OUZOUNIAN:

When you were asked to join the first season of the Stratford Festival, did you ever think that fifty years later, it and you would still be together?

HUTT:

Well, I don't think I ever thought in those terms. Until the Festival opened. I mean I didn't spend the, you know, the rehearsal period saying, "Do I think this is going to go on forever?" *(laughs)* I was too busy, you know, just absorbing everything that could be absorbed. But once we opened, and got into that first season, short as it was, I realized it was going to go on as long as its natural lifespan. Because it was such a huge project for this country, and created such a huge media blitz across the world, across the theatre world, that I couldn't imagine anybody in this country just letting it die.

OUZOUNIAN:

Any memories from the early rehearsals?

HUTT:

My first memory was *Richard III*. I played a very small part, the keeper of the jail, Brakenbury, and the first time I got actually to open my mouth, and say something, in rehearsal, I clearly remember thinking, "I've got to show them that I can speak Shakespeare." So I bellowed it. *(laughs)* and in that vast building that was echo-crazy, the noise was deafening. And I remember a rather startled look on Alec Guinness's face and his eyes shifted to where Tony Guthrie was standing, and I immediately knew exactly what the problem was. I was just talking too loudly. And I think Tony made some politic remark like "We don't need quite so much voice, boy. Thank you very much."

OUZOUNIAN:
What are your memories of working with Alec Guinness?

HUTT:
Here we have, you know, the international champion of reserve, of less is better, almost to the point of nothing being best. Doing his magic, and suggesting so many things, rather than imprinting them. And yet, he was never unfriendly or unapproachable, even given his natural reserve.

I remember a couple of things that Alec did that impressed me enormously. One was after the coronation when he says:

I must be married to my brother's daughter
Or else my kingdom stands on brittle glass.

He had a ring or two on his fingers and when he got to the phrase "on brittle glass" he did a gesture, and under the lights the way he moved his hand around, you could see a field of glass. And I've never forgotten that.

Another time was when he's talking to the whole pack of them, and says:

Let me put in your minds, if you forget,
What you have been ere now, and what you are;
Withal, what I have been, and what I am.

What he did with his right foot is just . . . squeeze it into the ground as if he were squashing a bug. I remember those things, which intrigued me.

Another thing I learned from Alec was rather embarrassing for me at the time. It was during a rehearsal of *All's Well That Ends Well,* and I was an eloquently silent chamberlain or something. And there were two others, and we were placed around, standing in the gutter, one here and one here. And I was right in the centre there. And Alec was in his wheelchair and he was delivering a long speech. First to this guy, that guy, and then that guy, just so he'd get the speech around to the house, you know?

As he was talking, Tony Guthrie decided he was going to quite quietly readjust a bit of the choreography upstage left behind Alec, so Tony tiptoed up and started to readjust it and my eyes wandered to this six-foot-four figure, adjusting the choreography, just as Alec got to me. And he dried . . . he forgot his line. He went on for a bit and then stopped and came back to me and he said, "Bill, I dried because you were more interested in what Tony Guthrie was doing than in what I was saying." And I've never forgotten that because it is absolutely vitally important on that stage all the time to listen to who's speaking to you. Because if your eyes wander, you throw them. And if they do the same thing to you, then you're thrown. And that's the wonderful part about that stage: you have to listen and answer.

OUZOUNIAN:

What was it like, working for all six-foot-four of Tyrone Guthrie?

HUTT:

Well, I think that I probably anticipated that this giant of the English-speaking theatre, with his huge international reputation, was going to descend on Stratford with an aura of impenetrable reserve and a cloak of aloofness. And what we got instead, was a six-foot-four firm but compassionate father figure, who was deeply respectful of both our talents and our shortcomings, never pushed us beyond what we naturally could do, because that would make us look phony. Whatever we had to offer, he just made it work. So, consequently we had a tremendous trust, a faith in Guthrie, and a deep abiding affection. His rehearsals were always . . . full of knowledge, improvisation, sometimes wild improvisation, certainly a lot of fun.

OUZOUNIAN:
You were in his famous production of Oedipus. *What do you recall from that?*

HUTT:
Well, the first thing I recall is how stifling it was. I mean those massive, heavy costumes, brilliantly designed by dear Tanya Moiseiwitsch, but oh God, they were awful to wear. And the tent was a steambath on hot days in the summer. And since we were all wearing huge bulky costumes in a steambath, we all lost pounds and pounds during that summer.

But I do remember, I remember Tony Guthrie right from the beginning saying, "This is a huge experiment, and we may just simply get trashed by everybody, critics and public. They may stay away in droves. But we're going to take that big chance and just do it."

I remember a moment as the leader of the chorus when we were rehearsing one day and he stopped and said, "I need a sound here from somebody, a howling sound, howling to the moon." So suddenly I just opened my larynx and howled at something. And he said, "Who did that?" And I said, "It was me, Tony." "Wonderful, keep that in. That's exactly what I want." And I felt enormously proud that I was able to howl to the moon to his satisfaction.

OUZOUNIAN:
James Mason played Oedipus. How did he fit in with all of this?

HUTT:
Dear James . . . I remember Tony saying at the first rehearsal,

"It's very, very generous of a major film star, arguably one of the most handsome of all film stars, to be willing to come up here and put a mask over his face to play Oedipus." And we all looked at the handsome man for some kind of reaction. He just did nothing. There's no hidden agenda in that remark of mine. He just didn't do anything.

Before Oedipus, we had all done *Measure For Measure*, and I made an entrance right after James. On opening night, before he went on, he said over his shoulder to me, "I hate this. I don't know why I do it." And he went out and the dear man couldn't be heard beyond about the third or fourth row.

And then when we got to rehearse *Oedipus*, I think he realized that he had to do something, and to the man's enormous credit, from the first rehearsal, he took voice lessons every single day. And ultimately he was fine. He was deeply, deeply moving at the end of the play, I found . . . 'cause I was able to, of course, sit there and listen to it and he was, he was very very moving. I liked James. He was a nice man.

OUZOUNIAN:

You stayed with the company, and soon found yourself working for Guthrie's chosen successor, Michael Langham. What was he like?

HUTT:

Very precise. I think he gave style to the company. Tony Guthrie's productions featured a lot of improvisation on his part and indeed on ours, and consequently, they seemed slightly to fall apart at the seams in the middle of the season.

Not Michael. He was very precise and very good at choreography. He seemed somehow to have the entire production staged in his mind before he went into rehearsals. And each picture wasn't just choreography for the sake of choreography, or movement for the sake of movement. It illuminated the text.

OUZOUNIAN:

Was there a downside to that?

HUTT:

If there was a downside, it would be that at times I felt I was a puppet. That I didn't always quite understand why he had me move. But I moved anyway because the director told me to. I suppose as time went on, I began to sort of fill in the blanks and say, "Well, it's up to me to find out why I'm moving. He knows why. It's up to me to do my homework and find out why he has me move there."

OUZOUNIAN:

Some people have used words like "chilly" or "overly intellectual" to describe working with Michael. Did that ever occur to you?

HUTT:

Well, he wasn't a hugger. *(laughs)* Yes, I think he was a bit chilly. Mind you, he started off not in the happiest circumstances and it wasn't his fault. But there was a group in the company who after Guthrie left, felt that God had deserted us and we were saddled with a not very intelligent Jesus. And they gave him a hard time. And didn't make him welcome. There was a certain little pool of resentment. And he was aware of it and I think it hurt him. And it may have influenced the way he behaved, particularly in the early years, by seeming rather chilly and standoffish. But you know, being an artistic director is not . . . not necessary a popularity contest.

OUZOUNIAN:

Christopher Plummer came along soon afterwards to star in Henry V. What kind of initial impression did he make on you?

HUTT:

Chris . . . I remember admiring him enormously. Sometimes he was a bit difficult to rehearse with because initially, in those days, he would be almost *sotto voice* in the early rehearsals until he actually knew what he was going to do. All of us would be bellowing most of the time, because we were trying to be, you know, really Shakespearean.

I remember one time, I was doing a scene with Chris and he was going "Mumble, mumble, mumble" and you could barely hear him. And I said to myself, "Is he doing this to piss me off? Why don't I do the same thing?" So I did exactly what he was doing and he looked at me and sort of pulled himself together and then started to give out.

What I've always respected about Chris is that he has enormous style and also a huge sense of danger, which is wonderful. You never quite knew what he was going to do, particularly in the early days.

OUZOUNIAN:

The next year, the Festival moved into its permanent home in the theatre here. How did you find the change from tent to theatre? Was it a positive one for you?

HUTT:

That question, in and of itself, is the understatement of the entire fifty years! I mean to get inside a permanent building was just heaven because, romantic as the tent was, it was impossible. I mean, it was not soundproof, it was hardly rainproof. And it was a steambath. So simply to get in a building whereby you didn't have to stop the performance because the rain was pounding on the roof, or stop the performance because there was a baseball game going on down on the diamond, it was wonderful. Just that.

OUZOUNIAN:

One of the first shows in the new theatre was Hamlet, *with Plummer as Hamlet and you as Polonius . . .*

HUTT:

. . . and the biggest memory I have about that first *Hamlet*, was the night that Polonius died of a heart attack. Michael Langham had organized the closet scene so there was no arras, there was no curtain. I was to hide underneath the balcony and, when I sensed danger, come running out towards the centre pillar. And Chris, who would be standing in the centre stage saying "How now! A rat? Dead, for a ducat, dead!" would put his sword out behind him and I would run on to the sword, and it would look like a terrible accident. And when it worked, it was really quite startling, because it did look accidental.

Well, despite the fact that it was a new building, it wasn't air conditioned, so it was still pretty warm on the very hot nights. And as I was running from way underneath the balcony towards the centre pillar, which isn't a great distance, I saw that Chris was having a difficult time getting his sword out, because the steel was sweating against the leather. And so what am I going to do? I can't walk out into the middle of the stage, and have him kill me there. Because it would be against the whole concept of that moment. And even if he just sort of brutally stabbed me he would still have to trample back and forth across this body during the scene with his mother, and since I was wearing a wig, if he had to drag me off upstage, my head would bump against the step that goes out. And my wig would fly off. And all these thoughts were flashing through my mind as I was heading towards the centre pillar. And by the time I got to the centre pillar he hadn't got his sword out, so I did the only thing that I can do—die of a heart attack. So I just put my hand on my chest and said, "Oh my God!" and fainted, just beside the centre pillar.

And then Chris finally got his sword out and he had the nerve to sort of poke me like an underdone chicken and say rather plaintively, "Is it the king?" *(laughing)* I was underneath screaming with laughter. I'm sure my costume was shaking. And that was the most vivid memory I have of Chris's Hamlet.

OUZOUNIAN:
Bill, there are several plays that you have a long history with through

the Festival's fifty years and one of them was King Lear. *When you look back on your various Lears, what do you recall?*

HUTT:

Well, the fact that I have actually played the role of Lear, one, two, three, four times, and survived it, I think is sort of an accomplishment in and of itself. I don't know of any other actor on the English-speaking stage who's done four major productions of *King Lear*. So I'm rather proud of just simply that fact.

The first one I did was with the Canadian Players back in the very early sixties. They referred to it as "The Eskimo Lear" or "Lear in the Parka," which was the design concept and a very interesting one. And I can remember in the middle of rehearsals simply walking offstage one day and saying, "I can't do this. I'm not ready. I don't know enough how to do this part. I can't do it." And, of course, everybody looked, and I looked at them looking and realized I can do this. I can't just walk away, because all these people are going to be out of work. But I actually felt that. And I just had to sort of do what they loosely refer to as climb back on the horse and do my best.

The second time around, it was easier because I learned that there are moments in it when I have to spare my energy for the larger moments. This was in the production that David William directed, and that we eventually took across Europe, to Moscow, Leningrad, Warsaw, Krakow, Holland, and Denmark. That production was what I would call full declamatory—what we would now call an old-fashioned knock-down, drag-out production, you know, full blast. And I think it worked extremely well for its time.

The next Lear I did was some sixteen years later. Robin Phillips had ceased to be the artistic director but had his own Young Company at the Tom Patterson Theatre at the time. And I saw the enormous talent he had in this Young Company, and I just took a chance and said, "Robin, what would you think of my doing *Lear* with the Young Company at the Patterson Theatre?" Because for some time I had been wondering what would it be like to do *Lear* in a small space, where you're not required to have the full-blown declamatory high-decibel performance—and consequently and possibly make the play and the role more accessible.

Robin agreed, and I can remember one day in rehearsals when he called the company together after the rehearsal, giving notes out and finally he got to me and says, "Bill, you're too loud, too loud, too loud, too loud, too young, too young, too young, too young. Do you get the point?" And I did get the point. You know, I was playing it too young and too loud. For that space. Even having wanted to do it, I was still too loud, you know? And so I began to tone it down considerably, just vocally. And started thinking internally rather than externally. Not how am I going to do this? But what am I going to be thinking while I'm doing it? And I remember after we opened, Robin would come and see at least part of the production, most evenings. And he came into my dressing room one night about halfway through the run and said, "Bill, I want you to take your subconscious onstage tonight." I said, "Sure. I understand what you mean." I mean by this time Robin and I had worked so closely together that we'd talk almost in telegrams. What he meant was my performance was becoming too self-conscious. I was aware of what I was doing."

I think it certainly started me thinking in terms of being able—that late in my career—to speak and phrase Shakespeare as if it were everyday conversation.

OUZOUNIAN:

You played Lear one more time for Richard Monette on the Festival Stage.

HUTT:

Well, by that time, I could talk conversationally on that stage and be heard. I was able to use what I had learned at the Patterson to a certain extent, but obviously some moments had to be slightly louder simply because you're dealing with a much larger space.

OUZOUNIAN:

We've talked about how your performance as Lear has changed over the years. Has what you think about the play changed as well? Do you still feel it's the same play to you?

HUTT:

I think obviously the older one gets, the wider one's emotional horizons are, and one's life experience is. And that comes, that is brought to bear subconsciously, no matter what happens. You can't help it, you know. I can't help being eighty-one and the eighty-one years that I have lived are richer by their longevity than they were, say twenty, thirty years ago. So that there are just more experiences to bring to bear on the role I don't think I could . . . I don't think I'll ever do another one. In fact, I'm quite sure I won't.

OUZOUNIAN:

In the midst of all these Lears, you also played the Fool to Peter Ustinov's Lear. What was it like to shift sides of the coin?

HUTT:

I found it very interesting. I had to sit back and observe what Peter was doing first before I knew what I was going to do. And what I observed from his Lear—and this is not to be interpreted as an unkind or critical remark—was that this Lear was not as intelligent as the Fool. Ustinov himself has a sharp brilliant intelligence, but he was trying to project a character who wasn't very smart. So I had to be smarter, which of course fits in with Shakespeare's concept of fools anyway. In practically all the plays where there is a fool, the fool is arguably the most intelligent person in the play. That's why he calls them fools.

OUZOUNIAN:

This pairing of you with Ustinov was Robin Phillips's idea. Let's open the Robin pages. You two first worked together on Measure For Measure. *What kind of experience was that for you?*

HUTT:

Slightly daunting. But I remember one moment when I began to realize how subtle Robin was, how accurate his perceptions were along with his subtlety, and that was the first time we rehearsed the scene where the Duke Friar goes to Mariana's place. The rehearsal took place just after lunch. I walked onto the stage and Robin and Daphne Dare, who was the designer, had just left the stage. On the stage were a wicker easy chair with a footstool in front of it, a little side table, and on the side table was a little silver platter and on the silver platter was a glass of champagne. And I looked at that. I said Robin is telling me that probably the Duke Friar has known Mariana in the biblical sense. Why would she do this if she wasn't used to seeing him? How subtle that was. The subtle message in the design concept showed me how to play the scene.

OUZOUNIAN:

Is that experience a metaphor for what it's like working with Robin?

HUTT:

Yes, it is. Robin seems to know what you want to do before you know yourself.

OUZOUNIAN:

Moving to more recent memories, the production of Long Day's Journey into Night *you starred in with Martha Henry remains one of the high-water marks of the Festival's history. Why did it work so well?*

HUTT:

It started off absolutely brilliantly by accident. For the first three weeks of rehearsals, Martha couldn't attend. She was busy finishing off directing *The Miracle Worker* at the Grand Theatre. So for those weeks, there was just me and Martha

Burns, Tom McCamus, and Pete Donaldson. So we rehearsed all the boys' scenes with me. So when Martha (Henry) turned up, it was just, it was, it was just absolutely perfect. Mother has just come back from the sanitarium. That's where she's been these three weeks, which was in the play. So that there was this sense of . . . welcoming her home, which was real, absolutely real.

The second thing was that we emphasized the fact that there is a very very strong thread of love and loyalty in most dysfunctional families. That however dysfunctional they are, somehow there is a sense of support and love that threads its way through. Because I know dysfunctional families and they're at each other's throats, but you know underneath that they love each other, because in times of stress, they come together and do something. And I felt very strongly that there was more love in this family than I had ever seen before.

And it was very easy for me to play that because I adored Martha and I adore her to this day. I'm in love with her and always have been. So it all just meshed perfectly.

OUZOUNIAN:
What would you wish Stratford for the next fifty years?

HUTT:
I do wonder if in the next fifty years, Stratford may find that it sometimes gets a little hungry, if not actually starving for talent. You see, if one examines what is happening to the young people today, first of all the age of the great stage actor is almost over. There are very, very few great stage actors left in the world today. You can count them on . . . perhaps one hand. Their era is fast disappearing. Fast disappearing. Also what is disappearing therefore is the young actor who wants to make a career of the stage. They want to have the springboard of the stage. They want to learn their craft on the stage. And if they can get hired sporadically on the stage, fine, but

basically they are training themselves, either consciously or subconsciously, for films and television. So, eventually, Stratford may just be starving a bit for qualified careerists on the stage. Therefore, maybe the answer for Stratford is: If you can't fight 'em, join 'em. Build a studio. Do your own films. Why aren't we filming our own productions? And if that's not possible, you know, if you can't build a studio so that you can do these things, then form an alliance with a film-producing company that's already in existence. That kind of thing, I think, is going to help keep Stratford alive. I can't visualize it just disappearing from the face of the earth. I can't visualize that happening.

OUZOUNIAN:

The last question. When I say "The Stratford Festival" to you, what images come to mind?

HUTT:

Home. It's where I learn. It's my school. It has been my support. It has been my mentor. It has been my pleasure to contribute to its success, and whatever, whatever national or international reputation I have is almost entirely due to Stratford, and I can't imagine a better picture in my life than that.

Lloyd Bochner as Cassius in the 1955 production of Julius Caesar.
Photograph by McKague, Toronto.

Lloyd Bochner

Lloyd Bochner was a part of the Stratford Festival for its first five seasons, playing roles like Clarence in *Richard III*, Cassius in *Julius Caesar*, and Horatio in *Hamlet*. He then went on to a long and successful career in American film and television, including continuing roles on the series *Dynasty* and *Hotel*. I spoke to him in Los Angeles in February 2001.

OUZOUNIAN:

How did you wind up getting to the Stratford Festival?

BOCHNER:

Mavor Moore was a good friend of mine and he phoned me one day and said, "They're starting a new theatre in Stratford. I think you should come up and meet the director." So I came to Toronto, and in the New Play Society offices, there was a tall, impressive man named Tony Guthrie. I fully expected to read him a speech from Shakespeare. But no, all he wanted to do was to talk to me and we talked about many things. When we finished, he said, "How would you like to join the company?" And it sounded a little harebrained at the time I must admit. But I said, well sure, it sounds very interesting. And before I knew it, I had a contract to go to Stratford. In March, my wife and I drove down to Stratford just to see how the land lay. It was a rainy, cold, miserable day, and I met Tom Patterson. He talked about all that was to happen in Stratford, all of which seemed most unlikely. And I said, "Well, where's all this going to be?" He drove me down to a park and took me all around this dank, forlorn area, which was muddy and miserable. And he said, "We're going to build the tent over there." And I thought, "This is one of those great ideas, which wasn't going to go very far." Little did I realize how impactful this would be on the Canadian scene.

OUZOUNIAN:

In Richard III, *Guthrie entrusted you with the very major role of Clarence. What was it like to work with him?*

BOCHNER:

There was a great contradiction in the way Tony approached us. Perhaps I shouldn't call it a contradiction, but a mixture of directorial elements. For example, he was intent on our doing what came to be known as seven lines of Shakespeare on one breath. This, in Tony's opinion, would give a flow, a rhythm, to the poetry. And at times it was very difficult to achieve, especially since you were belting out these lines to reach the back row of the theatre. Seven lines is quite an exercise.

At the same time, he wanted us to give a note, more than a note of reality to the performance, to what we were doing. But in contradiction to that, one of Tony's favourite expressions was "Make it showy, dear boy, make it showy." Now what he meant by that was, make it larger than life. Make it stagey, if you will. And so at times we were left in some confusion.

He was a great showman. He was theatrical to his eyebrows, and his productions were marvellous because he brought all this drama, all this imagination, all this excitement to them. And at times I guess we were confused by this. He had a great sense of style and theatricality. He exercised our imaginations to the nth degree as he prodded us constantly. And it was terrific.

OUZOUNIAN:

You initially said that you thought Stratford was a wonderful idea, but you didn't know if it would work. At what moment in the process did you realize it was *going to work?*

BOCHNER:

I think when the tent went up and all the physical elements came together, suddenly there was a realization that this indeed was going to work, that this cast of Canadians had been amalgamated into a very strong company under Tony's influence.

Yes, there were problems, and the tent was hot, and it leaked, and the trains kept running by at inopportune moments. But the company rose above all that. This was an epiphany for those of us who had struggled through the beginnings of theatre in Canada, through summer stock, or inadequate theatres and low wages, and suddenly it was all happening and we were part of it. We had the best. We had Alec Guinness and Tony Guthrie and Irene Worth and we were privileged to be there.

OUZOUNIAN:

After the triumph of the first year, what were things like in the second season?

BOCHNER:

Guthrie turned over the production of *Measure For Measure* to Cecil Clarke, who had been his production manager, and it made for a wholly different feeling. In the first year, we were so dependent on Tony; we gave ourselves over to him; he was our leader. There was no question as to the way the production was going to go. In the second year, we found ourselves more dependent on our own resources and though this was challenging, and a way complimenting, it was very dangerous. And towards the end of rehearsals, we felt we needed Guthrie to come in. We approached him, a number of us who were playing leading roles, and explained our weaknesses, our problems—not the problems of the production, but rather we personalized the situation. And Guthrie said, "Oh that's fine, dear boys. That's fine. Just work your way through." This went on for about two weeks and we became more and more desperate, because we recognized that the magic of Guthrie, which we felt the production and the theatre deserved, wasn't there. Finally, he came in with about, I think, ten days to go. The first thing he did was to attack the last scene, which was the important climactic scene, of course. And then he worked backwards and doctored it.

But our idea was that the theatre and Tony were one. And when he finally stepped aside, it was a bit of a shock to us—although he found someone who gave us a shot in the arm to have them with us.

OUZOUNIAN:

Did you have any feelings when the theatre moved from the tent into the permanent building that this could have been a bad thing?

BOCHNER:

Certainly, there were problems with the tent. The major difficulty in those years was the terrible, terrible heat that was generated. We had to have huge blocks of ice which had fans aimed at them and that was the air conditioning. I remember losing so much weight wearing these magnificent but heavy costumes, and they were soaking wet all summer.

But still, there was an adventure, there was a romance about working under the canvas. It felt like a new enterprise, which indeed it was. Even though it didn't have the substance that bricks and mortar has, there was an adventure to it. And those of us who were involved felt that we were part of a creation of something new and exciting and dynamic. But when it became solidified, if you will, with those bricks and mortar, we felt that perhaps it was becoming more of an institution than an adventure.

OUZOUNIAN:

One of the first productions in the new theatre was Hamlet, *where you played Horatio to Chris Plummer's Hamlet. Are there any specific moments that you remember?*

BOCHNER:

I admired Chris's Hamlet enormously. It was very moving. I remember when we were on the stage together and he was doing the "Alas poor Yorick" speech, it was so moving. And his death was so touching that when I stood over him and said "Goodnight, sweet prince" the memory of it still brings tears to my eyes.

OUZOUNIAN:

What was it that touched you so much?

BOCHNER:

Chris has a way of bringing a reality to a part. He's so believable in what he does. He has the knack of bringing to life the poetry that he's speaking. Not that he ignores the rhythm or the sound of the poetry, but he makes it understandable and real to an audience. And real to his fellow actors.

OUZOUNIAN:

What would you wish the Stratford Festival for its next fifty years?

BOCHNER:

I wish it nothing but the best for the coming years.

OUZOUNIAN:

What comes to your mind when I say "The Stratford Festival"?

BOCHNER:

A milestone in my life. Without the Stratford Festival, I have no idea where Canadian actors would be today. It gave us a feeling of confidence, of security, of belief in ourselves. That we were not simply stock company performers, that we were capable of more. And indeed, many of us have gone on and ventured into theatre and television and film around the world. And I think without Stratford that might not have happened. We brought with us an aura of success, and that was all thanks to Stratford.

Timothy Findley. Photograph by Michael Bedord.

Timothy Findley

Besides being one of Canada's finest novelists, Timothy Findley was a young actor who appeared in the first season of the Festival and then later returned as a playwright with works such as *The Stillborn Lover*, *The Trials of Ezra Pound*, and *Elizabeth Rex*. I spoke to him in Stratford in the summer of 2001.

OUZOUNIAN:

What's the very first thing you remember about the Stratford Festival?

FINDLEY:

Tyrone Guthrie. I remember being summoned to meet him at an old studio where I had studied dance, which was above some shops on Yonge Street, just south of Bloor. And I remember . . . I remember this so vividly, Richard, going up the steps and the way the stairs made their noise . . . and of course the floor was a floor for dancers. So it had a certain give and take to it. It was wonderful. And Guthrie was very clever. Because it was a studio for dancers, it was quite long and narrow. And Guthrie sat at the far end, at a table, and you had to walk in and present yourself all the way down to the table, when you did your entrance.

Well, I was cast. And I was given a wonderful role in *Richard III*, of Catesby, who is one of Richard's henchmen. I remember the first rehearsal, up where the market is held, in a big tin barn. And you couldn't hear anything because when the rain came down, it just pounded on the roof. And the swallows and the sparrows kept flying around shitting on everybody as we rehearsed, you know. *(laughing)* It was crazy.

It was a sit-down readthrough of *Richard III*, and the cream of the Canadian acting community had been hired. I mean really, unbelievable. And Guinness and Irene Worth and Tanya Moiseiwitsch and Guthrie all sat up on a sort of raised level, and read from there. But we all sat in seats like an audience, and read our roles from there. I remember when it got rolling. I just happened to look up at Guinness and he turned to Guthrie in that moment and went—"wow"—like that. I mean Tony knew whom he hired, but they weren't quite prepared for the level of professionalism and the level of talent that was evident in that readthrough.

OUZOUNIAN:
What was your first impression of Alec Guinness?

FINDLEY:
Shyness. It was all absolutely true about the person in hiding. He wasn't there. It wasn't like a defensive hiding; it was just absolute shyness. "What? I'm not anybody. You know, I'm just me." That kind of thing. And we got to know each other extremely well. In fact, he became my mentor and he took me to England and sent me to theatre school and all that.

One day he said, "How would you feel if you came and heard my lines?" And I thought, jeez . . . I've got to sit down in a room with Alec Guinness and listen to his lines, and correct him when he's wrong. That's not easy. But it went terribly well and I read all the other roles in the scenes that he was rehearsing. And I think I must have done that with some accomplishment, because as he walked me back to where I was living we stopped under a lamp and he said, "Ducky, how would you feel about coming to London to study, because your voice needs help? And I think you have talent and I think it's worth getting the voice right as early as possible." So I nearly died. I mean how do I say no? But at the same time, it's very intimidating. But I went, and it all unfolded from there into this magical journey, all because of Alec.

So a full circle happened in my life, from when I first arrived to come to play at Stratford all the way through to the production of *Elizabeth Rex* in the season of 2000, when I had become a playwright and was no longer an actor. And what a wonderful circle that has been! For me. I feel so privileged and I won't say lucky, but you do have to be in the right place at the right time, and when you're there, you have to be ready. Very early on, Alec took a book he gave me—essays by Harley Granville Barker about the plays of Shakespeare—and he wrote in the flyleaf "The readiness is all. Hamlet." And that's the truth. You have to be ready for it to happen. You can't not be there when the moment presents itself, as it will if you stay long enough. You have to be willing to give your whole life to what your talent asks of you. And my talent has been to be a good actor and then a playwright. And one fed the other, but I always made certain that I was ready for whatever it was that was going to happen. Be there. Be there. Be there.

OUZOUNIAN:
That very first summer, what was it like working with Tyrone Guthrie?

FINDLEY:
(laughing) He was beyond belief! And there are no more giants of his kind, no more giants of the classic mould like Guthrie. They're gone. We had the best of them in our time. We had the very best.

Guthrie was incredibly tall, but he didn't look down his nose at you. He never bent his head to look. He looked out at everything. And he discovered early on in rehearsals that I had been a dancer and that I had some athletic skill. Now, my character Catesby had to come on in *Richard III* at the moment when Richard is alone on the stage saying "A horse, a horse, my kingdom for a horse!" And the whole stage was in darkness except for one spotlight on Guinness, as Richard. And Guthrie said, "How would you feel, Findley, if you jumped off the balcony. We want a surprise entrance." Jump off the balcony in the dark? With only this spotlight, and I knew I had to miss that because there stood himself. So I had to go up the stairs in the dark at the back of the balcony and then break through the curtain, run onto the balcony and leap. I had to do it like that. I couldn't look. I couldn't do anything. Well, I never landed on Guinness and I never broke my legs, but it was really scary.

But Guthrie asked of you that you do things like that. He didn't shy away from saying "Look, come. Come up. Be better. Do more." And he taught us wonderful things about language. He was a magical character.

OUZOUNIAN:
What was Irene Worth like that first summer?

FINDLEY:
She was the most generous, wonderful person, and as an actress, she was a revelation. When you saw her doing Mad Margaret, this sweet lovely woman became a vessel of rage, and it was just extraordinary to watch her haul out the guns and fire them all. But the thing about both her and Guinness as the two leading figures in that season was what you learned as an actor from both of them. You learned what control was. You learned what range was. You learned about getting it just to *there*, and then letting the audience do the rest.

There's a wonderful story that Bill Hutt tells about that. We had seen a performance of *King Lear* that was awful. It was awful because it was . . . it was Donald Wolfit time. You know, hanging on the curtain and real tears at the end of the play with Cordelia and so on. And I said, "Bill, why doesn't that work? Why didn't it work?" And Bill said, "Well, he just went 'do re me fa so la ti do,' but the actor's real job is to go 'do re me fa so la ti' and let the audience go 'do.'" Isn't that wonderful? And that's what you learned from Guinness and Worth. The power was there, but it didn't spill over.

OUZOUNIAN:
When I sat watching Elizabeth Rex, *I thought Guthrie would have liked this play. Did you ever think of him when you wrote it?*

FINDLEY:
Oh yes. You always do. I mean whenever you're writing for the theatre, you think of all the people that you have cherished. Yes, I wondered what he would have done with it, and it made me more adventurous. Because you have to leap into the dark the way I did. Because if you wait to make sure that everything is perfect underneath you, that you're perfectly safe, then to hell with you. The theatre is about danger. That's what it's about. And if there isn't danger, it's worthless.

OUZOUNIAN:
What would you wish for Stratford for its next fifty years?

FINDLEY:
That it just keeps going the way it's going.

OUZOUNIAN:
Give me some images or words that come to mind when I say "The Stratford Festival."

FINDLEY:
The tent. Unforgettable moments with Guinness and Worth and Guthrie.

And how right it is that in the moment Richard Monette happened, he was absolutely the very best person for that moment. Once again, aren't we lucky?

Irene Worth as Helena in the 1953 production of All's Well That Ends Well.
Photograph by Peter Smith.

Irene Worth

Irene Worth was one of the stars of the Festival's initial season, appearing in *Richard III* and *All's Well That Ends Well.* She later returned numerous times to play roles like Rosalind and Hedda Gabler. I spoke with her in New York City in April 2001. It was the last interview she ever gave. Ms. Worth died on March 10, 2002, at the age of 86.

WORTH:

Shall I tell you what I remember of how my part of it started? Alec Guinness said to me, "You know they're going to build a new theatre in Canada. We don't know what it is or anything about it, but Tony Guthrie's been asked to direct it and create it in a way. He's asked me to join him, and I'd like you to come as well, if you would. We both would like you to come."

I said yes, of course I would. We were always, even at that time, very idealistic and our dissatisfaction with the theatre was just beginning. There was upheaval all over the world at that point in dissatisfaction with the classic theatre. We wanted a new kind of theatre and now was our chance. Alec said, "You've got to come because this will give us a chance to start a real revolution in theatre. And not in the round. It's going to be a hundred and eighty degrees." And so, of course, naturally I was thrilled to be asked.

But then the most terrible thing happened. Alec rang one Sunday. He said to come to lunch because Tony's going to be here and there's an awful lot of trouble now. And perhaps we can't go to Canada, after all. And I said, "What?" And so we all talked and Tony told us the situation. There was a tremendous financial crisis. And the money had not come in. I really didn't know the details of that, and well, it wasn't my business to know. Anyway, Tony said, "I'm afraid it's all off." And Alec said, "I have to go to New York for some business. I'll just go over into Canada and look around, see what's really happening, what the situation is."

I rang my agent immediately, who said "I'm afraid it's off. You can't go if there's no guarantee. They have not deposited a penny for you." And I said, "Well, I don't know, but Alec has shown good faith. I think I've got to show good faith as well." He said, "No, no, no!" I was sitting on my packed suitcases at that point. I said, "What shall I do?" And he said "Unpack." And I said, "I can't do that. I have to go."

And so that's how it happened really. We just went . . . with pure blind faith. And why not? Tom Patterson had faith. He had the strength of purpose and vision, and then he had the wit to choose a very brilliant man. Tony Guthrie, who was also a man of instinct. Not only talent, but instinct and faith. People in the theatre will take a chance; we'll risk a great deal many times just, just to see that perhaps an idea or a vision or something could come through.

So anyway we did, we did go. Alec came and then I arrived and I remember the afternoon when the whole town of Stratford came out to welcome us, and we stood on the top of a hill, and shook hands with, I think everybody in the town of Stratford. And, in fact, then there was a little reception after that. We were all parcelled off to various houses. It was extraordinary. You see, the community had already enveloped the actors. The friendship we made were friends for life. One never loses those old, old friends.

And we rehearsed in the exhibition grounds hall, with a tin

roof. And, of course, as it was the spring, all the little birdies were getting ready for their families. And these eggs used to fall out of the nest, and we'd find these mashed dead little baby birds everywhere. It was a nightmare. And the storms were so terrible that we had to stop rehearsals sometimes because the noise was incredible.

OUZOUNIAN:

What was it like when you moved to the tent?

WORTH:

The wonderful Skip Manley, the gentleman who was in charge of the tent, finally appeared and the tent went up. Well, that was a great moment. You can imagine. And we all went in and looked around and rehearsed in it. And then we began very serious rehearsals. I remember one night so clearly. I was sitting on one side of the tent and Tony was on the other, and neither of us could hear. We couldn't hear a thing. And I went 'round to sit with Tony, and I sat on a pile of rope—very, very thick rope. And all of a sudden I said, "Tony, I can hear the actors." And he said, "We've got to cover these steps." So he went immediately to the trustees and said, "I'm afraid you'll have . . . I know you have no money but you have to, we have to buy some coconut matting and all these steps have to be covered because the acoustics are nil." And so that's what they did. The trains went all night with coconut matting. And they covered it. It made all the difference in the world.

OUZOUNIAN:

Is it true that the people of Stratford thought the great British theatre stars were probably going to have to have limousines to take them everywhere?

WORTH:

Yes, that's the tale. I never knew about it, but Tom says—and I believe it—that my agent had said that I had to have a limo, a hairdresser, a manicurist, and, I don't know, various other things I suppose. And so I think Tom came by for me the first day to take me to rehearsal, and I said, "Are you supposed to do this every night?" And he said, "Oh yes." I said, "Well, you don't have to do that . . . couldn't I have a bicycle?" So Tom gave me a bicycle and I always bicycled all over the place. And the most lovely thing . . . I can remember so clearly, bicycling down the main street in the mornings and on the way to rehearsal, and people saying "Hello, Miss Worth. Hello. Hello. Hi, Tom. Hello, Bill . . ." And we all knew each other and wherever you went, you were welcomed.

OUZOUNIAN:
What about the end of the season, when this wonderful thing was coming to a conclusion? What did you feel like?

WORTH:
I think we left with such a euphoria that I don't think it ever occurred to us that it could have been a failure because on the opening nights, the applause was thunderous, and the audience stood to their feet and it was such an amazing experience of a genuine outpouring of affection, not only from the people who came from Canada but from the many who came from New York, as well. So it never occurred to us that it couldn't go on and wouldn't continue to succeed.

OUZOUNIAN:
Did you think Stratford would be here fifty years from that first season?

WORTH:
Oh yes. I mean it never occurred to me it wouldn't. The only trouble with an establishment that starts at the top, as it were, is that it's very hard to build on something that has such a legend from, from its first year. And I would . . . I can't imagine what could happen to it in fifty years' time. Because time moves. And people change. Cultures and visions change. And there's nothing you can do about retarding that. Nothing will

stop movement and change. The only thing I think one has to keep in mind is why was Stratford made in the first place. Quality. Simplicity. Purity. That's what's important in the theatre. And as long as actors can continue to create for that one season, for that, and not for themselves but for it, I think that then, you know, you'll have an incredible establishment that will . . . continue to inspire people.

I don't get worried about success, but I get very nervous about success. I think it's the search, not the finding that's important. And so perhaps as long as we all go on searching at Stratford it will, it will keep its marvellous buoyancy. I always think of Stratford. The first time I ever walked into Stratford, I thought this is a town that is expecting something. I felt, I felt an absolute calm and that calm, that serenity, is very important in whatever you're doing.

OUZOUNIAN:
Do you have a single memory that sums up Stratford for you?

WORTH:
The swans. I once saw the swans during the mating season, I suppose. Or they were watching their nests. Two swans that sailed around each other without ever moving their bodies from each other. Early one spring, I came back and I made Bill Needles come with me and we had to pick up swansdown. I was determined to have a Stratford swansdown pillow. We picked up all the swansdown and I, I still have that old swansdown pillow. It's very small but it's Stratford.

OUZOUNIAN:
Any other images, pictures, words, you want to say if I say to you "The Stratford Festival"?

WORTH:
The tent. I think in a way they were very clever in not changing the feeling of a tent. That tent, oh how hot it was! But it was so wonderful. And I think to act in a tent like that

was a great invention. It was very clever of them to start out with a tent, wasn't it?

I came back seven years later when the permanent building had just been done, and I came back with a friend and I took him through the front door purposefully, and into this darkened theatre, with just the lights on the stage. And he said . . . 'It's like church. Like being in church." And I said, "I'm glad you said that. I'm glad you feel that because the theatre is a holy, a holy invention." And originally it was, it was used to glorify life and the gods. And if art is not that, then there's no point in having art.

I think of Stratford, and I realize that nothing like that could happen again, because of its purity. Nobody was looking outside for fame, glory, money. I felt in a way as the early Elizabethans must have done when they began to gather their players around. We were all working for each other. And no one was working for himself. It was for the theatre. And because it's a very intoxicating thing, you know, the idea of a plan, a vision. And that's how the great leaders of the world had always begun because they had this vision. And if you have a strong enough vision—and Tom Patterson had that strength and that absolutely undiluted concentrated vision, and he knew how to get it going.

So I have the greatest respect and admiration for that theatre. I love it very much. I know it's changed, but I've changed too. Everybody changes.

Dawn Greenhalgh as Heloise in the 1978 production of Heloise and Abelard.
Photograph by Robert C. Ragsdale.

Dawn Greenhalgh

Dawn Greenhalgh has been part of Stratford for many years. As a young girl, she appeared in the two initial seasons, and then returned and married Ted Follows. She was pregnant with her daughter, Megan, during the run of *Antony and Cleopatra*, and later did work for Jean Gascon and Robin Phillips, as well. I spoke to her at the CBC Broadcast Centre in the spring of 2001.

OUZOUNIAN:
Dawn, how did you first hear about the Stratford Festival?

GREENHALGH:
I was in Montreal going to high school. Been in some high school plays. I had a wonderful teacher by the name of Eleanor Stuart, who had been invited to go to the first year of Stratford. And she recommended me to Tony Guthrie. Now Tony didn't audition people, he just met them. And this is all very exciting. So I met him at Montreal High and he said, "Right, you've got a great voice. Just what I need—you're in." And there I was—it was my first professional stage job.

OUZOUNIAN:
What is it like for a high school kid to be suddenly walking into rehearsal every day with people like Alec Guinness and Irene Worth?

GREENHALGH:
Well, you had to be very careful with Sir Alec. He didn't like any movement going on around the hall. He would be distracted easily, so you had to be very careful and quiet. It was

amazing. Irene, well, I just thought this is magic. I just thought this is perfection. I love everything about her. She is so fabulous. And we even looked a bit alike which is kind of interesting. She's had an enormous influence on my life.

OUZOUNIAN:
When she did Helena, which is potentially such an unlikeable role, she must have brought that great inner glow she has to it. Do you recall what she was like?

GREENHALGH:
She'd stand on the middle of the stage when she was suffering as the character. It was like her whole body would just sort of shake like a leaf. She was so vulnerable and beautiful in this wonderful yellow gown and it was just spellbinding. You know? Absolutely, she's one of the greatest actresses I've ever seen.

OUZOUNIAN:
What was it like to work in the shadow of Dr. Guthrie? And I mean a large shadow, right? He was how tall?

GREENHALGH:
Six foot, four inches, and he'd wear this old raincoat and his language was absolutely appalling. It used to shock everybody but I loved it. He'd pay such attention to detail. He loved it. So that even though I was just in the crowd scenes and understudying, he'd still say it was very important. And you'd be asked to do certain things right on the centre of the stage just as part of the crowd, which is what made it really exciting. You really had to be on your toes. He didn't miss a thing. So, in that respect it was, it was very exciting.

OUZOUNIAN:
When opening night came, did you know it was going to be wonderful or were you just too young to be terrified?

GREENHALGH:
Well, I knew that I personally wasn't going to make or break it!

(laughing) Let's face it. It was just so exciting to be a part of it and when we finally got it going, and it was on, it was just so thrilling.

OUZOUNIAN:

You stayed with the company and the second year . . .

GREENHALGH:

Yes, but the second year I was doing much of the same sort of thing and I was getting frustrated because I wanted to do more. And, so I left after the second year of doing much that I, that I did the first year, which was understudying and . . . you know being part of the crowd. And all of that.

OUZOUNIAN:

You went away for a while, but then you returned. What brought you back to Stratford?

GREENHALGH:

I got married at Stratford, believe it or not. I mean the first marriage that Stratford had in the company was mine to Ted Follows. We got a lot of publicity—Stratford marriage and all of that. And I remember Jason Robards gave me for a wedding present, his script of *Long Day's Journey into Night*. God, I should find it, shouldn't I? Can you imagine?

OUZOUNIAN:

That was the first time you got to work with Michael Langham. How did you find him?

GREENHALGH:

(laughs) He didn't miss a thing. Not a thing. No matter what you were doing, you know, if you were just in the crowd, if you weren't doing what you were supposed to do, "Dawn, what are you doing there?"

OUZOUNIAN:

A few years later you were in his production of Antony and Cleopatra, *playing Cleopatra's handmaiden, Charmian, and understudying Zoe Caldwell as Cleopatra. What was that like?*

GREENHALGH:

Oh, I loved Zoe. She was extraordinary. What I admired most about her was that she had such daring. She'd just do anything onstage. She was never afraid to make a fool of herself. She'd just go overboard as she needed, and then pull it down because ultimately she was very, very serious about what she was doing. But at the same time there was that enormous energy and courage, which I found so exciting.

OUZOUNIAN:

What do you think brought the two of you so close together?

GREENHALGH:

I don't know. But it's true, we were very, very close. Well, of course, I was there all the time. So she would say, how am I doing? And how are you feeling? So we really had a rapport together. You know Cleopatra spends much more time with Charmian than she does with Antony.

OUZOUNIAN:

Speaking of Antony, what was the chemistry like between Chris Plummer and Zoe?

GREENHALGH:

Oh, I think she shed a few tears now and then . . . I mean they're both extraordinary, what can I say?

OUZOUNIAN:

An added complication for you, besides doing this great emotional play with this great actor and actress, was that you were pregnant with your daughter, Megan Follows.

GREENHALGH:

Oh yes, which meant there were a couple of rather embarrassing moments of having to get off the stage fast and throwing up in those tunnels, which they call the "voms," appropriately enough.

OUZOUNIAN:
A few years later, you go back to Stratford and the child you were carrying during Antony and Cleopatra *is now playing Juliet on the Festival stage. What did it feel like for you?*

GREENHALGH:
Part of me was scared. I mean Stratford's quite the place, you know? It's tough. Let's face it. There's a lot of pressure. So part of me was like, you know . . . I hope she's doing her best. *(laughing)* And then lots of notes for her afterwards. She wasn't too pleased to get them at first, but I noticed that by opening night she'd incorporated all of them.

OUZOUNIAN:
If you could wish Stratford anything for the next fifty years, what would it be?

GREENHALGH:
I hope it just goes on forever.

OUZOUNIAN:
And when I say "The Stratford Festival" to you, what words or images come to mind?

GREENHALGH:
I guess I'd have to say "family" because not only did I grow up there, but my children did as well.

William Needles as Petruchio in the 1954 production of The Taming of the Shrew. *Photograph by Peter Smith.*

William Needles

William Needles was a part of the first season of the Festival, playing Norfolk in *Richard III*. Since then, he's been part of forty-two seasons at Stratford, as one of its most versatile performers, playing everything from the Chorus in *Henry V* to Merriman in *The Importance of Being Earnest*. I spoke to him in the Festival Theatre in the winter of 2001.

OUZOUNIAN:

Do you recall the first time you met Tyrone Guthrie?

NEEDLES :

(laughs) Oh yes, indeed I do! I went to the New Play Society on Yonge Street, just below Bloor. It was a tiny office. And they had Guthrie seated at a little deal table in a tiny chair and he was six-foot-four, you know, and he was all curled up. He was so cramped. And he looked up at me and said, "I understand you're interested in being with us this summer?" I said, "Yes sir." "You're willing to accept the same salary as the rest of us?" I remembered it wasn't very much, but knowing that they were approaching people like Guinness and Worth, I said, "Oh yes sir." "You'll learn your lines and do as you're told?" I said, "Yes sir, I will." "Very well, you're hired." I said, "Don't you want to hear me read something?" "No, I understand you're very good. Now get out!" Little did I realize that I was being hired for the next forty-two years. *(laughing)*

OUZOUNIAN:

Do you have any memories of the first day of rehearsal?

NEEDLES:

A very vivid memory really, because we were out at the Fairgrounds in front of the Pig Palace. That's where we were rehearsing. Well, the beams, the ceiling of the place was all open. It was filled with birds, twittering and pooping away. And that's where we had our first rehearsal. I remember how very, very nervous we all were, because we Canadians at that point hadn't had that much experience with Shakespeare. We'd had a lot of experience in radio and television, and very good experience, too, but we weren't trained Shakespearean actors and here we were with people like Guinness and Worth. So it was awe-inspiring, to say the least.

OUZOUNIAN:

What was it like when you moved into the tent?

NEEDLES:

I suppose my most vivid memories of that are sitting outside, watching them raising the tent over the Tanya Moiseiwitsch stage, which was just beginning to appear. And little did we realize how much that tent was going to mean to us.

We had absolutely no idea how important it was all going to be. There were lots of difficulties in the beginning—financial and otherwise, and appeals had to be made. And threats were made, as well. *(laughs)* But I think the most vivid time I had realizing that it might not work was one afternoon after rehearsal, when Guthrie came out of the tent looking terribly tired, and I said, "Dr. Guthrie, would you like a ride home?" because I was one of the few people with a car in those days. Guthrie sighed, "Did you see it written in letters of fire on my forehead? Yes, dear boy, take me home."

So we got over to his place on Norman Street and he said, "Come in!" So I went in. And back in the kitchen was Judy Guthrie, stirring a big pot of Irish stew with a cigarette hanging out of her mouth and the ashes dropping into it. *(laughs)* She said, "Tony, it's going to be a few minutes until supper is ready. Sit down and have a drink." So Guthrie and I sat there and suddenly he turned to me and he grasped my arm and he said, "You know, Needles, this whole thing could be the most dreadful disaster." And he roared with laughter. I thought "My God, what a great man he is!" He saw that it could fail. But that wasn't daunting him one little bit.

OUZOUNIAN:
That night with Guthrie, you saw the possibility for failure, but when did you know it was going to be a success?

NEEDLES:
Not until opening night. The place was packed, of course. And *Richard III* was a marvellous show. Guinness was stunning in it. So was Irene Worth as Mad Margaret. I can still hear her curses ringing in my ears. She was so fantastic. At the end there was the most stunning applause, and people were shouting, and we were laughing and crying. And I thought, "This is going to work. It really is!"

But when that season closed, I remember walking out the gravel driveway there crying because I thought, "That's it. It's all over. It may never happen again." And it might not have happened again. But had I known, I might have been crying for another reason. *(laughing)*

OUZOUNIAN:
What was Guthrie like as a director?

NEEDLES:
It was an experience that one could never forget, and I've been an actor for sixty-two years now. He could be terrifying in rehearsal, absolutely terrifying, and shout the most dreadful things. Some of which are not repeatable in mixed society. But he was dead on every time. He knew exactly what he wanted and how he was going to get it.

I remember during one rehearsal for *Oedipus*, he arrived

wearing a mackintosh with a scarf around his neck, looking quite dark. And he was racing up and down the stairs, shouting things like "You're overacting terribly. Back. All right. Never mind. All right, on. Stop. Come forward, you ladies. Can't see. Well, you silly, come forward!" And suddenly he came belting down from the auditorium, he ripped the mac off on the way down, and he had nothing but a tiny little pair of shorts on underneath. Well. He was a vast man, you know. And it was a terrifying sight, this *thing* coming hurtling toward us. And everybody was in fear and trembling. But on one of his trips back up to his wife, who always sat with him during rehearsals, she whispered to him, "Tony, do put your mac on. You're upsetting the company."

But despite the fact that he could be critical, he could also be enormously supportive. After rehearsal when you felt that you'd been belted for fair by Tony, you'd come out of the tent, dejected, down, fallen . . . and suddenly this great figure was beside you with his arm around your neck saying, "Didn't go very well this afternoon, did it? Never mind. Go home. Rehearse in the shower. The voice always sounds better there. And then come in and amaze me in the morning." *(laughing)* And you knew that he'd forgiven you.

OUZOUNIAN:

In the second season, Guthrie fired Mavor Moore early on in rehearsals of The Taming of the Shrew *and turned to you. How did that happen?*

NEEDLES:

I came out of the tent one day and there was Cecil Clarke, Guthrie's right-hand man. He said, "Dr. Guthrie would like to see you at his house for lunch." I was playing some minor role, so I said to myself, "Well he can't fire me, because I'm not doing that much." I got over to his house. He said, "Here, sit down, boy. Have a drink. I think you're going to need it. Here it is. You're playing Petruchio." Well, I nearly fainted on the spot, but he said, "Never mind, learn the lines, do as you're told and you'll be very good." Well, I wasn't very good. I've read about it in theatre books since. And they say "not a very remarkable performance." The whole production was played like an American Western, and Guthrie saw me as Harold Lloyd. But once we started rehearsing, I found that certain scenes just didn't work that way, so I came to Guthrie and I said, "Dr. Guthrie, what do I do when I have a problem?" And he said, "Well, when in doubt, dear boy, go faster." *(laughs)*

OUZOUNIAN:

A few years later you played the Chorus in Michael Langham's famous production of Henry V, *where all the French roles were played by francophone actors from Quebec. What was that like?*

NEEDLES:

Oh, it made the play work so wonderfully! They came in gleaming and shining in silver and blue, and they were the exact reverse of what we were. Poor condemned English. We certainly *were* the poor condemned English. And they were simply marvellous in the parts. I remember Guy Hoffman, who was one of their leading character actors. He was playing the governor of Harfleur. It's a tiny part. There's only four or five lines to it. But I have never forgotten him in that role because he didn't speak English. So they had to teach it to him by rote. And he was held up there on the balcony by two guys and he was trembling from head to foot, to remember it in English. But his energy and passion made it so enormously effective.

OUZOUNIAN:

Later on in your career at Stratford, you left the Festival for a while, and then returned when John Hirsch was here. How did the two of you get along?

NEEDLES:

Well, I was very close to John. I liked him very much, and I had the very good fortune of being invited over to his place occasionally. But once you were there, he didn't like to talk about the theatre. He would talk about other things, and his background was so vast and so terrifying. What he'd been through during the Holocaust was beyond belief. He would tell me the stories of how he fled from Hungary across Europe after he lost his entire family. They all died at Auschwitz. He said, "I ran, clutching a box of photographs. It was the only thing that I had left of my family." He finally made it to England, and it was there that he was adopted and taken to Canada. He was a very complex person and I know that there were a great many people who didn't like him. But I found he gave one of the most inspiring speeches I have ever heard in my life about what theatre means to the world today, where it belongs in our lives, and he was just speaking off the cuff. Because of the genius of him, all the rest was forgotten in the long run. Every now and then, people got angry with him, you know? Yes, he could make people very angry, but he was a genius.

OUZOUNIAN:

After Hirsch came John Neville. What was your experience during the Neville years like?

NEEDLES:

It was quite wonderful. I said to him early on, "John, do you think you're going to be able to use me?" He said, "Bill, as long as I'm here, you're going to be here." Well, just that one sentence put my mind at ease. Because with a family of five children and fifteen grandchildren, now it was nice to know that you had something to go to, that was in one place. Travelling around, when you have a family is not that easy, although I've done a lot of it in my lifetime, but I had this as my home base and I've always been extremely grateful for that.

OUZOUNIAN:

How do you find things now with Richard Monette?

NEEDLES:

Well, of course, I've known him since he was eighteen years old. And I've seen him do some very wonderful things that remain in my mind. I've always admired him as an actor or person, and the place is going marvellously now. He's subject to criticism; of course, anybody who is in that job is, but he does get poked at all the time. And I don't envy him that. It's an enormous job with enormous responsibility, but he's resilient as all get out.

OUZOUNIAN:

Do you have any wishes for Stratford's next fifty years?

NEEDLES:

I'd like to think there's a new generation that's ready and capable of taking over, and the place will go on to more and more success. And it's wonderful to have been able to live this long, to see it happening.

OUZOUNIAN:

When I say "The Stratford Festival," what do you think of?

NEEDLES:

Prospero's wand, which waved over a simple provincial town and made magic happen.

Bruce Swerdfager. Photographer unknown.

Bruce Swerdfager

Bruce Swerdfager came to Stratford in 1953 and acted during its first four seasons in every show, winning the first Tyrone Guthrie Award at the end of his fourth season. He later went on to a distinguished career in arts administration and management, returning to the Festival as a member of the company in 1986. I spoke to him in the Festival Theatre in the winter of 2001.

OUZOUNIAN:
Do you remember the first time you heard about the Stratford Festival?

SWERDFAGER:
I was in Ottawa, that's my hometown, and some people at the Ottawa Little Theatre mentioned that Tyrone Guthrie was coming to interview people about this Stratford Festival. I said, "Stratford Festival?" and they explained what was going on and all about Tom Patterson and so on. And I said, "I'd love to meet Guthrie, he's one of the greatest directors in the world," and so I was able to organize it that I had an interview with Guthrie. And it was just that—an interview. He didn't audition people.

OUZOUNIAN:
What did you and Guthrie talk about?

SWERDFAGER:
I told him about some of the Shakespearean parts I had played and mentioned that I was a salesman for Remington Rand at

the time, in the office machinery business. Guthrie asked, "Well, if I offered you a place at Stratford, what would you do about your job?" I told him I thought that maybe I could organize a leave of absence, and he said, "It's going to be eleven weeks, you know, with rehearsal and playing." And I said, "Let me see what I can do." So I went back to the office and told my sales manager, who in turn phoned the national sales manager, and I remember his reply, "Oh, let the young man do it. It'll be broadening for him." So there I was. Coming to Stratford. *(laughs)*

OUZOUNIAN:

What was the feeling about the Festival? Were people afraid it was going to fail?

SWERDFAGER:

Oh yes. Everyone was wondering if this thing would work, you know? Would it really come off? I mean wow, what are we all doing here and in a tent? Come on. Everyone sort of wondered if the whole darned thing wouldn't just fall apart.

OUZOUNIAN:

Was there one particularly dark moment?

SWERDFAGER:

Evidently there was a dark moment with the administration and the raising of funds at one time. There was a great shortage of funds to be able to carry on. But they did a weekend blitz and were able to get some major donations. The First Mutual Insurance here was one of them. And the other was from the Massey family.

OUZOUNIAN:

Having survived all that darkness, when did you start to think it was going to work?

SWERDFAGER:

Oh, on opening night. Opening night was the most incredible

thing you ever saw. I don't think Canadians ever saw anything like this before. They had gone to Broadway, but this was still better than that. It was better than anything they'd ever seen. And right from the moment Guinness jabbed his dagger and said, "Now is the winter of our discontent," right until the end, it was a magnificent audience. Then at the end, it was instant. They stood and they did not stop applauding. I recall we used to come out in a group and then the next group and so on. And we all stood and while they applauded, it went on and on. And then finally Guinness came out, and then there was a bigger roar than ever. And then we would all peel off and I remember running down the tunnel, and round and back up and then the stage manager—who was Jack Merigold, I believe—said "On!" And on we'd go and do it all again. And they still applauded and cheered. Off down the tunnel, up and around. And I recall after three times or so, Guinness saying, "They've got to stop!" And we went on again, and the applause just continued, continued, continued. Finally, Guinness stopped them. And he said a few words. He thanked them for coming to the opening of the Festival and what a wonderful kickoff it had been and so on. But he wanted to thank the one person most responsible for all of this. And I said to myself "I wonder if it's going to be Guthrie or Patterson. Who will he really pick?" And he said "William Shakespeare." *(laughs)* It was the perfect end to a magnificent evening.

OUZOUNIAN:
How important did you feel Guthrie's contribution was?

SWERDFAGER:
Well, he was probably the key to the whole success. You know it was a time in his life when he wanted to do something new—he wanted new horizons and was always looking to be challenged. And the idea of doing Shakespeare on a stage similar to that which he wrote his plays for, he thought was

very challenging indeed. And in the end, the idea of Shakespeare in the middle of the cornfields of Ontario I guess appealed to him a great deal indeed. *(laughing)*

I think of that incredible personality and dynamic that he had, his ability to direct people, and to inspire them at the right time. We were very lucky to hit him at the right time. I mean there was more than luck to it all. Don't misunderstand me. But it was still amazing that it worked when you think of all the things that could have gone wrong.

I remember at the first rehearsal, he spoke to us and said, "Now I do want you all to have your opinion. I want to hear everything you say and I want you to be certain to speak out . . . just so long as I have the last word."

OUZOUNIAN:
How did you feel at the end of the season?

SWERDFAGER:
Well, near the end of the season, I got a big cheque from Remington Rand, even though I was on a leave of absence. It was the commission on a whole roomful of typewriters I had sold to the High School of Commerce in Ottawa just before I started working at Stratford. All of a sudden, I received this wonderful amount of money. More money than I'd made all season from the theatre. And I said, "Am I crazy? Do I really want to go into this business?" And I did. I wanted to try it. I would never have been happy if I hadn't.

OUZOUNIAN:
So you came back to Stratford?

SWERDFAGER:
I was in all the shows the first four years. I was fortunate enough to become one of the first Tyrone Guthrie Award winners—along with Bill Hutt.

OUZOUNIAN:
What would you like Stratford to do in the next fifty years?

SWERDFAGER:
I would like it to carry on as it is. It has learned to do things other than Shakespeare and that's very important. Back when Michael Langham added a fourth play to the season when we used to do only three, I was company manager at the time. I said, "Michael that's going to be an awful lot of additional costs to do another whole show." And he said, "Bruce, Shakespeare has his valleys and his hills and he goes up and down. If this company is only known for Shakespeare when he's down, then they're going to be in trouble. So we have to know how to do more than Shakespeare." And he was so right.

OUZOUNIAN:
As somebody who started out here as a young actor, has lived here, and seen the Festival over all the years, what words come to mind to describe Stratford?

SWERDFAGER:
Caring. The community is a caring community. It's a wonderful community in which to live, and the Festival, of course, is superb.

OUZOUNIAN:
When you think back on fifty years, what comes to mind?

SWERDFAGER:
When I left my job selling something solid like typewriters to work for something as shaky as the Stratford Festival, everybody thought I was crazy. Well, look at things now. Who would have guessed that the Stratford Festival would outlast the typewriter?

William Shatner as Lucentio in the 1954 production of The Taming of the Shrew.
Photograph by Peter Smith and Co.

William Shatner

Although best known as the intrepid Captain Kirk from *StarTrek*, Montreal-born William Shatner's career began on the stage in Canada. He first appeared on the Festival Stage as Lucentio in the 1954 production of *The Taming of the Shrew*, and he also played Gratiano in *The Merchant of Venice* and Gloucester in *Henry V* during the three seasons he spent at the Festival.
I spoke to him in Los Angeles in February 2001.

OUZOUNIAN:
What's the very first thing you remember hearing about the Stratford Festival?

SHATNER:
I was asked to be in the first season of this new theatre that was taking place west of Toronto, but I'd also been offered a job at the Canadian Repertory Theatre in Ottawa. Well, I decided to go with the CRT, thinking that it was more likely to survive than this new Stratford thing. My judgement has not improved since then.

OUZOUNIAN:
But did they open the door again for you to come back for the second season?

SHATNER:
Indeed. The second season they asked me back and this time, I accepted.

OUZOUNIAN:
When you met Tyrone Guthrie, what was your first impression?

SHATNER:

I've a very vivid recollection. We seated on the stage, on the first day of rehearsal, I quivering with excitement and nervousness, seated on one of the steps, that surrounded the thrust stage. I believe it still is the same construction. But at that time it was a tent. And the rake of the auditorium was very steep. And the flap of the tent—this giant circus tent that was opaquely lit by the sun—the flap opened up and it was as though somebody had shot a beam of light down through the staircase, and I was the recipient of the beam of light. And shadowed coming down that steep rake, came Zeus, preceded by Zeus's belly and then Zeus's nose, for those were the two most prominent features of Tyrone Guthrie. And he was, he was six-foot-four, I think. He was a tall man and I was immersed in Greek mythology at the time. And so it was to me somebody coming off Mount Olympus as he descended. I never got over that impression.

But he could also be very down to earth and enjoy a good laugh. I remember that when I played Lucentio in *The Taming of the Shrew*, he had them dress me in a straw hat, white pants, and black patent leather shoes. Now I'd been an athlete in school, so balance on the balls of the feet was natural to me. And my feet were always moving. The black patent shiny leather shoes were always moving. You can see yourself moving, and there's a pattern of light, a pattern of motion in the, in the patent leather shoes. Guthrie loved watching me moving around like that. It made him laugh, and he told me that I had "happy feet." I always remember that.

OUZOUNIAN:

How did it feel to join the company in the second season?

SHATNER:

I had no classical background at all, and I felt intimidated by all these people who knew each other. And had all this theatre background and . . . and they spoke so well, I knew nothing. I was a raw kid out of Montreal who had acted in amateur theatre and college, and then that one season at the Canadian Repertory Theatre. I didn't know very much and I didn't know anybody. I didn't know the gossip. I didn't know who was doing what to whom in that intricate gossip pattern that existed among the very tightly knit group of people who were at Stratford. I was on the outside looking in almost the whole time. For me, almost the whole time. I never really became a member of the pack, and I remember that ostracism to this day.

OUZOUNIAN:
The leading actor in your first summer was James Mason. What do you remember about him?

SHATNER:
I remember his struggle with the role of Oedipus. Here was a man whose physical beauty was just incredible. As a young leading man on film, he was just beautiful. And then as he aged, he aged so well. I mean he was just a glorious man to look at. So here was a guy who'd made his living with his face, and to cover him up with a mask as Guthrie did in *Oedipus Rex*, meant that he had to rely on his voice, which he really wasn't accustomed to using. So it was a struggle for him.

He was very kind to me, though. I remember him very fondly, and at the time it meant a great deal to me to be accepted by someone in his position. It taught me a lesson ever since: the lasting impression you make by just saying "Good morning."

OUZOUNIAN:
Guthrie was known for giving challenges to his actors. What's the most outrageous thing he ever asked you to do?

SHATNER:
He asked me to spit on Frederick Valk. Frederick Valk was a noble, bald-headed, renowned, international actor, playing

Shylock in *The Merchant of Venice*, and I was playing this tough street guy, Gratiano. And we had a crowd scene together where I was reviling Shylock, and one day Guthrie called out, "Spit on him. Spit on him, Bill." I said, "Spit on him?" So I made this half-hearted attempt and went "Pffft," and Guthrie was furious. He said, "No Bill, I said spit on him. *Really* spit on him."

So, in performance, I cleared my throat, hauled off and went "Aggggghhhhhhhhhhhkkkkkkkkk!" Now, Frederick Valk had a leonine head and he used to emote with his mouth wide open. He'd stand there with his jaw just hanging open. And I watched this thing from my mouth go "wh wh wh wh wh wh whap" across the stage and land right in his mouth. Guthrie never asked me to do it again.

OUZOUNIAN:

The next season, Chris Plummer joined the company. Did you know him from Montreal?

SHATNER:

Peripherally. Everywhere I went, every theatre I went to, he had played in. And everyone would say, "Oh, you should have been here when Chris was here. He was so wonderful!" I was always following him, even at the Canadian Repertory Theatre. Christopher Plummer. So he was a magical name to me and when I met him, he lived up to all his publicity.

You have to understand how glamorous he seemed to me. He played the piano. He played tennis, wearing those tennis sweaters and shorts, and he had these great legs and he was slick and he was an *actor*, in the Barrymore tradition. Just like Barrymore, he had this marvellous profile, and he always turned it sideways towards you. He came from three streets away from where I did in Montreal, but he somehow had acquired all this *panache*. I don't know where he got it from. But he got it. He was the great young actor. He was the great young promise. And he was there to play Henry the Fifth.

OUZOUNIAN:
What was his Henry like? What do you remember from it?

SHATNER:
It was full of the verve and excellence and enunciation and drama and style that Chris always has. All those things. He was extraordinary.

OUZOUNIAN:
That summer, Plummer got sick, and you were his understudy, so you had to play Henry the Fifth . . .

SHATNER:
. . . and it was one of the highlights of my life. I look back on it and I think, "What in heaven's name was I doing?" *(laughs)* I was playing Henry's brother, Gloucester, and when they offered me the part, they said, "We'd like you to understudy Henry the Fifth, as well." I said, "Wow, understudy to Chris Plummer? I'm not sure about that . . ." and they assured me "This is just a courtesy, because understudies do not go on for twenty-five hundred people who have paid a lot of money and come from all over the world to see Christopher Plummer, so I wouldn't depend on going on, young man."

Well, I kind of loved the role and before I came to Stratford, I used to study my little copy of the script and I'd learn the lines: "Once more unto the breach, dear friends . . ." Then, once the season opened I asked, "When do we have the understudy rehearsals?" And they told me they did them after we opened the third play, in about three or four weeks' time. So I'd go home to my little digs, and I'd *really* learn my lines. I'd say them out loud in the toilet 'cause that's the best place, quietest place. If you have a room, if you're renting a room from somebody in Stratford, there's a whole family, you know, so the only place you have any peace and quiet is to occupy the john. So I learned my lines on the toilet.

Sometimes, I'd take walks with another young actor in the

company named Don and he'd help me with my lines. He had a phenomenal memory, and any time anybody fumbled with a line in any play, instead of the stage manager prompting you as needed, Don would know exactly, and he'd give you the words. Don knew every word of every play we were doing.

Anyway, one day I was in the village somewhere and I got word that they wanted to speak to me in the office right away, urgent. I rushed down wondering what I had done, and they said, "Plummer is sick. Are you capable of going on as Henry the Fifth?" I said, "But we've never had an understudy rehearsal." In fact, I'd never even seen the whole play, only the scenes I was in. But I took the chance and said, "I think I can go on."

They tried to call a rehearsal right away to show me the staging. It's now about four o'clock in the afternoon. So they started calling around, but they couldn't find most of the actors, so they abandoned that idea. So seven o'clock, seven-thirty, I'm in the theatre. And they're dressing me. And Chris's clothes were not quite wide enough in the shoulders and too loose in the belly. But somehow they made them fit. And I remember Michael Langham coming up and saying, "Can you do this?" "I can do this." And on I went.

And the muse was with me. I just went on and said the words in the way I had remembered them in the bathroom. And it worked out. And I have no idea how. I have no consciousness. I was not nervous, except at the end of the battle of Agincourt, when I suddenly dried. I couldn't remember the next line. And I'm in the middle of a thrust stage. And there's nobody around that can help me. Then I looked over. I saw my friend, good old Don who knew every line. He had taken over my part, Gloucester, Henry's brother. So I walked over to him, put my arm around his shoulders and whispered, "What's the line?" He just looked at me—I remember he had long blond eyelashes that went up like that—and his eyes just rolled back in his head and he was tongue-tied. So I thought, oh my God, there's no help here. I turned around and walked back and then the line came to me. And off I went and played right through to the end of the show without a hitch.

There happened to be some critics in the audience, and the next day, there were write-ups all across Canada: "Understudy goes on for Plummer." It was a big thing. And some of them even mentioned the great piece of staging, when an exhausted Henry the Fifth goes over to his brother, puts his arm around his shoulders, and then walks away.

(laughs) Oh, the gods were with me!

OUZOUNIAN:
Do you have any wishes for Stratford's second fifty years?

SHATNER:
My memory of everyone connected with Stratford is one of great enthusiasm, of passion, of love for each other and for the work at hand. If they could retain and sustain those passions, that'll keep the theatre in the limelight.

OUZOUNIAN:
What comes to your mind when I say "The Stratford Festival"?

SHATNER:
Joy. Music. Tinkling of bells.

Michael Langham

Photograph by Peter Smith.

Michael Langham was brought to Stratford by Tyrone Guthrie in 1955 to direct *Julius Caesar* and he stayed through 1967 as artistic director. He has been behind some of the Festival's greatest productions, including *Love's Labour's Lost*, *Cyrano de Bergerac*, and *Antony and Cleopatra*. After years in charge of the Guthrie Theatre in Minneapolis and the Julliard School in Manhattan, he has frequently returned to Stratford, both as a guest director and as the first artistic director of the Young Company.

Helen Burns

Helen Burns as Marjory Pinchwife in the 1964 production of The Country Wife. *Photograph by Peter Smith and Co.*

Helen Burns came to Stratford with Michael Langham, her husband, and first appeared as Nerissa in Guthrie's production of *The Merchant of Venice*. Some of her other memorable roles include Jaquenetta in *Love's Labour's Lost*, Hermia in *A Midsummer Night's Dream*, and Mrs. Pinchwife in *The Country Wife*.
I spoke to them in Los Angeles in February 2001.

OUZOUNIAN:
What made you come to the Stratford Festival?

LANGHAM:
Tony Guthrie. It was at a time in our careers when things were going very well for both of us, particularly for Helen, in the British theatre, and I wasn't doing too badly as a young director. But Tony persuaded us that we should go to Canada. We didn't know anything about Canada, but he made us feel this something that was really unavoidably our responsibility to do.

BURNS:
Yes, it was hard to resist him. We didn't really know what he was talking about. I mean it sounds rude to say this but we didn't know where Stratford, Ontario, was. And the idea of doing Shakespeare in the middle of Ontario scared us, but Tony went on and on until we almost felt that Canada would collapse if we didn't go and save it.

OUZOUNIAN:
Michael, when Tony talked to you about coming over to Stratford, had he made it clear he wanted you to succeed him after his time there?

LANGHAM:
Yes, and that was a tremendous honour, because I'd admired him so much, not only as a human being but also because he was a sort of icon as a director for me. And that had a huge effect on our decision: will we go for it? Well, we did, and we had regrets sometimes, I mean, they weren't the happiest of years to start with, they were very difficult years. We were highly suspect. The British Raj coming in and all that. Also, Tony was a difficult person to follow. You know, he'd been sort of the paternal figure over there but here was this young man coming in, and I had to learn about the stage and I'd never worked fully on a thrust stage.

When I got to Stratford, I found that stage very, very difficult and I fought it for the first years. I resisted it, and it took me quite a few years I began to realize that I had to accept it and go with it and sort of marry it.

OUZOUNIAN:

People now speak of you as the master of working on that stage and understanding it. When did the breakthrough come?

LANGHAM:

I guess it came with *Love's Labour's Lost*, when I really began to feel that I could meld it to my own purposes and realized really that it would serve me, it would serve what I wanted to do. And from then on I enjoyed it. But the initial years were tough.

BURNS:

I found it a wonderful piece of wood to act on. And it meant you really had to listen, because whether you were listening or talking, you were in full view of the audience. And so people who listened had to really exert a great deal of energy listening, and understanding. And wanting to communicate. It was an extraordinary experience.

OUZOUNIAN:

Once Tony had left and you were well and truly in charge, what drove you those first few years?

LANGHAM:

To save it from collapse. I mean it had its birth, which was spectacular. And then it had to go through natural teething problems. As Tony used to say, "You know, one day it will be a cat. While it's a kitten, people will be very attracted by it. But after that, be careful."

Well, it was very attractive in the tent. The tent had a romanticism to it in itself. But it was a question of surviving when the sort of wonder was over. It had a lapse and I was in charge at that time. And that was hard to fight. We just had to stick to it.

The first year I was in charge, we did the *Henry V* that other people still talk of with a great deal of affection, partly because it was a romantic interpretation of the future of Canada. The peace conference at the end of the play was about the two nations marrying each other and really coming together, the two national cultures. I did another production of *Henry V* ten years later, when the whole atmosphere of Canada had been completely changed, and we did the peace conference at the end of the play with real sort of venomous snakelike animosity between the two nations, because that seemed to be reflecting the country we were in.

OUZOUNIAN:

That first Henry V *marked the first time you worked with Christopher Plummer, but over the years you did a lot of his hallmark shows—* Hamlet, Cyrano de Bergerac, Antony and Cleopatra— *why do you feel you and he worked together so well?*

LANGHAM:

I admired him and I thought I was able to exploit certain aspects of Chris that I find attractive. I've always said to him that he's probably ideally cast as the victim of events, rather than the master of events. And he's such a genuine romantic.

There was one moment when he played Cyrano that I'll never forget. It was just one moment, but it was a magical moment. It was when the doors were thrown open at the end of the first act and Cyrano sees Paris.

And Chris at that moment was utterly breathtaking. Well, his communication of the vision he saw of Paris was one of those moments you think—this is, this is always to be remembered, this magic.

OUZOUNIAN:

Cyrano de Bergerac *is one of those shows that you've gone back to many times over the years. Why does it speak to you so much?*

LANGHAM:

It appeals to me to do a play about someone who has standards and doesn't believe in the cheap route of most commercial life. Cyrano does stand for a certain philosophy, highly romanticized certainly, but resolute in its anti-phoniness. And it doesn't matter if you're ugly, as long as you're true to yourself. A human being's outer part, the skin, however beautiful, is nothing. It's the content that was interesting. And that was why he's written as a sort of ugly man in a way.

OUZOUNIAN:

Why do you think Love's Labour's Lost *is another one of your "signature" plays?*

LANGHAM:

Probably because it was the first play of Shakespeare's that I directed ever, where I felt I could hear, genuinely hear, the voice of the author. And felt I was able to hear it in the production I was putting on.

We did all the rehearsing in the small room upstairs at Stratford. We didn't bring it onto the stage for a long time. I felt it was so delicate, I didn't want to go into the big space, because everyone will start pushing like mad to reach the back seats, and I just wanted the thing to settle down on that stage and to breathe more deeply and to reach the back seats without any pushing of any kind. The play and the production were much loved by all of us and it made the world of difference to my confidence. And that was a turning point. After that, things changed and it became a glorious place to work in, and a very good company, very rich company, developed in all ages, and they were very good years.

OUZOUNIAN:

Was there a downside as well for the company during those years?

LANGHAM:

There seemed to be in those years the need for a lot of drink to be consumed. It became part of the Stratford scene for the actor. It was a macho thing. Well, there wasn't much to do outside the work. And so what could you do but just develop your capacity for the amount of booze you could hold. And this became a bit of a problem.

It wasn't just a problem with the actors; it was a problem with first night audiences, as well. In fact, we used to have a debate at board meetings as to whether it was better to have the party before the show, which if you did, meant the actors were faced with half an audience that was dead drunk. Or whether we should have the party afterwards, in which case, the road accidents were increased. And I facetiously said my contention was to get death out of the theatre and back on the roads where it belongs.

BURNS:

It was strange, the business of the alcoholism. It became . . . was sort of like a proud defiance. It was as though it was saying, we're tough.

OUZOUNIAN:

Did the Festival take a personal toll on you, as well?

LANGHAM:

Stratford was a difficult mistress to work for, to be responsible for. And it didn't do very good things for our private life. You can't say Stratford broke up our marriage. I broke up our marriage, but the pressures of Stratford were part of the picture behind that event. We got married again since. We enjoy getting married to each other very much.

BURNS:

In fact, we would like to do it all over again.

OUZOUNIAN:

What made you finally decide to leave Stratford after being the artistic director for eleven years?

LANGHAM:

I had actually wanted to leave earlier, but there was a disagreement over the succession, and I agreed to stay on for another three or four years after that.

BURNS:

It was too long.

LANGHAM:

Yes, it was a bit too long, but everything was going very well, was making money, without doing things on the cheap in any way or putting on potboilers. When I did finally leave I was proud of what we had done.

OUZOUNIAN:

Helen, what would you like to wish for the Stratford Festival for its next fifty years?

BURNS:

I think it needs passion and a dedication to the playwright. If you're going to be doing Shakespeare, then the job is to be true to the playwright and true to the audience and making flowers flourish where before there were none. It's a matter of gardening, planting the right seeds. I'd love to see many young people associated with the theatre. Small productions . . . and the schools being brought in. So that they learn that they actually do possess something that is of value. That's what I'd like to see.

OUZOUNIAN:

Michael, your wish for the next fifty years?

LANGHAM:

I think what Helen says is difficult to better, but this is another thing to put beside it. I think that Shakespeare—and Stratford is primarily meant to be about Shakespeare—does go in and out of fashion. We have been through a fantastic period of development in the past seventy years, of rediscovering

Shakespeare in a way that was closer to what he was about in his own time than anything that ever happened before that. And that was amazing.

But now it's time to waken a new excitement, and that will be the challenge of the next fifty years.

OUZOUNIAN:

What do you think of when I say "The Stratford Festival"?

LANGHAM:

When Tony Guthrie asked us to come to Stratford, we thought, "The middle of Ontario? What are we going to find there?" Well, we found enormous love and creativity.

Tony van Bridge as Falstaff in the 1967 production of The Merry Wives of Windsor.
Photograph by Peter Smith.

Tony Van Bridge

Tony Van Bridge came to Stratford in 1955, and worked there frequently over the next twenty-one seasons. His greatest roles included Falstaff in *Henry IV*, *Parts 1 & 2* as well as in *The Merry Wives of Windsor*, Bottom in *A Midsummer Night's Dream*, and Dogberry in *Much Ado About Nothing*.
I spoke to him in Niagara-on-the-Lake in the spring of 2001.

OUZOUNIAN:
Do you recall how you first actually came to the Stratford Festival?

VAN BRIDGE:
I was one of the last people who came on a boat, I think, to start with. And I wasn't really coming to the Stratford Festival. I was just coming to Canada. It was one of those . . . one of those dramatic moments in your life when you think—what am I going to do? So we immigrated, came to Canada, and one of the first people I met when I arrived was Tony Guthrie, and he invited me to join the Festival.

OUZOUNIAN:
By then, it was the third year in the tent. What was it like performing there?

VAN BRIDGE:
(laughing) It was hair-raising sometimes. A storm or a strong wind would blow and you really thought the whole thing was going to fall on you sometimes. It was really quite alarming, I must say. And old Skip Manley, the tent master, every now and

again, he'd go around the tent with something that looked like a sword blade. Sort of slashing at it, to let the water through. I mean, he treated it like a ship. If there was a pool of water gathering in an ominous place, he'd just jump up and slash it then and there, even in the middle of a performance. He knew his tent, I must say. He was very good with it.

A lot of people were sentimental about the tent, but I think it was a good job when we got rid of it. Because everything came through . . . trains, rain, wind—the whole lot!

OUZOUNIAN:

Your first show at Stratford was Julius Caesar, *which you worked on with Michael Langham, and you did a lot of shows with him over the years. How would you describe your relationship?*

VAN BRIDGE:

It was very good. I got on very well with him. He was tough at times when he wanted to be. But always with good, good purpose. He never ranted for any particular bad reason. And he'd always have some nice little turn that would help get you into your role. I was in *Troilus and Cressida* for him, playing Ajax, and I wasn't getting it right. So he came onto the stage in rehearsal one day, with a perfectly straight face and said, "Tony, rehearse it with a monocle." I said, "What?" "A monocle, you know, put a monocle in your eye and rehearse it." And I did. Everybody thought it was screamingly funny and all that. But it started me working with a different tone of voice, a whole British send-up. And it turned out to make the plot work.

Langham was a unique kind of chap. He was shot down very early in the war, and spent years in a horrible prison camp. That's where he started working on theatre, directed *King Lear* with the prisoners. He had years to do it, so he would work it out carefully in his mind, one piece at a time.

Calm, methodical, precise—maybe just a bit frosty.

OUZOUNIAN:

You were also being directed by Guthrie at the same time in The Merchant of Venice. *Was that a different experience?*

VAN BRIDGE:

Oh yes, it was. Guthrie was a showman, and when he was directing he would make a show of it. I don't mean to say that it was insincere. It wasn't, but it was his way of directing and he would have all sorts of wonderful little lines that he would come out with. His famous line to any actor who couldn't think fast enough on his feet was "Well, think of something and astonish us with it in the morning." And so the whole thing had a showmanship touch about it.

Whereas Langham was more as if he was still in that prison camp to a certain extent. It was what he had spent the war working out. He always walked about with the text of the play, but he knew it absolutely inside out. And appeared to be very serious when he was directing, a much more direct attitude towards the play than Guthrie seemed to have. And yet, one wouldn't put one before the other in any sense. They're both extraordinarily valuable people to have had in the theatre. And for Stratford to have had Guthrie to start with, followed on by Langham is one of the most, greatest pieces of luck I can think of. It was interesting, of course, because Guthrie picked Langham to follow him and they were different, complementary, it was maybe like we begin with the fire and then we'll go on to the music, that sort of thing.

OUZOUNIAN:

How was it to be a part of Guthrie's production of Oedipus Rex*?*

VAN BRIDGE:

It was very interesting. I enjoyed that. Very much. He's very good to work with. I played the old shepherd who came in with an important piece of news. And I remember it was the first thing of any substance that I'd done at Stratford, so I was really nervous. And I had—in true Guthrie fashion—to make an entrance, not from the back stage or anything like that, but from the top of one of the aisles at the back of the audience so that the whole entrance was down a flight of steps. I was in a long woolly gown and I used to think, "Oh Lord, I'm going to finish up like a ball of wool in this thing, at the bottom of the stairs" but I didn't. It was all right. I was wearing a big mask, too, and that thing was covering everything. Could hardly see out of it.

But my real nervousness, I have to confess, was because the cast had told me that the part had the only laugh in the play, and they kept pulling my leg about it saying "You've got to get the laugh, you know?" So I came in, not only encumbered by this gown and the mask and everything, but also by this terrible feeling. I felt I wanted to run away from the theatre immediately. However I got onto the stage, I opened my mouth and I said this line, which I can't remember now at all. And it got an enormous laugh and I don't know whether I grinned or what I did but I was so pleased I forgot to act for about two or three minutes . . . and Guthrie would have said that was a good thing.

OUZOUNIAN:

When the company left the tent and finally moved into the permanent theatre, how did you find that?

VAN BRIDGE:

I found it good to play in. I found it easier to play in than an ordinary theatre, because Tanya's stage is so centring. It's really a very small stage. The thing that makes Stratford work is the fact that this tiny little pill is the centre of everything, and it concentrates everybody's attention on the actor. It's very important when you're doing Shakespeare to know that everybody can see you and that they're all looking at you.

OUZOUNIAN:

A few years later, you played one of the greatest roles in the theatre: Falstaff in Henry IV, Parts I & II. *Do you recall how it came about?*

VAN BRIDGE:

It was first offered to me by Michael in the corridor outside the canteen in Stratford. He came up and said, "Oh Tony, wanted to see you. We're going to do *Henry IV* next year. I'd like you to play Falstaff, okay?" By the time I couldn't recover myself enough to say "Yes," he's gone. *(laughing)* That's an incredible line to say to an actor—"I want you to play Falstaff." But then he scooted off as if he'd just said, "I want you to play the third soldier on the left" *(laughing)*.

It was one of those parts that you could get frightened by, but the size of it stops you from getting frightened. The length of the part and the size of it. The fact that it's always there through both plays. He's at his hottest in Part I, and then in Part II he's simmering down because he's getting really a bit past it, and he's no longer as funny to the prince as he was, all that kind of thing. So that by the end of that, while he's banished by the prince, told to just get out of his way and all that, it hurts him enormously and he tries to pretend it's not there.

This man who was always saying "Here I am!" is suddenly pushed aside by everybody, and it's not difficult to play but it does tend to make you cringe a little as a person because you really feel that there's nothing left. There really is nowhere, nowhere else to go. I often likened it to an old actor who's played a lot of big parts but doesn't get them anymore. Now I'm half jokingly likening it to myself, but it's not a pleasant experience for that to happen to a person, to somebody like Falstaff who was an actor, who was a big actor. He knew it. Everybody loved his performance in the early part. He was much loved by, by the riffraff that he surrounded himself with.

And they tried to pass it on to the lords in the second part too. Tried to make everybody think that he was a wonderful man. And his own discovery of the fact that he's not, is really the death of him. It's a part that I enjoyed playing more than anything else.

OUZOUNIAN:
What would you wish the Stratford Festival for their next fifty years?

VAN BRIDGE:
All the best, of course, naturally. And I wish that they continue to give us Shakespeare on a good scale, and keep it in balance with whatever else is done.

OUZOUNIAN:
When I say "The Stratford Festival" to you, what words come to mind?

VAN BRIDGE:
Guthrie. Langham. I was extremely lucky to have had those two men following each other in that theatre.

Christopher Plummer as Antony in the 1967 production of Antony and Cleopatra.
Photograph by Douglas Spillane.

Christopher Plummer

Christopher Plummer first appeared at Stratford in 1956 in the title role of *Henry V*. He later went on to star in *Hamlet*, *Macbeth*, *Cyrano de Bergerac*, *Antony and Cleopatra*, and *Barrymore*. In the Fiftieth Anniversary Season, he returned in the title role of *King Lear*.

I spoke with Plummer on the stage of the Stratford Festival Theatre in June 2000. He sported his trademark tan and was casually elegant in a charcoal sweater and grey slacks.

OUZOUNIAN:

Do you recall what you thought the very first time you ever heard about the Stratford Festival?

PLUMMER:

I was astounded. I think everybody was. And everybody across Canada immediately wanted to be here, because for the first time we had an international kind of theatre of our own, and we all wanted to work with the great Tyrone Guthrie.

I was already an actor. I was earning a good living in Montreal on radio as well as stage, but I auditioned for Tony Guthrie for the second season. A friend of mine, Dick Gilbert, and I did a scene from *Julius Caesar* at our high school and Guthrie came and he was very nice. We worked on it like hell and we thought we did pretty well because we were both experienced actors and we threw our hearts into it and he said at the end, you know the way he speaks *(imitating Guthrie)*, "Very nice, very good work, we'll let you know, thank you."

So we all went away hopeful, but then many months went by and they didn't even answer or say that we saw your audition, thank you very much, perhaps another year . . . nothing. And then I realized that an old radio producer in Montreal who I'd worked for, who thought I was having an affair with his wife, had spread such terrible rumours about my behaviour and lack of discipline and that I was a drunk. "Don't use that young man, he's just totally unreliable!" That sort of thing.

Guthrie took this to heart, he took it seriously, as I suppose anybody would, for God's sake, since half of it was true. Except I was not having an affair with that man's wife. I *was* having an affair with a lot of other people, but not his wife. This man, by the way, was a well-known radio producer for the CBC—I will not mention his name, but many people will know whom I'm talking about—and he was very useful to Guthrie in casting plays because he knew every actor in Canada. So, of course, Guthrie listened to him.

So that was my opening experience with Stratford and it wasn't until I had a success on Broadway, three years later, in *The Lark* with Julie Harris that they finally came around and it was Michael Langham actually. That was his second year and he came around and said, "Come on, I want you to head the company as Henry the Fifth for next year," which I was much readier for three years later than I would have been initially.

I was actually the first young Canadian to lead the company, because up to that time they had stars come over like Alec Guinness, Irene Worth, James Mason, Frederick Valk, and all those sort of people from England. But I was the first time they had a Canadian leading man and I had that scary responsibility.

OUZOUNIAN:

You performed in the last year of the legendary tent. What were the pros and cons of working in it?

PLUMMER:

Oh, I adored the tent, and unfortunately, when it left, I still think an awful lot of the adventure and excitement and spirit of this place went with it. I don't mean to say that it isn't marvellous now, or anything like that, but those early years were glorious years because it was new. It was an experiment. They didn't know if it was ever going to take off. Even in 1956, with me walking onto the stage it certainly could have closed. *(laughs)*

But I wouldn't miss those days for the world because the tent represented a not-permanent feeling, which made us work all the harder and better, I think, and made us compete with each other like being in an arena, and the spirit was extraordinary.

Also, that last year of the tent we had possibly the best season that Canada has ever seen in the theatre with the French Canadian company, Le Theatre du Nouveau Monde, and the English boys on the same stage at the same time—they talking their own language at times and we talking in English—it was perhaps the last time that we were ever to see the formation of a truly national theatre in this country.

Boy, that was an emotional year! The two languages on the same stage—not only politically, but emotionally and nationally—it was an extraordinary feeling. When we took it to the Edinburgh Festival, it didn't have quite the same impact, because the people there probably couldn't care less about the differences between the French and English here.

Sadly, it has been repeated here, but not to that extraordinary extent, and I wish to God that it would come back, and one day, we *must* have a National Theatre here, with both languages playing at different times in the same theatre.

OUZOUNIAN:

Were the audiences receptive to it?

PLUMMER:

Oh yes, oh God yes! They got it. Don't forget we had a very international audience in those days, because it was all new and novel and it was covered by all the press. The critics from New York—the *Times*, the *Herald Tribune*—the *Times* from London. We had critics from all over the world coming to our opening nights. That doesn't happen anymore, sadly, but it did then.

And a lot of New York and London were sitting out there in the audience. I mean, all the people from the theatre certainly were. And so this was like an audition platform, because you were actually acting in front of Broadway producers who were sitting out there. Alan Jay Lerner used to come here all the time and Alexander Cohen, all the top guys came here. Roger Stevens came to see my Hamlet the next season, the year that this theatre was built, and I was determined to give him a good Hamlet to bring to New York. And I thought, "Here I am, the Dane of the moment!" *(laughs)*

Of course, Roger had gone to one of those disastrous opening night parties the night before and he was still over with Siobhan McKenna in her house celebrating the next day. We had a matinee of *Hamlet*, which he entirely missed because they were still celebrating the party of the night before, drunker than lords, all singing Irish shanties to each other while I was working my butt off on this stage. Those are good, good early years.

OUZOUNIAN:
With Henry V, *what kind of interpretation did you and Michael Langham work out in 1956?*

PLUMMER:
Well, the last big Henry before mine, I suppose, was at the Old Vic with Richard Burton, who was a kind of a young and surly prince, and the other one before that was Laurence Olivier's movie in the forties, which still sort of hung over everyone as the definitive *Henry V*. So, it was hard to cut across with a new kind of interpretation only ten years later. But we did succeed

without ruining the trumpets and drums that it demands, because vocally it's a huge part.

I was, thank God, able to do that, and still play him in the early part of the play as a rather angry young rebel, which was very popular at the time because Osborne and Wesker and all those playwrights had just formed a new kind of theatre and *Look Back in Anger* was sort of *the* play of the time. It was a whole new moment and *Henry V* fitted rather well into that pattern.

It develops him from a rebellious youth (which was still hovering through the early part of the play) into a very scared young king before the big battle of Agincourt and then he realizes during the prayer that, of course, he becomes a man and a soldier and a king all at the same time. He grows up before the battle begins. So it did have a nice build.

OUZOUNIAN:

You were the first Hamlet of the Festival during the initial year of this building, did you feel that was a bit daunting?

PLUMMER:

(chuckling) Oh, just a bit . . .

OUZOUNIAN:

What's the first thing you thought about? How you were going to do the soliloquies?

PLUMMER:

Well, *Henry V* had taught me how to talk to the audience and that gave me big confidence to be able to do Hamlet. I also knew the play pretty well—as we all do—not just from school, but because one has seen so many productions. I had already seen a lot of Hamlets, Olivier's and Gielgud's, and so I was able to pick little things from them and try to, not imitate them, but certainly be influenced by them.

No, I was not that daunted, because, you know, you're pretty arrogant when you're twenty-six and you've already had a success. Fear doesn't seem to enter into things. I barrelled ahead. I was much better later when I played it again, but I think you can't play Hamlet properly until you're probably seventy years old, because it needs a whole lifetime of wisdom and technique and maturity and a kind of calm thing that can bring out those words and make it totally believable that someone of twenty-six could never speak like that, for God's sake, in reality.

Can you imagine at the pub, sitting around with Rosencrantz and Guildenstern and they're all getting drunk and Hamlet delivers that extraordinary speech, "What a piece of work is man . . ."? They'd say he's out of his mind drunk, get him out of here, nobody speaks like that. Where did he learn to speak like that?

OUZOUNIAN:
How did you and Langham approach the play together?

PLUMMER:
Michael was extraordinary, because he had such an academic mind that took care of all the intellectual part of it. And he had an enormous fund of knowledge about the part, because he'd been in the war and he sort of . . . well, Michael kind of took on the look of Hamlet, you know, as certain directors do when they're really close to something, they become the part.

So you had two Hamlets there, me and Michael. Michael, as I said, had been a prisoner of war, but was also very aesthetic like Hamlet. So he was an aesthetic soldier, which was an interesting combination, and he could certainly understand a speech like "How all occasions do inform against me." So he was an enormous help.

He was also able to show me how to build vocally in certain parts and then take others lower because it's such a huge part. You must orchestrate it with great variety, otherwise the audience would be driven out of their minds. Vocally, it's a strain because there's so much emotion going through it that fights your technique, so you have to balance both very carefully so that one doesn't spill over the other.

I'll tell you the most important thing Michael told me about Hamlet. You know, Hamlet kvetches a lot, as they say, and he bitches a lot, and if he was played without humour or irony and somebody just said the lines it could be a real moaner. I mean, he's always saying how Denmark's a prison, and he's always complaining about the weather, and about "Oh that this too, too solid flesh would melt." *(laughs)* I mean, he's so discontent!

Well, Michael had a wonderful trick. He said when you come to passages like that, which could be taken as rather offensively self-pitying, just think of the phrase, silently before you say them, just say "Isn't it extraordinary?" to yourself, as a great aesthetic would, as an intellect would. "Isn't it extraordinary how ill this world is?" and it changes the whole. It's wonderment at each thing, so that even his death—"the rest is silence"—is an extraordinary discovery. You know, it's something I wanted to tell you, it's just *(he pauses)* extraordinary.

It got rid of the complaining note and that was a wonderful piece of direction. For the record, I did not keep saying "Isn't it extraordinary?" out loud. *(smiles)* That was a silent thought.

OUZOUNIAN:

Let's talk about some of the actors you worked with in that production, such as Frances Hyland . . .

PLUMMER;

What a great Ophelia! I think she was one of the greatest Ophelias of this century, and Brooks Atkinson in the *New York Times* said so. She was tough. She wasn't just a little porcelain doll—which she looked like—but underneath that fragile, overbred creature was a sort of animal, a demon inside, a turbulent soul, fighting, fighting, fighting for her love and her position in that strange decadent court.

And her speech about Hamlet—"Oh what a noble mind is here o'erthrown . . ."—I used to listen to it every night offstage. Frances had extraordinary technique, apart from her beauty, and when she got to the end of that speech where she says "blasted with ecstasy," on the word "ecstasy," she let her voice break and it rose to a very strange and rather ugly note, like a broken violin string . . . iiiiieeeeee. And that little soul died before your eyes. You just knew she was going to go mad.

That moment was absolutely riveting, and I've never seen anyone else do that. She did it every night because she had such vocal technique, Frances, that she was able to recreate that same reality at every performance and it never looked like technique. It was just, you know . . . amazing.

OUZOUNIAN:
Bill Hutt was your Polonius, and is it true that one night he had to die of a heart attack because something went amiss with your sword?

PLUMMER:
I think it got stuck in the arras, if you'll pardon the expression. I mean I just jabbed it and it stuck and I heard Bill going "Mumble, mumble, mumble," and then as only he could, he died like this . . . *(he collapses flamboyantly)*. The audience, thank God, did not fall about with laughter.

And then there was the matinee when Hutt went on as Hamlet for me because I'd broken my foot. Tanya Moiseiwitsch had made me a wonderful fibreglass cast that I could walk around on and I got more sympathy from that damn cast than anything. I mean I kept it on even when the foot was better, because you just walk onstage with a cast and they say "Oh my God, poor guy!" and you hardly have to act at all.

Well, Bill went on one matinee while I was bedridden and I kept lying there gnashing my teeth with jealousy saying, "God, I hope he's not better than I am!" And there were two guys whom I paid like moles to watch the performance and give me a full report. And they came back and they said, "He was absolutely marvellous!" I thought, "That bastard . . ." And they went on describing how much quicker he was in the part than I, and that the curtain came down at least half an hour earlier, and that the audience went out wanting more, and I thought I was going to kill those two traitorous bastards.

Then one of them said, "Except, there was this one mistake he made. Utter nerves, perhaps, but just one." I said, "What was it? What was it? Tell me!" And he said it came at the end of the part where he tries to kill the king. The lines are "Here, thou incestuous, murderous, damned Dane, / Drink off this potion. Is thy union here? / Follow my mother." And he pours the poison drink down the king's throat.

But that afternoon, in clear William Hutt perfect diction tones he said, "Here, thou incestuous, murderous, damned Dane, / Drink off this potion. Is thy union here? / SWALLOW my mother." I thought "Great!" The Freudian implications were immense and I was a happy camper again. *(laughing)*

OUZOUNIAN:

Hamlet *was one of the first plays performed in this new theatre. Was that a big change to go from the tent to all this bricks and mortar?*

PLUMMER:

Yes, and in one way the adventure and spirit were slightly gone, because it was all permanent now. You had the feeling of permanence, and perhaps you were all right and taken care of, and you didn't have to work so hard, but it was a relief to be covered with a roof on rainy nights, for example, because in the tent you couldn't possibly hear yourself speak. *(laughs)*

And then there was that damned train that we changed the time of! It always happened during the quiet soliloquy before Agincourt, on the same line, the softest line in the speech every damn night, and I'd try to hurry it up so that I'd get there before the train whistle, and no, the train would be a little earlier that night and go wheeeeeee right on my line.

So I yelled at Tom Patterson. I said—you know, arrogant young actor—I said, "Change the time of the train, you fool, or I will not go on again." And he did. He called the station, good old Tom, and he changed the time of the train and they didn't whistle anymore. How extraordinary what you could do in those days!

What did we lose when we left the tent? All we lost was that first fine careless rapture of adventure. That, and a kind of small band of soldiers trying to fight it out against the elements, which gave it an enormous excitement.

Michael, through this new building, regained that excitement, of course, and he built the company from Tyrone's extraordinary flourish and grandeur. Guthrie left, and it was Michael who had the tough job of keeping the standard high and developing the company, and we *were* all getting better because we were getting more experience. He matured this company into a kind of rich burgundy, where before Guthrie had made it a kind of champagne. But now it was a real, solid, trustworthy and good wine . . . and rich.

OUZOUNIAN:

*You also worked with Langham on various Shakespeare comedies—*Much Ado About Nothing *was the first—what was he like on those plays?*

PLUMMER:

In some ways, I think he was probably more suited as a director to high-style comedy than he was to tragedy. The sort of refined thing Michael has in his makeup, and his wit, which is extraordinarily quick, suited him to direct Restoration plays better than anyone else, as well as very high comedies such as *Much Ado*.

A few years later, he did the most enchanting and miraculous soufflé of a production of *Love's Labour's Lost*, but it was also real, it wasn't just style. There was heart underneath, which Michael had too, so the combination of that heart and that style, I think, were his finest contributions as a director.

He did the same very stylish kind of thing with *Romeo and Juliet* many years later, which I played Mercutio in, along with Bruno Gerussi and Julie Harris as Romeo and Juliet, and Kate Reid as the Nurse. He gave it a kind of lightness of touch, and Lou Applebaum—bless his heart!—wrote the most witty and beautiful little score for it. Langham used his light comedy touch in a tragedy and it worked extraordinarily well, because suddenly you were doubly jolted out of your seat when things got very black.

OUZOUNIAN:

Your next major production was the Macbeth *that Peter Coe directed and it caused a great deal of controversy. It didn't get terribly good reviews and it wasn't even well perceived within the company. What do you recall about it?*

PLUMMER:

It had a very Breughel-like look, I remember. Coe would have people in tiny, knotted groups all over the stage, and he had us kneeling all the time, so ever since I blame that production for my state of arthritic pain. He wanted a sort of cave-like atmosphere of early Britain and I thought that was an excellent idea.

Strangely enough, it was very ahead of its time, because it was also very Brechtian in approach—Brecht being rather fashionable at the time—and Peter was a bit of a disciple of Brecht. It had a bleakness and irony and wildness about it, which I felt was perfectly right. I mean, you felt he wanted to give the impression that these people never washed—which they didn't—and that their castle was something made out of part of nature. The thanes were just more successful peasants; they weren't particularly aristocratic and they didn't have any educational refinement.

I thought all those ideas were extraordinarily good and we bought into them like mad. The critics didn't like it, but it was provocative—we sold this place out every night. They came to see it either to boo or to watch a new idea. *(chuckles)* I think now it would be counted quite old-fashioned, but then it was ahead of its time.

OUZOUNIAN:
Another controversial aspect was that your relationship with Kate Reid as Lady Macbeth was perhaps more Oedipal than usual.

PLUMMER:
Well, it would be easy to give that impression in any scene you played with Kate, because she had an overabundance of warmth, but I think it's true that Lady Macbeth is Mommy in an awful lot of the play. Her influence over him is prime. How could he go through all that without her? And boy, does he know that! And he's lost. He goes into a catatonic state of almost mystic despair at the end of the play because he's lost her.

You know, I said that the critics panned that production, but I should be specific. It was panned by a lot of the Canadian critics (not the bright ones), because they hated to see Canadians making a success of themselves in the theatre. You see, this had already become a kind of Establishment by then, and those anti-Establishment journalists took advantage of it and started to decry it.

The interesting thing is that after the *New York Times* would give a production rave notices then the Canadian critics would change their reviews over the season and rewrite them in a favourable fashion. We always had the *Times* reviews put in the Green Room in great prominence . . . and the local papers? Well, you had to use a telescope to see them.

OUZOUNIAN:
That same season, you had one of your greatest triumphs, a part you played many times since: Cyrano de Bergerac. Did you know from

the start that it would be one of those parts that opened up something inside you?

PLUMMER:

No, I didn't. In fact, Peter O'Toole was supposed to play the part. I'd just played his part of Henry II in *Becket* in London, which he had relinquished to go and make *Lawrence of Arabia*. I was very happy because I won the Best Actor of the Year in London, in *his* part, so I thought, "God, Peter, I owe you a lot."

Well, he came back when I was still in *Becket*, and he came into my dressing room and the first thing he did was take his pants off and show me his bum, his bare bum, which was lacerated in the most horrible way and he said, "There you go, that's what it's like to ride on a camel!"

Then he congratulated me on my performance, I thanked him, and he said, "It's all right, you can have Cyrano." I said *(deadpan)* "Oh God, thank you." Because now I was lumbered with both Macbeth *and* Cyrano.

At first I thought, "This play isn't going to work in 1962. It's so old-fashioned and melodramatic and how are we going to make the audience swallow this?" Oh boy, was I wrong! I mean, Edmond Rostand was a master at knowing his theatre. I think he knew how to weave a theatrical piece better than anybody. It's just tailor-made, and I think anybody that can act that's at all good, or decent, or knows his craft can play Cyrano. It is a gift from the gods.

OUZOUNIAN:

A gift, perhaps, but not an easy one. Look at that scene where you're improvising a poem and plotting revenge while you fight a duel with de Guiche. How did you put all those things together at once?

PLUMMER:

You rely on the words. It's all there in the words. And I must also salute Paddy Crean who was our wonderful fencing master. We brought him over from London and that was his first season, although he was to stay for many years. He designed a fabulous duel for *Cyrano*, all orchestrated precisely to the words and I give him full credit for that sequence because he took care of both the text and the swords and handled them brilliantly.

OUZOUNIAN;
Do you have a favourite moment in the play?

PLUMMER:
I think it's the final scene. It's such a beautifully written, emotional scene, but I had to learn *not* to cry when I was doing it, because as a friend said to me, "You can't cry at your own death!" But actually, it's the happiest death in all theatrical literature, really, because his whole romantic dream has been affirmed at the end. He's got what he wants. Roxanne knows it was him who wrote the love letters. She knows that he loved her and she sees that. And so he dies ecstatically, which makes it doubly moving, because he dies a happy man and the audience shares in that happiness.

OUZOUNIAN:
Is it better to do a play like Cyrano*, which the audience loves, than* Macbeth*, where—no matter how marvellous you may be—they won't embrace you at the end?*

PLUMMER:
I don't know how the hell they can. No, that's not possible. Playing Macbeth is the most masochistic exercise anyone can have. Nobody except Larry Olivier made a big success in it, and he did it simply because he played it black and white. Everybody else over history had been working their butts off to make him human and try to help the audience understand what motivated this evil man. Larry just took the script and said, "I'm going to play him like a villain. Period. Enough of this psychological rubbish, I'm just going to play him down and dirty." And it worked.

OUZOUNIAN:

You briefly mentioned Langham's Romeo and Juliet *before. It seemed to have an extraordinary effect on audiences. What was the magic of that show?*

PLUMMER:

Michael's knowledge of how to make it rather like a fairy tale which then becomes ugly and real, combined with the great passion of the cast, is what made it work. Julie Harris brought an immense conviction to her Juliet even though she was much too old to play the role—she was in her late thirties, I think—but she always had that kind of gamine, little girl quality and that breathless kind of wonder in her acting that made you believe she was fourteen. I'll never forget when she takes the poison and has that horrible, hallucinatory drug-filled speech, she really put hackles down your spine. You saw the ghost of Tybalt just like she had. I'll never forget that.

OUZOUNIAN:

It would seem that she and Bruno Gerussi, her Romeo, were from two different worlds. How did they work together?

PLUMMER;

It was amazing. Bruno—such a good comedian and such a good character actor—suddenly playing handsome young Romeo. But Bruno's Italian anger worked for him very well in the fiery scenes. You believed that. And he wasn't the sort of conventional-looking Romeo with the long, lank hair, which I was sick of anyway. They all looked like ballet dancers. He was a man and a soldier and perplexed with love and that was kind of marvellous.

OUZOUNIAN:

In 1967 you appeared in Antony and Cleopatra*—what would prove to be your last Festival appearance for almost thirty years till you came back to do* Barrymore*. The anticipation of seeing you and Zoe Caldwell together caused the entire run to be sold out before it* *opened. Does that kind of situation put pressure on you?*

PLUMMER:

Oh no, I'm very thrilled to know that it sold out, thank you very much. I would like to know that there are going to be asses in the seats; I think that fills you with confidence. It also fills you with a desire to work harder, because your responsibility is that much greater.

My friendship with Zoe Caldwell started that year and she was an extraordinary Cleopatra. I was much too young to play Antony. I loved the part and I'd love to do it again now that I'm the right age. I could give them that ruined look that comes so easily to me now. *(laughs)* In those days, I had to sort of draw in the bags under the eyes and pretend to be wizened and drunk and ruined, but I was in much too good physical shape. I wasn't even forty then and he really should be in his late sixties.

OUZOUNIAN:

What did Zoe bring to Cleopatra that was so special?

PLUMMER:

She brought an extraordinary humour. The part is filled with laughs and she got more than was to be expected. But it was her flashes of humour and anger together that made her Cleopatra so successful. Some critics dared to say that she "wasn't regal enough" and I wanted to ask them if they had known Cleopatra personally.

Anyway, what does that word mean, "regal"? Cleopatra was a Macedonian, a very rich but totally different kind of animal in those days. The word "regal" has nothing to do with Victorian England or even Elizabethan England as we know it. Shakespeare certainly had the instinct to make her a kind of frantic beast. And here we had a Tasmanian devil playing the part, and they were made for each other. Her grief over the death of Antony was unbelievable. She had such wonderful vocal power. She keened. She could have come from any wild European country. There was nothing Anglo-Saxon about her performance at all.

OUZOUNIAN:
Was it a good play for Michael Langham to direct?

PLUMMER:
Yes, I think he understood it very well. He understood the nobility of failure, which is an extraordinary thing to talk about. It's a play that is very sophisticated and has great poetry in it. Such a wonderful play, and yet it's never really popular with audiences. Why? Because it's about two magnificent failures and nowadays audiences only like plays about mediocre successes. But I think it's an extraordinary look into the tragedy of ruined greatness. Actually, it's just about his best play, I think. It's absolutely extraordinary.

OUZOUNIAN:
Years later you came back to Stratford to play John Barrymore. He would have been a wonderful Antony . . .

PLUMMER:
You're right, what an Antony he would have made! That's why I put the words of Antony into the play just before the curtain went up, because they absolutely refer to his life. You know, "let's have one more gaudy night." That's the philosophy of Jack Barrymore right there. Even in dying he would have wanted them applauding, you know.

OUZOUNIAN:
You keep coming back to Stratford. What magic does the Festival have for you?

PLUMMER:
Well, it's my home, because I grew up here. I spent so much of my young professional life growing up in the theatre here. This was like a family to me, especially when I think of the tent.

Under that tent, one felt very much like a close-knit family battling the elements, and that never leaves you.

OUZOUNIAN:

If you think of one moment from all those years here, what would it be?

PLUMMER:

I'd have to go back to *Henry V*, with the English and French Canadians on the same stage at the same time, because that's hardly happened ever since, and it should. It should be a part of our future. It should be a part of now.

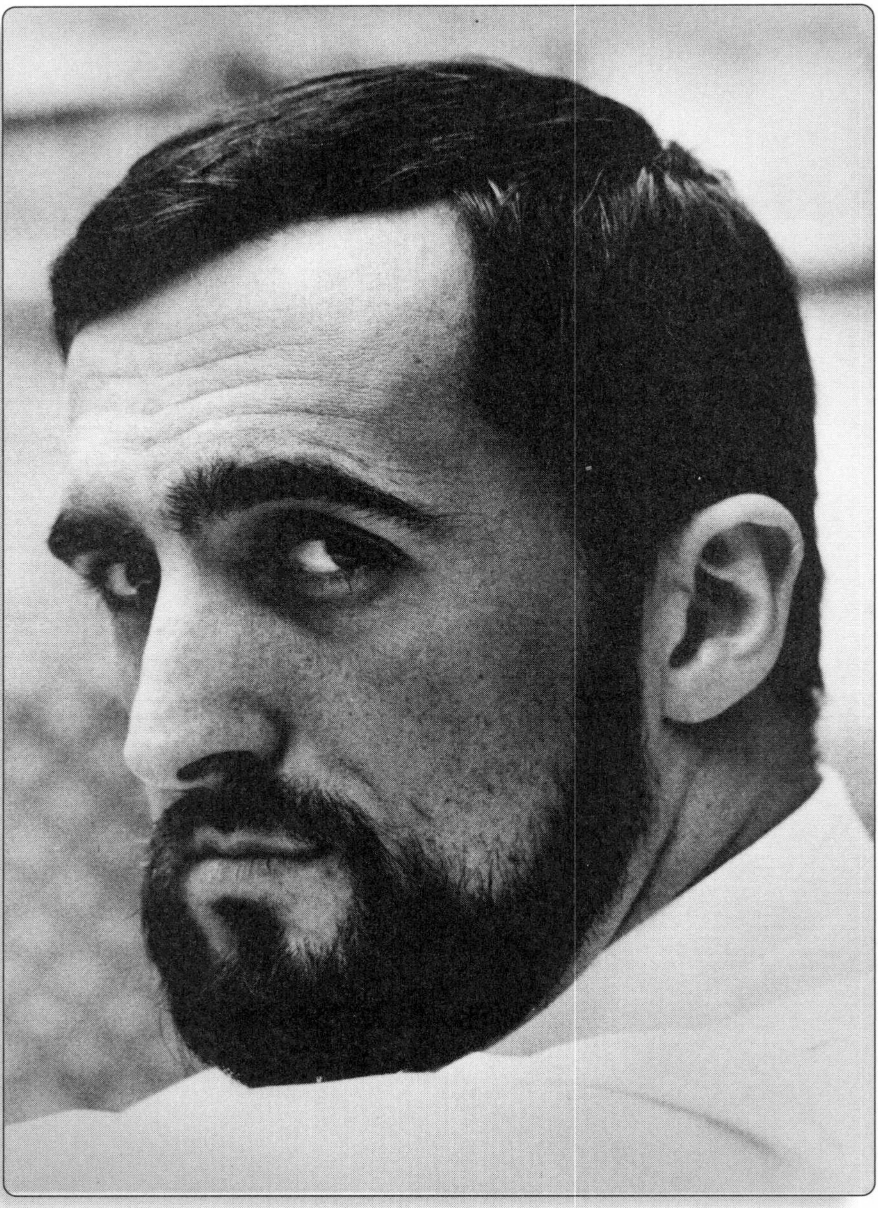

Desmond Heeley. Photographer unknown.

Desmond Heeley

Universally regarded as one of the most influential classical theatre designers of the last fifty years, Desmond Heeley first came to Stratford in 1957 to work on *Hamlet* for Michael Langham. Over the years, he has designed dozens of successful shows for Stratford, including recent triumphs like *Camelot* and *Amadeus*.
I spoke to him in the Festival Theatre in August 2000.

OUZOUNIAN;
What brought you to the Stratford Festival in the first place?

HEELEY:
Michael Langham. I designed *Hamlet* for him at the Memorial Theatre in Stratford, England. It was very controversial and it was the first and only time I designed costumes in what was called "no period." They looked like early *Star Wars*. It was pretty dreadful, but Michael seemed to like me, and the following year I remember him at a tea shop in the Strand in London asking me about coming to Canada. Then I found I was here and I think I was twenty-five years old, and I said, "Oh my God, what have I done? Now I better be really a grownup."

I'd worked with Tanya Moiseiwitsch for a long time in helping, assisting, and suddenly now I was going up the ladder and it was nervous-making. I grew up in a theatre workroom, props, wardrobe, scene painting, and my calling cards were these. I could make things, you know? And I was useful. And I think that's sort of what got me started with Michael, as well as Tanya being in the background about this all happening.

I was a little alarmed when I got here because it was, I think, late February, early March. The snow's on the ground and we came to the theatre, and only half the roof was on. And I remember thinking, "They're going to have a play here in June? What optimists!" What was thrilling about being here then was pioneering, that's what it was. And I realize that Guthrie himself and Langham had invented minimalism in the most wonderful way.

It was very exciting theatre. And with Michael, who I think—apart from being a wonderful director—is perhaps the best choreographer I've ever come across, it began a lifelong obsession with me about the traffic on the stage, not just design. Not the beautiful costume, the beautiful set. What I got really intrigued with were the segues, how the scenes moved into each other.

Langham knew how to make the audience do a great deal of work without them knowing it. When we were working on the first Cyrano de Bergerac, he said, "I think each act should have a spell. I think Act One should be greasepaint and Act Two . . . bread-baking and Act Three . . . jasmine. And then gunpowder for the battle in Act Four. And damp leaves for the final sequence." The wit, the understanding!

He had an incredible head for detail. In *Love's Labour's Lost*, there was a series of letters, a lot of letters, and they're very confusing. So Michael wrote this paper called "Postal Congestion in Navarre," describing all the letters in detail. "This letter," he wrote, "should be small, badly written, much folded, tear-stained. The next one, very flowery, open, petals should fall out, perhaps ribbons." And so on. It was a lovely paper to read, a wonderful one to keep, heaven for the actors and terrific for props. Details like that are very special. He taught me a great deal over the years, an enormous amount. Enough for me to take on directors who perhaps weren't as skilled as he.

OUZOUNIAN:
How would you describe what a designer does?

HEELEY:
I provide a platform for the actors to present the play. Often the actors *are* the scenery here, that's why I like to know who they are, who's there, who's doing it? What you've got? Once you know all the bits and pieces, then it's easy. What's hell is to go in half-baked and say, "Oh, okay, now we'll work."

One of the things that used to be marvellous about this place that's changed a bit is the way that the stage, the dressing rooms, the workrooms, all used to be on the same level—the most brilliant combination ever. The fact that the workrooms were next to the stage was useful for several reasons. The actors knew what we did. We knew what they did. We saw them every day. Wigs and small wardrobe, big wardrobe, design office. Props down below. So you're in constant flow. We all knew each other and once that's removed, even by a floor, a little barrier goes up, you know? And you do less and less. It meant that we could mock up things and there was no upstairs to say you can't do it. We could mock up things, take them on the stage, look at them, bring them back, do it. In a funny way it saved time. It saved money and it was, you know, another piece. But once the department moves somewhere they cut down trees forever to do communications.

OUZOUNIAN:
You've been here for most of the first fifty years of Stratford, what would you say to someone who came here for the next fifty years?

HEELEY:
Have an enormous amount of energy in giving. Don't expect anything back. But giving and giving and giving. To a director or an actor or anyone in the production who needs your energy and ideas. In my book, a designer is responsible for a number of people's lives for a few months. You can make them happy

or you can give them hell. You can be prepared. It's your job to help the ones that are not quite so bright, to smack down the ones that are too confident, and have Plan B, at the back, should Plan A go wrong. And you have to wear this all very lightly. It's all fun. It takes a tremendous amount of energy but I love it. Always have done.

I have no blood family, and yet from day one, I have the most incredible family scattered all over the world, largely to do with Stratford. You never know where the next layer's coming from. It's only now, looking back, I realize how lucky I am. I took it all for granted. Come to Canada? Sure. For the first ten years, I had no contract. I just came. And I'm glad I did.

Roberta Maxwell as Rosalind in the 1983 production of As You Like It.
Photograph by Robert C. Ragsdale.

Roberta Maxwell

Roberta Maxwell began as an apprentice at Stratford in 1956 and has returned many times over the years to play roles like Nina in *The Seagull*, Lady Macbeth in *Macbeth*, Rosalind in *As You Like It*, and Elmire in *Tartuffe*. Her distinguished career has taken her to all the major theatre centres of the world, as well as to prestigious work on film and television. I spoke to her in New York City in the fall of 2001.

OUZOUNIAN:

Your first Stratford credit was as Ursula in Much Ado About Nothing. *What was it like to encounter Michael Langham, Christopher Plummer, and that stage, all at once?*

MAXWELL:

I just crossed my fingers and prayed. Everybody was terribly kind and very attentive and, of course, I learned a tremendous amount at such a young age: I had my seventeenth birthday that summer. All my experiences in those early years, and really in my latter years as well, were about learning from the extraordinary actors who I had the great privilege of observing and working with.

OUZOUNIAN:

The word that a lot of people use to describe Plummer onstage is "dangerous." Would you agree?

MAXWELL:

I would say that would be an understatement. And I'm sure there are actors on many continents across the world who would back that statement up. I understand that at one point in his career they had to take his sword away from him and give him a rubber sword during one of his performances because you just wouldn't know where your ears might land. But he was always on his best behaviour when working with Michael Langham.

OUZOUNIAN:
What was Michael Langham like to work for?

MAXWELL:
He was so handsome. He was a killer actually. He was witty and wry and, of course, brilliant, I mean that's a given. He was the director who followed through for me on what Guthrie said about the reason for theatre and the function of theatre in a society. You could sit in any seat in a Langham production, and never be cheated. You always got your money's worth. Because he understood the energy of that stage. And he understood the relationship of the actors to every seat in the house, and how important it was. I used to, when I wasn't playing on the stage, I used to buy six-dollar seats and sit way up in the corner, and that's how you really knew if a director understood what that stage was there for.

Tyrone Guthrie, my first year there, once stopped me while I was doing something on the stage and he said, "Do you see that seat way, way up there?" "Yes, Dr. Guthrie." "And do you see that seat way, way over there?" he said, pointing down at the front. "That's the dynamic that creates theatre. The people up there are working desperately to get into the seats right down here, so they can reach out and touch the silks and satins that the kings and queens are wearing."

Guthrie was huge. A beacon. A standard. So kind, certainly to me, and I found to anybody who I observed him deal with. He was a great Freudian presence. He explored text. You went forward and conquered and experienced your life as a hero, and he did that, of course, with Shakespeare, but with the Greek myths as well. He was the great pillar on which Stratford was founded.

And then, swinging into the seventies, Robin Phillips, who explored and brought to the stage the subtext. Dr. Guthrie was the Freudian and Robin was the Jungian, the exploration of what's behind the gesture. Giving up the text and allowing the actor to go deeply inside, not only the character, but himself, to come up with this other reading of text.

OUZOUNIAN:
What do you think Guthrie would have made of Robin Phillips?

MAXWELL:
I think he really would have loved him, because they were both great adventurers, and great spirits.

OUZOUNIAN:
You yourself have come and gone from the Festival numerous times over the years . . .

MAXWELL:
But I always came back. It was always my spiritual home. And for a time it was my physical home because my father and I had a house there. It had, it had such an important influence on my early years. I have always thought that I would go back and retire and live there as an elder, senior person. Not necessarily working. The area itself was enchanted. It's a world that's gone. But still in a person's mind it remains, it remains elusive, because it can never be re-created. But you go back always to try and find those moments of magic that were so important in your life.

OUZOUNIAN:
You came back in Michael Langham's final season and played opposite Alan Bates in Richard III. *What was he like in that role?*

MAXWELL:
It was the role of a very accessible and human and very attractive man. You could see his power was in dealing with and seducing people. It would have been a pleasure . . .

(*laughing*) . . . the *first* night. After that . . .? *(she shrugs and laughs again)*

The way he died, like a horribly wounded animal, causing his own death, was such a magnificent, frightening end. I think it was among John Hirsch's finest work. John brought the real dark side of humanity to the Festival. And that was such a shock, I think, for the actors and for audiences. Because we'd had Guthrie, the great mythmaker, and Langham, with his bright heroic work. And then Hirsch came in with the exploration of the darkest and blackest sides of human perspective. And he, in his most successful pieces, really asked us to come to terms with that. In himself and within the texts.

OUZOUNIAN:

You worked with Hirsch again years later, but next it was Robin Phillips and Nina in The Seagull.

MAXWELL:

Of course I jumped at the opportunity. I was as mad as a hatter, I think. I can only say this in hindsight. But my grip on reality was not as firm as it should have been. In fact, I don't think anybody shared the same reality with me. I was going through a very stressful time. And Robin really understood it and was able to make me feel safe in the exploration of this really very frightening world that I was occupying in my mind. He allowed me to explore my subtext and the character's subtext. The wonderful thing about Robin Phillips is that you can go anywhere. He's a total artist. As long as you are committed to your work, he will let you go anywhere. But you are not alone. He will go into the scariest places of you, yourself as an artist, and be unafraid. And be able to support it, and use it, and take it and bring it into the light.

OUZOUNIAN:

But during all of this personal exploration, you were also working with people like Brian Bedford and Maggie Smith . . .

MAXWELL:

Well, they had their hands full also with their own parts . . . (*laughing*) . . . and with each other. Robin builds a family of people who respect each other. So I certainly felt that I was very much supported by everybody else. We were a part of the same world, we were all on the same page, which is what he has such an eye for. He wants everyone to be there in the same room at the same time, at the same place. He wants everybody to feel safe enough to go into those places. With each other. And with yourself. Because he's there. He, he is never farther than a millimetre of an inch from you psychically, or emotionally.

He sees the whole thing. He understands where you have to go and he will take you there. But it isn't mapped out. It happens intuitively. His intuition as he's listening with his mind and his heart to you. And you slowly begin to reveal your colours. And he says, "I'll take this one, and I'll take this one . . ."

OUZOUNIAN:

Is there any downside to working with Robin?

MAXWELL:

Well, yes. You have to give yourself totally. And one hundred and ten percent or your life is not worth the paper it's written on.

OUZOUNIAN:

It's time to come back to John Hirsch. When you returned to Stratford—having last been there in the final Phillips year—how did you find the Festival had changed?

MAXWELL:

Well, in the director's house on Douglas Street, all the furniture was different. (*laughing*) When Robin was there, it was filled with exquisite furniture, everything was white and beautiful green palms; and when you went to visit John, everything was stripped and covered with . . . Persian carpets were on the walls and it was a very kind of European feeling to it. The meals were very different as well. John served goulash. And as he said about Robin, "He gives you three peas on a plate and a little garden salad; you need goulash." John was a feeder of actors. He would take you, and before a show he would make sure you were stuffed with things to give you the energy to go onstage.

OUZOUNIAN:
Do you think that came from his childhood in Hungary, with all of the deprivation?

MAXWELL:
Everything came from his childhood. One of the most extraordinary directions I received from John was in *Andorra*, and Heath Lamberts was playing a boy tied to a stake who was about to be shot. And John said to Heath, "Look up and see a bird flying," and it's one of those images that has resonated throughout my entire life. People who are trapped and may be about to die. And that must have been something that he experienced in his own life.

OUZOUNIAN:
What kind of tension arose when you have the John Hirsch view of the world colliding with a show like the one you starred in for him, As You Like It?

MAXWELL:
John wanted me to be bright and glamorous. But I was forty-two years old and the great Irene Worth had also been forty-two when she played the part, but her Rosalind had been very mellow. And then, of course, there was the great Miss Smith, and she too was forty-two when she played it. And Robin had allowed her to be the pining, languishing Rosalind. But Hirsch wanted me to move it, to be joyous, to be less of what I internally truly was. In many ways, I suppose after Robin my work changed, and how I wanted to work, and what I felt I could bring to a part—it all changed. So John and I were in

constant battle. Real insane battle. And I think he felt that I had betrayed him. I was old enough, and had invested enough in my own life to say no, and oh John didn't like to hear no at all. "What is she doing?" he would cry. And we battled openly in front of the company.

After the season was over and I left, John took all my pictures off the wall. He had me completely blacklisted in that theatre. Oh, he was terribly angry with me and as I say, he felt betrayed.

OUZOUNIAN:
Did you ever resolve it with him?

MAXWELL:
We did. In his illness I called him on the phone. Immediately when I heard that he was ill. It's one thing to fight with an enemy, but to fight with a friend and to understand that they are mortally ill, and that you have the chance to come back and tell that person how much you cared. . . . I had to do it. And he immediately responded. Just like that. There was no question that he withheld his love for me.

OUZOUNIAN:
You came back to Stratford again, but it wasn't the same for you, was it?

MAXWELL:
I was very happy to be in Stratford, in the place, in the town. I always feel that I'm at home in the town. But I never got past Robin . . .

OUZOUNIAN:
When you look back on your time at Stratford, or all the various things you've done, is there a golden thread that goes through it for you?

MAXWELL:
That stage. That magic place. To stand in the middle of that stage is what it must have been like to be standing on one of the great Greek stages. It's a place on the planet where there is

a total sense of being in the right place. Not too many places you can say that about.

OUZOUNIAN:
What would you wish Stratford for its second fifty years?

MAXWELL:
To quote Tennessee Williams, "Happiness and good fortune."

OUZOUNIAN:
When I say "The Stratford Festival" to you, what comes to mind?

MAXWELL:
My career. It gave me a career. I am the actress I am because I began with Dr. Guthrie at the Stratford Festival.

Norman Campbell. Photograph by Dale Barnes.

Norman Campbell

Norman Campbell has one of the most distinguished careers as a director and producer in the history of Canadian television. He set the standard for the award-winning work that brought the Canadian performing arts to an international television audience. From *H.M.S. Pinafore* in 1960 through *Romeo and Juliet* in 1993, he brought many of Stratford's greatest hits to CBC Television.

I spoke to him, naturally enough, at the CBC Broadcast Centre in the spring of 2001.

OUZOUNIAN:

There's been an appetite over the years to take Stratford and put it on television. Why do you think that has happened?

CAMPBELL:

I was part of that appetite. I kept urging the CBC to go and shoot more Stratford. I think Stratford belongs to the people of this whole country, and it's a shame that only a few people living within several hundred miles of Stratford get to see it.

OUZOUNIAN:

The first full production broadcast from Stratford was a Gilbert and Sullivan operetta that Tyrone Guthrie himself directed. Did you get to interact with him at all at that point?

CAMPBELL:

Yes. Guthrie came to Canada the second time, after having founded the Festival—the tent days were over—to direct Gilbert and Sullivan. I had, by that time, done many Gilbert and Sullivans myself, some in New York and many of them in Toronto. So I invited Guthrie down to the CBC studio and played him a few of the bits of shows that I had done. And he was wonderful. So a few months later, I was doing *H.M.S. Pinafore* with him for television.

At the time, we didn't think we could do it from the stage of the Avon Theatre, so we moved the whole company down from Stratford into CBC Studio 7, and I had plotted all the shots and worked them out ahead of time. Now, Studio 7 was big, but not that big. It was only a half of the Avon. Or even a quarter of it. But Guthrie insisted we had to place our maestro in an orchestra pit. Well, Studio 7 didn't have a pit, just a concrete floor. So Lou Applebaum is there on his knees on a pillow conducting and I shot him over the waist and you see all the people out in the background shot over Lou's conducting beautifully, and then he gets up off his knees and disappears after the shot!

OUZOUNIAN:

Now a couple of years down the line, you actually directed one of the Gilbert and Sullivans at Stratford yourself from scratch.

CAMPBELL:

Yes, Michael Langham had seen some of my television productions, and he asked me to direct *The Mikado* for the stage. So I directed it at the Avon Theatre and Alan Lund did the choreography.

When the curtain went up, I took as my clue the alternative title that Gilbert gave the show, "The Town of Titipu," and I made quite a thing of the life of the town. We saw Pooh-Bah being shaved, people selling fruit, somebody going through with a squid dangling its tentacles . . . that kind of thing. We had a great deal of fun.

OUZOUNIAN:

In subsequent productions, they were later to rewrite Gilbert's lyrics to make them more pointedly political. Did you dare to do that?

CAMPBELL:

No, I wouldn't do that. I still wouldn't do that. I didn't like it.

OUZOUNIAN:
You were responsible for doing this version of The Mikado, *onstage and then you brought it to television.*

CAMPBELL:
Yes, but I had great fights with the director. *(laughing)*

OUZOUNIAN:
When you have to take an existing stage show and bring it to the television screen, do you try to compromise as little as possible or do you find there's some things you just have to request that they change?

CAMPBELL:
I've tried to do the Stratford productions without requesting change. We've been helped by having seven or eight cameras. You're able to shoot the show from different angles and that helps a lot with some of the problems.

OUZOUNIAN:
A few years later, there was a series of Gilbert and Sullivans that you also did for television. These were the Brian Macdonald versions, which were sometimes a little more revisionist and certainly very splashy and effective. Did you find it sometimes a little strange to go from the more traditional ones to those?

CAMPBELL:
Working with Brian was a special honour in a way because I admire his work very much and he was a very inventive guy. When he did the overture, he would contrive actions that could be going on. He would invent the whole cast arriving at the Avon Theatre, some of them on skates, and they would all be coming to the stage door and going into the theatre. It built up an appreciation of these characters, and all of this was compressed into the overture.

OUZOUNIAN:
Did you feel that you got a chance to capture the live feel of Stratford enough in your television versions?

CAMPBELL:

I love the live feel of Stratford because you go in knowing that . . . when the cannon goes off, you're into it. And you are running for your life. But this is true of the whole crew. We have cameramen and sound men and everybody knows their job and they're all working, but none of them can look back. You cannot, you don't dare think about what just happened. You've got to keep going. Got to keep going. In a television production from Stratford, like on the main stage, I might have 580 shots. That's a lot of shots, when you consider what a feature film would have, and a feature film takes many months to shoot, but we go up and we shoot it in a couple of days.

OUZOUNIAN:

Television time is different from stage time. Do you ever have to adjust or do you keep it as close to the original director's vision?

CAMPBELL:

Well, that's an interesting question. A stage production is . . . just sort of sits there. It's a beautiful thing for an audience to see. You sit in your seat in the theatre and watch it from wherever you've been placed. If you bought a ticket that had you over to the side, you see the entire show from that side. And the dramatist is able to stir your emotions.

When you're shooting it for television, you just have to use different techniques. Sometimes you can heighten things by use of closeups. You can be in a medium shot and then gradually tighten. As you do, the audience feels uh oh, something's happening. Often you can see things with a TV camera that the theatre audience isn't aware of. Little subtleties, and the actors know this. And they know that a little more subtlety in a performance will go a long way towards making a moving television moment.

OUZOUNIAN:

What would you like to wish Stratford for the next fifty years?

CAMPBELL:

I would like to see Stratford do some Canadian shows without regard to the American influx. To have a big American audience is very important to Stratford, and I completely acknowledge the necessity of favouring them, but there's an awful lot of Canadian theatre that should be seen by the Stratford audiences. And I think this can be increased as, as the years go by.

I wish them well in the next fifty years. I think they'll be very solid at the end of that. There'll be a hundredth anniversary and we will still be here celebrating that. Hundredth Anniversary of Stratford. Amazing.

OUZOUNIAN:

What images come into your mind when I say "Stratford"?

CAMPBELL:

I think Stratford is a castle. It's a beautifully designed building with a setting that is so romantic. You walk through a bunch of swans on the way up the hill to this great castle and you see the flags on the rooftop and then suddenly you hear the Lou Applebaum fanfares drifting around the corner. They're in the distance. Ba ba ba ba ba, ba ba ba ba. You hear . . . this sends a chill through you. A wonderful anticipatory chill. And you walk up closer to the theatre and go in the door. Your expectancy rises and rises and rises. And you know you're going to see a great show, whenever you go to Stratford.

Zoe Caldwell as Cleopatra in the 1967 production of Antony and Cleopatra.
Photograph by Douglas Spillane.

Zoe Caldwell

Internationally famous Australian-born actress Zoe Caldwell first came to Stratford in 1961 as Rosaline in Michael Langham's landmark production of *Love's Labour's Lost*. She returned in 1967 as Cleopatra, Mistress Page, and Lady Anne, and in 1979 to direct *Richard II*. I spoke to her in April 2001 in the glorious mountaintop home that she shares with her husband, producer Robert Whitehead, on the New York–Connecticut border.

OUZOUNIAN:
How did you first get involved with Stratford?

CALDWELL:
Well, when I was at Stratford on Avon, I knew that there was also a Shakespeare Festival in Stratford, Ontario, and that it was very high class and started with a tent, and that's about as far as I knew.

And then I was in London, asleep, and the phone rang and a man said that he was Michael Langham and he was the director of Stratford, Ontario, and would I be interested in coming to do Rosaline in *Love's Labour's Lost* and I said, "Oh yes, that'll be fine. I'll do it." And he said, "How soon can you come?" I said, "Who got sick?" He said, "Toby Robins is pregnant." I thought to myself, "Poor little thing. I must knit her some booties or something," and then I said, "So when do you want me?" And his answer was, "How soon can you get here?"

Well, I started with the company and I was truly amazed because they were so incredibly strong and clean, and their speech was very—I felt—Shakespearean. And I thought this is going to be marvellous.

OUZOUNIAN:

Michael Langham feels that was the show where he first really felt he found his voice.

CALDWELL:

Well, I'd never worked with him before so I had nothing to compare it to. I just thought he was like some sort of a magician, understood the stage and its environs and the company, and was our leader. I took it for granted that he knew exactly what he was doing. For he did.

OUZOUNIAN:

A few years later, Langham asked you to come back in his final season to play Cleopatra, Lady Anne, and Mistress Page. That's quite a plateful . . .

CALDWELL:

Oh, I was ready for that year! When I was a little girl of twelve in Australia, I had seen Vivian Leigh play Lady Anne and it stayed in my mind. *(imitating Leigh's Mayfair voice)* "Set down, set down thy honourable load." And I thought that's what you did with Anne. But when I started rehearsing—John Hirsch directing, Alan Bates playing Richard the Third—I realized that that wasn't it at all. That scene between the two of them over the bier is such an incredible scene and she's fifteen! That little Lady Anne is fifteen, with all the hormones piping in. Oh, that was some scene Alan and I had! Must have been thrilling for Richard, too, to have a young hot teenage girl spitting obscenities across a bier with a corpse that's still bleeding. I mean that's a lot of terrific stuff. If they filmed it like that today, it would have to be Johnny Depp or somebody like that. But my God, what a film that would make, eh? Anyway, I found that incredibly sexy and thrilling and stimulating.

And then in *The Merry Wives of Windsor*, I played my mom when I played Mistress Page, and it worked. I studied Hollingshead for Anne, Plutarch for Cleopatra, and I just tucked Mom in for Mistress Page. I rang her and told her, "Mom, you were a terrific success as Mistress Page." *(laughing)*

OUZOUNIAN:
What made you think of using your mother?

CALDWELL:
Well, Mistress Page is a suburban lady and with all the same things and all the same concerns about "Well, I hope the neighbours never find out about that." So that's how I played her.

OUZOUNIAN:
So you were in Richard III *and* The Merry Wives of Windsor, *but the big deal had to have been* Antony and Cleopatra.

CALDWELL:
I was preparing for Cleopatra for about three months before starting rehearsals, getting my body into really proper condition, and my voice, and my emotions. I had brought some spectacular blowups from a book from the Cairo Museum of Egyptian gods, goddesses, kings, queens, everything. I had a little house in St. Mary's, which was absolutely chock-a-block of everything that was Egyptian and erotic. Then I perfumed the little house so I was almost drowning in Cleopatra. And I worked out a special makeup for my entire body and I perfumed the makeup. So I was living with her for a long time.

And then Chris (Plummer) came. He was late because he was doing a film of Oedipus in Greece, and we had to start without him. Didn't matter 'cause I had such a great group on the Nile—Jimmy Blendick and the most wonderful Charmian that has ever been, Dawn Greenhalgh. I hope that Cleopatra had as good a Charmian. And we had such a good time on the Nile, because Cleopatra's court was some extraordinarily free court. So anything was possible and we had a swell time.

One day Chris finally arrived. And we were all pale 'cause we'd been rehearsing like mad and we were all sort of a little, you know, funky. But he came in dressed in white, with brown wonderful glorious skin, and just took me in his arms and took possession of me. So I knew that everything was going to be swell. *(laughs)*

OUZOUNIAN:
I know the part I remember so vividly of your Cleopatra was the final scene, your death scene. What made you play it that way?

CALDWELL:
By the time you get there, she does become a sort of . . . immortal person. She transcends all the stuff that has been going on that makes her join hands with all women. She sheds it, I think, there. You see I was always so stunned how so much of the relationship between Antony and Cleopatra could be enacted in anybody's house. Their fights, their mistrust, their "forgive me, forgive me, forgive me," the many, many different aspects of man, woman, living together.

You know, when we were doing the school matinees, they asked me if I would put a piece of material over my breasts because they were children. And I said no I would not because I know the children would sense that we were hiding something from them and they would be crushed. They wouldn't trust anything we did if they thought, oh, they're just trying to bring it down to us and cover up.

So Chris and I didn't bring down our performances one tiny bit and those kids behaved like a marvellous Elizabethan audience. They were quiet. They were raucous. They were bawdy. They were just sensational. Except for one performance. And then they were so rude that I got angrier and angrier and angrier and angrier until I had the asp at my breast and I thought, that's enough. So I stopped and I walked forward and said, "You are incredibly rude. And I am very, very tired. I have to play Mistress Page tonight. Now we have two choices. Either we stop right now or we continue. Under different circumstances. The choice is yours; you must make it."

No noise, no sound. And then eventually a tiny little voice said, "Please continue, Miss Caldwell."

OUZOUNIAN:

The years pass and you're invited by Robin Phillips to direct Richard II *at Stratford, but with one hitch: there's going to be three different Richards . . .*

CALDWELL:

I think it was a little funny test that Robin was making because I had said something about him to a reporter on the telephone. "What do you feel about Stratford under Mr. Phillips?" he asked, and I said I thought it was being run like a communist state. Because when I went backstage, and I'd say, "How are you?," all the actors whom I knew, most of them reasonably well, they'd say, "I am very happy and Robin is a genius." Well, that's the answer you get when you go to a communist state.

So I think Robin was sort of in a "Gotcha!" moment and said, "We'll do this multiple *Richard II* and ask Zoe Caldwell to direct it." So they did, and when I asked about casting, his assistant said, "Oh, it's already cast, Miss Caldwell." I said, "It's already cast?" "Yes." I asked, "Well, who's playing Richard?" *(laughs)* And they said, "We've got three Richards. *And* three Bollingbrokes." And I said, "Onstage at the same time, all of them?" And they said, "No, no, no! Alternate performances." And it was already designed. Everything had been done for me.

Well, I thought the only way to do this is to become the most terrible authoritarian. I started with punctuation, because I believe punctuation is the playwright's score. So I made the actors sit down around a table and read the play for punctuation. And I read the play for punctuation. We must have spent a good week doing nothing but read the play. Then we gradually began to talk a little. But not about subtext, which Robin loved to do, because I don't think Shakespeare has subtext. The thing about Shakespeare is he has *text.*

And then, when we got on the stage, I would not allow anyone to look at anyone else, unless given permission, because I had grown so sick of everybody's slapping each other on the back. So I thought no, let's just be still. When you watch those big political things in the Rose Garden and you watch those big big important leaders of the world—they don't slap each other on the back and they don't even give each other their eyes. And when they do, the power goes from them, to the person they're looking at. And so if you're just sort of casually looking around, where is the power? But if you contain that power, and only look at a person when you really need to, it's terrific.

Anyway, the actors didn't like it and I don't blame them, but it was very good. And then Robin had the most glorious retaliation by taking me to dinner one night and saying, "I know you once said Stratford was being run as a communist state, but from what I hear of your rehearsals, it is now being run as an Islamic state, and you are the Ayatollah Khomeini." Isn't that a splendid answer? I adored that.

OUZOUNIAN:
What did you do in rehearsal after that meeting?

CALDWELL:
What did I do? Kept doing the same, of course. I had to.

OUZOUNIAN:
In the end, did you feel that this Richard II *was stimulating?*

CALDWELL:
For me, yes. Most probably irritating beyond belief to the company. But for me it was thrilling.

OUZOUNIAN:
What would you wish Stratford for its next fifty years?

CALDWELL:

Just more of the same. I mean, good actors, good plays, and people coming from all over the place to have the thrill of being there.

OUZOUNIAN:

If I say "The Stratford Festival," what do you think?

CALDWELL:

Theatre—the theatre. The theatre that was a tent and became solid. The miracle of it happening at all. And St. Mary's. I loved St. Mary's. I had a yellow Jeep with a red top, and I drove like billy-be-damned to get out of the house that was so full of Cleopatra. *(laughing)*

Martha Henry as Mary Cavan Tyrone in the 1994 production of Long Day's Journey into Night. *Photograph by Cylla von Tiedemann.*

Martha Henry

Martha Henry first appeared on the Stratford Stage in 1962 as Lady Macduff in *Macbeth* with Christopher Plummer and as Miranda in *The Tempest* with William Hutt. Over the next forty years, she has delivered some of the Festival's most memorable performances, including Isabella in *Measure For Measure* and Mary Tyrone in *Long Day's Journey into Night*. She has also received acclaim for her direction of *Richard II* and *Elizabeth Rex*. In 2002, she will be directing the Fiftieth Anniversary production of *Richard III*.

OUZOUNIAN:
What first brought you to the Stratford Festival?

HENRY:
I first came to the Stratford Festival when I was a teenager, like so many other teenagers, in the back seat of a station-wagon. We were coming from Michigan to see Christopher Plummer in *Hamlet*. And I remember going back home to Michigan in the station-wagon and all the other girls were either asleep or they were giggling at each other and throwing things, and I was sitting in the back with my copy of Shakespeare, open to *Hamlet* trying to figure out how Christopher Plummer had made that language sound like speech, like conversation. It was just fascinating to me. I thought that I would never get a chance to work at Stratford, of course, because that was just beyond anyone's imaginings, especially as a teenager, but I knew that I wanted to get as close to it as I could, and I wanted to work in the country that could produce a Stratford Festival.

At that time in the States, there was nothing like that, at

least nothing that I knew of. And it wasn't even that so much. It wasn't even that it was a Shakespearean Festival. It was that the work was unlike anything I'd ever seen. I felt transported and I felt as though I were in a magic place.

OUZOUNIAN:
Was there something to you almost holy about that space, that stage?

HENRY:
Oh yes, there is. The first year I was here I was playing Miranda in *The Tempest*, and my Ferdinand was Peter Donat, who had been here before. They used to have then a gathering for all the people who were about to start rehearsal, and we were upstairs, having a glass of wine and I was introduced to Peter, and he said, "Have you seen the stage?" And I said, very knowledgeably, "Oh yes, I've seen plays here for years and years and years." And he said, "It's not the same thing. Come with me."

And he took me into the empty theatre. The lights happened to be on, on the stage, and he said, "Just sit there and watch that stage for a while." And so I did. I sat and I looked at the stage, and the stage without people on it seemed as though it was breathing. I could actually see it rise and fall. I could see the wood going up and down. It was, again I suppose, propelled by my own excitement and consternation of actually being here for the first time, so it was all quite, quite heady. But I swore that that stage was a living space. And I have never been in that theatre since then without feeling the same thing. It seems to me that the stage itself is capable of holding actors that treat it well, and of throwing actors literally off it that don't treat it well. And by treating it well, I don't mean being polite to it. I mean the actors who, who treat that stage with vigour and discipline and respect and creativity and often wildness, but still are connected to that stage, are the actors that the stage embraces.

OUZOUNIAN:

What was it like the first time you actually went on to that stage yourself?

HENRY:

Well, of course it was very exciting. My first entrance as Miranda was made from the house right tunnel. And I had to run all the way up to the balcony, where Bill Hutt, playing Prospero, was standing. So I didn't really see them, the audience, until I turned around, which was a good thing. All those thousands of eyes focused on you can be an overwhelming experience. But by that time I got to my place, the exertion of running all that, that way, and being concentrated on Bill took care of me. He's amazing that way. He not only plays with you, but especially for a young performer, he's very protective. He manages to embrace you onstage, as if to say, it's all right. You can be perfectly free. Go ahead. I'm here and nothing will happen to you. You won't go wrong, because you're with me. And he's always done that.

OUZOUNIAN:

Do you still kind of have that relationship today?

HENRY:

Well, he demands more of you as you become more capable of giving more back, but I've always felt with Bill, as though there was an extraordinary onstage connection and that I could do anything with him, because, of course, he can counter anything. You don't have to be afraid of hurting him or breaking him up or even upsetting him in any way, because he is so incredibly skilled that he can take care of anything you do and he, he uses it to, he plays with you. So it's wonderful being onstage with Bill. It's very freeing.

OUZOUNIAN:

Michael Langham was the artistic director when you first came here. What are your memories of him?

HENRY:

I was quite frightened of Michael. He was very intimidating but I thought he was amazing and I wanted nothing better, of course, than to please him, and be one of the young actors that he thought enough of to invite back. And indeed I got the chance then to work with him the next year in *Troilus and Cressida,* which was an alarming experience for me, but thrilling.

I'm not sure that I ever went through with Michael the journey that meant that we were friends, or that I was ever anything less than terrified of him. I think I was too young to finally get to the point where I could work with him as a friend and equal colleague. I just don't think that was possible at that time. But I eventually realized that he . . . he probably wasn't as terrifying as he seemed to be to me. And in the years that I have seen him and spoken to him briefly afterwards, he's been extremely kind and generous to me. So perhaps he wasn't aware that I was scared to death of him.

OUZOUNIAN:

Much of your work in the late sixties and early seventies was away from Stratford, but you had returned by the time Robin Phillips arrived. How would you describe him?

HENRY:

Robin is, of course, a very complex man, and can be a very difficult friend to have and a complicated director to work with, but he is, without a doubt, the most thrilling and brilliant director I think I've ever worked with, and I don't think that will ever change. After you've worked with Robin, working with other directors seems to be slightly pale in comparison. Which is not to say there aren't, there aren't lots of other really wonderful directors but Robin— I think it's because Robin is such an extraordinary teacher. And it doesn't matter what age or what experience you are at, he uses the rehearsal periods to teach you about acting in a way that I have never known any other director to do.

OUZOUNIAN:

The first show you worked on together was Measure For Measure, *and after one scene of incredible sexual tension, you plunged your hand into a jug of water and splashed it on your face to relieve what you were feeling. Where did that come from?*

HENRY:

(smiling) Well, it's hard to know where things come from with Robin. My memory of this is that in rehearsal one day, on the desk, he simply put a jug of water. And then everything else he talks to you about makes it inevitable that you will put your hand in the jug of water and splash it on your face. He doesn't tell you to do something. He helps lead your thought processes to a point where no other choice is possible.

I had the extraordinary privilege of being assistant to the director, when he was directing *Cymbeline* and he sat with me several months before rehearsals ever started, showing me what his preparatory work had been. I'd never seen anything like this. He, of course, is a . . . consummate artist, a set designer. He can make wigs. He can design costumes. He can make costumes. He can probably make sets. He can do everything there is to do in the theatre. And he showed me some sketches he had done for *Cymbeline*. They represented crucial moments over the course of the whole play, and he had done these on the winter before we started rehearsals in the spring.

But one of them I remembered specifically because of what happened to it. He had drawn Iachimo, the character that Colm Feore was playing, with a yellow bath towel thrown over his left shoulder. And there was another sketch of Colm lying down on the yellow bath towel.

Well, we started rehearsals and I watched the evolution of

this. And I'd sort of kind of forgotten about these sketches. But one day when we were in the theatre, I saw Colm walk onto the stage in exactly the way that Robin had drawn him in the sketch, with the bath towel thrown over his left shoulder, and he put the bath towel down and lay down upon it. But I don't remember him getting there. I don't know how he got Colm to do that. Because he never said to Colm, "Come in, walk there, go over there, and lie down on your bath towel." But he seems to be able somehow to guide the rehearsal period so that the actor finally has no choice but to do what Robin has in his head. And I don't mean that in a militant way, I mean that every other possibility gets pared away. It's not unlike Michelangelo's sculpture: he simply pared away the stone to find the shape inside. And Robin seems to do that with a play. He pares everything else away and reveals the inevitable inside. But as long as I've worked with him, I don't know how he does it.

OUZOUNIAN:

You were one of the four-person directorate that the board of directors fired back in 1980, and after that, you kept away from the Festival for fourteen years until your old friend and colleague Richard Monette persuaded you to return. How did he do it?

HENRY:

When Richard asked me to come back and do *Long Day's Journey into Night*, I thought, "Having stayed away for that length of time, if I'm going to go back, then I would rather go back for Richard than for anyone else." And so I did.

OUZOUNIAN:

Did you have any idea that production would prove to be so successful?

HENRY:

I don't think I go into rehearsals with a preset notion that something's going to be a wonderful experience or not. I knew all those people extremely well. They had been rehearsing without me for quite some time, while I was directing a play in London. The boys were working without me. And so then eventually when I came back, Pete (Donaldson) and Tom (McCamus), who played the sons, said it was exactly as if Mamma had been away in the sanatorium as she was indeed in the play. And I think I felt that way too, that they all had achieved a kind of sense of themselves as a family in the house.

And I was coming back into rehearsals not being a part of that house, which is exactly what Mary Tyrone feels when she comes back from the sanatorium. She feels they've all been talking about her, and that nobody trusts her, that she has been excluded. She's been the outsider and everyone is watching to see if she's going to go back to the morphine. But no one is open with her. And that they all have their own secrets. So despite the fact that I love and respect all the others in the cast enormously, they still had been in rehearsals for a time without me. And that makes you feel a little like— all right, so what have you been doing that I haven't been a party to?

I don't know if it was that. I don't know if it was the fact that indeed we all knew each other so well. I had played Bill (Hutt's) wife many times. I had played his daughter. I had played his physician. (*laughs*) I had played Tom's mother before that. I don't think I'd ever played Pete's mother before that, but I'd certainly worked with him many times. And so we in a sense, we were like a family. We were like a theatrical family. And it was being directed by Diana Leblanc and I've known her since we were both at the National Theatre School together. So in that sense it was very close, the relationships. And that atmosphere of almost incestuous atmosphere somehow replicated the atmosphere of O'Neill's play, so all those things seemed to contribute towards making something extraordinary. And, of course, in the last analysis, all that stuff is indefinable. You can look at it afterwards and say this must have been a success because of this and this, but you never know.

OUZOUNIAN:

You've had an interesting relationship with the Stratford Festival in that you've often gone away—sometimes for a short time, sometimes for a very long time. Do you always feel that it's been a part of you when you've been away?

HENRY:

I don't know. I guess when I've gone away for short periods of time, I've felt it was a part of me. But when I left in 1980, I didn't think the Stratford Festival was a part of me, or wished to be a part of me. And so being away for fourteen years was a very good thing. It was like a divorce. And it caused me to look at what had been I think a too-close attachment to one theatre. I had thought that Stratford was my home, and that we had a sort of special relationship. Well, I learned that's not the case. That is never the case. It can't be the case with any theatre. A theatre is a place that hires you, if they can use you, and you're very lucky to be hired. And if they can't use you, they don't hire you. And you can go and find work elsewhere. There isn't an artistic organization anywhere in the world that owes you a living. And it was a big lesson for me to learn that Stratford didn't owe me anything. I felt much freer when I came back to Stratford again. I didn't feel that I was coming back to a relationship in which each side needed the other side. I felt I was coming back with something to contribute if I could, with full heart and joy, and delight, but without need.

OUZOUNIAN:

If I woke you up at three in the morning and said "Stratford," what would you say?

HENRY:

(laughing) "Am I late?"

Barry MacGregor as Earl of Richmond in the 1967 production of Richard III.
Photograph by Peter Smith.

Barry MacGregor

British-born Barry MacGregor came to Stratford to portray Jack Point in *The Yeomen of the Guard* in 1964, and he has spent twenty seasons at the festival since then, playing everything from Oberon and Sir Toby Belch to Charles Surface and Algernon Moncrieff. In the Fiftieth Anniversary Season, he will be playing the Fool opposite Christopher Plummer in *King Lear*. I spoke to him in the Festival Theatre in the winter of 2001.

OUZOUNIAN:
What brought you to the Stratford Festival?

MacGREGOR:
I was in New York, doing Peter Brook's production of *King Lear* on tour, and I went to a party and was introduced to Bill Ball, who was going to direct *The Yeomen of the Guard* at the Stratford Festival and didn't have a leading man. He asked me if I sang. Well, my father's philosophy was "Say yes until you sign the contract and then worry." So I went for a singing audition and they mustn't have heard a word I sang, because I got offered the job.

It was very frightening because I'd never sung in my life before. And if Lou Applebaum had not been in the pit as the musical director, I think I probably would have just screamed "Help!" on the first note, because I was so scared. So scared. But I seemed to get through it all right and I enjoyed it . . . afterwards. And that started my twenty seasons with the Stratford Festival.

OUZOUNIAN:
This was during the Langham years. How did you find his directing?

MacGREGOR:

I think he talked theatre language but he frightened you. I mean he was, he was a bully. I remember in *Henry V* he gave me a note—and I still haven't worked it out—which was "You seem to have a mental block there, Barry. Get rid of it." And that was the note. And I still don't know what it means. I have never had the courage to ask him. But years later, I was at a cocktail party, and I looked at him and said, "My God, you don't frighten me anymore." And he doesn't but, of course, I've never worked with him since, which is typical, isn't it? *(laughs)* But he was wonderful. His ability to communicate with an actor was just astounding.

OUZOUNIAN:

You were part of the famous production of Antony and Cleopatra. *Any memories of that?*

MacGREGOR:

Oh God, yes. I remember that Chris Plummer was shooting a film and showed up after the rest of us had been rehearsing for a few weeks.

He was wearing his very velvety shoes with "C.P." on the toecaps, looking very elegant in a blazer and cravat, standing in the middle of the stage back there, staring, while all the rest of us, with everybody knowing exactly where they were going, carried on with mad Egyptian passion. Chris watched it all in total disbelief, finally turned to Langham and called out, "Michael, are they going to be doing this while I'm trying to perform?" And Langham said, "You will be part of it." And Chris quietly said, "Oh." It was like the poor man had been dropped into a zoo.

But Zoe Caldwell said it was wonderful when he finally arrived. And they clicked. They were great together. They had a terrific rapport and sexiness and she was amazing. So was he. It was fascinating to watch him on the stage because his instinct was so phenomenal.

Caldwell was fun. She was a very basic lady and she told you exactly how it was and you just said "Fine, Zoe." I mean, remember she was playing Cleopatra, so one had respect for what she was doing and for her. But you still weren't prepared for her kind of absolute statement of fact. And she didn't suffer fools gladly. She had the situation where the audience was very rough here, one matinee of kids, and when it came to the final scene, as she picked the asp up and shoved it onto her breast, the giggles started and she just stopped and said in a deep Australian accent, which she had not been using as Cleopatra, "I've been very tired all afternoon and I have to play another part tonight, and if you're going to behave like this, I'll go home early and that's it. You have the choice." And someone stood up down there and said, "Oh please continue, Miss Caldwell, please." And she looked at them and said, "Thank you, darling." And we went on with the play and finished it. It was a wonderful production.

OUZOUNIAN:
That same season, you also played Richmond in John Hirsch's production of Richard III, *which meant you were the one who was supposed to kill Alan Bates as Richard. But you didn't . . .*

MacGREGOR:
I never understood quite why, and I still don't to this day, why it ended that way, but I trusted John totally—I mean, one had to trust one's director—but, here's what happened. I had won, I had disarmed Richard, and I was about to kill him, and then he grabbed the dagger out of my hand, and stabbed himself, and I never got the chance to kill him, which was most disheartening you know.

OUZOUNIAN:
What did you find Alan Bates was like to work with?

MacGREGOR:
He was wonderful. I remember sitting till about four in the

morning drinking, as one did in those days, more than one certainly does now. And saying, "You know, I don't like that helmet that I wear. I feel so bloody stupid in it." And he said, "Just take it off and throw it away, nobody's going to stop you. You're up there on your own." And I thought about it and I did. And it was great. I suddenly was able to do the scene properly, because I wasn't worried about this tin thing that seemed to be wobbling about all over the place. No, he was a very sharing actor and this is something I believe very strongly: that if all actors give on a stage, then they all receive. And if they all receive, the audience will receive a hundredfold.

OUZOUNIAN:
What was being directed by John Hirsch like?

MACGREGOR:
Insane and wonderful. I can give you a demonstration of what I mean, the year before *Richard III*, John directed me in *Henry VI* as the Duke of York, Richard's father. There were five people onstage. One leaves. Four talk about how to kill the one that's left. This one leaves. These three talk about killing this one and so on, until eventually I was alone with a soliloquy where I pondered how to kill Powys Thomas, who played the Cardinal in this giant red robe. And I didn't know what I was doing. I really didn't. I was just lost. And Hirsch said to me, "Barry, Barry, Barry. I want you to think of Powys in his big red frock, sitting on the toilet at nine o'clock every morning with the *New York Times*, and he's doing the crossword while doing his natural functions, and when he has finished the crossword at exactly quarter past nine, he leans up and he pulls the cistern, and you've put a bomb in there." And I fell about, with laughter. And he said, "That's how you should do the speech." And every time I did that speech, I had this image of Powys with the *New York Times* and his big red skirt up over his head, flushing and pulling and blowing up. So one had this joy of killing somebody,

which was exactly what Hirsch wanted to capture.

OUZOUNIAN:

What was Hirsch the man like?

MACGREGOR:

You know, when he came to Canada he had two suitcases . . . and was told that one had to be left behind, so he brought the one with books and family photos and left his clothes behind. I remember watching him eating a boiled egg. Now that may seem very mundane, but he cut the top off and then ate the egg. And when he finished, there wasn't a crumb left—not a piece of yolk or white in the eggshell. It was completely clean. It was like watching a surgeon eating. It was so precise and careful, full of respect for the food. And that relates very much to the misery and hell that he went through during the war in Budapest as a Jew and being without food and terrified. He didn't talk about it much, but one day he told us about watching people cutting up a horse that had fallen dead in the shafts of a cart somewhere in the streets. For food.

OUZOUNIAN:

You were also around during the Jean Gascon years. What was his management style like?

MACGREGOR:

(laughing) Gascon's policy here was no policy. And it was wonderful. He just did plays. He would direct you by saying things like, "Barry, you know you need more wah wah wah. Take a chance, baby." It was very big. It was very Gallic. When we were doing *The Duchess of Malfi*, it was my first time actually playing my own age, which was then in my early thirties, and at the end of the first week of rehearsal, Jean said to me, "Barry, you're so fucking juvenile." And I thought, "God, I'm juvenile." The next week I worked hard, and at the end he said, "Barry, you're not only juvenile, you're boring." I thought, "God, I'm juvenile and boring." But at the end of the

third week it was, "Eh Barry, you have the balls." And the fourth week was, "Eh Barry, the balls are heavier." So that was how he communicated, and you understood him. I think because English wasn't his first language, he was able to direct you in a much more direct way because the language was totally straight at you. I adored working with him. He was amazing. He was fun. He was as big as the building. And he loved theatre.

OUZOUNIAN:
It must have been quite a change when Robin Phillips came in.

MacGREGOR:
Absolutely. Jean had led us into a very rich and visual style, full of luxurious period costumes, and then Robin came along and moved us into the nineteenth and twentieth centuries. He brought back suits and uniforms and people were finding it easier to absorb visually so they could hear the play. Suddenly the play, the words, the story was becoming more predominant. And that was one of the great things I think that was happening here at that time.

One of Robin's great qualities is that he teaches as he directs, and I think that is so exciting. I've seen him get stuff out of Martha (Henry) and Bill (Hutt) and you just think, "My God, where's that been?" And it's been there, but he just went right in and pulled it out.

OUZOUNIAN:
You were the company manager under Phillips, so you were right in the middle when all the trouble happened in his final season. What was going on?

MacGREGOR:
I have no idea. I've read the books, and I've gone back in my own mind, and it's still not clear to me. I do know that I was very hurt by it all because one had given so many years of one's career to this building, and it suddenly was folding in, and I think the destruction that took place so quickly was a demonstration of how easy it is to prick a balloon and explode

it. There were a lot of things going on that nobody knew anything about. And in the end I think one began to wonder who was telling the truth. And what was the truth? And if there was a truth, who has it?

OUZOUNIAN:

After many years away, you were able to come back here. What made you return?

MACGREGOR:

I have great respect for this institution. That maybe is the wrong word to use, but in a way, it has become an institution. And I've come back to be a part of it and hopefully to contribute to it. That's not to say that one feels superior because one has a little bit more experience than the next person, because you never stop learning in the theatre. The day you think you know it all, you should leave. I think it was Henry Irving who when he was past seventy said, "Oh dear, I'm just about to die as I think I am beginning to understand a bit about the theatre." And it's very true.

OUZOUNIAN:

What are your hopes for Stratford's next fifty years?

MACGREGOR:

To not become too settled and too complacent with what one does. It's very easy to become comfortable. I think the theatre needs to keep changing every four or five years because the world that it represents keeps changing as well.

OUZOUNIAN:

What comes to mind when I say "The Stratford Festival"?

MACGREGOR:

Watching Maggie Smith in *As You Like It* as she changed from Rosalind to Ganymede. She'd run out of her dressing room, out of the stage door, and run right across and round the park, the football field, and come back in and bring all that air and freshness with her as she came onto the stage and the whole building just lifted.

Richard Monette. Photograph by V. Tony Hauser.

Richard Monette

Richard Monette first came to the Festival in 1965 as Dardanius in *Julius Caesar*. He achieved leading man status in the Robin Phillips years as Hamlet and Henry the Fifth. John Neville later brought him back into the company as a director with the 1988 production of *The Taming of the Shrew*. Since 1994, he has been the Festival's artistic director. I spoke to him in the artistic director's office in the Festival Theatre in the fall of 2001.

OUZOUNIAN:
Richard, what's the very first thing you ever remember hearing about the Stratford Festival?

MONETTE:
I came here, with a friend, to see *As You Like It* and that was it. I decided I wanted to be an actor. I decided I wanted to do Shakespeare. I decided I wanted to stay in this theatre and pursue a career.

OUZOUNIAN:
How did you get here?

MONETTE:
Well, I auditioned. I auditioned three times and, finally I guess, I was so persistent they just said oh, okay, come on in.

OUZOUNIAN:
What was it like for you the first time you stood on that stage?

MONETTE:
It was extraordinary, and I remember that vividly as well because I walked out and William Hutt was sitting down in the auditorium and he got up and shook my hand and he said, "Welcome home." And I've been home ever since really.

OUZOUNIAN:

After serving your apprentice years and going away to England for a while, you returned to the company to play leading roles, and Robin Phillips was in charge. What was it like to work for him?

MONETTE:

He took the acting company on a very interesting journey. You know, before him, the style of acting was bigger and more rhetorical. With Guthrie and Langham and with Jean Gascon. And then we turned a corner there, and the style in the seventies was very much more muted, everybody was doing more kind of naturalistic conversational work. So it was interesting for the company to veer in that direction. I learned a lot about acting from him. A lot about acting.

I remember once in a play called *The Devils* I was in with Nicholas Pennell, and the prose is very purple in that play, so we were acting our socks off. We were just going at it, you know. And Robin was watching this dreadful acting and all he said was, "You know this scene takes place at night. And at night you can hear sound so clearly." So, of course, we played night and we started to talk to one another instead of screaming. And the scene got a lot better.

OUZOUNIAN:

I want to talk to you about playing Hamlet for Robin Phillips. There were two of you, right? Robin picked you and Nicholas Pennell to both play the part. He loved to double cast shows, but why did he do things like that?

MONETTE:

I don't know why he did it. The best reason, I guess, is that he thought perhaps both of us had earned the right to do it. And we were very contrasting actors as well as good friends.

OUZOUNIAN:

What was your favourite part about playing Hamlet? What did you like doing the most?

MONETTE:

I liked the journey of Hamlet. Where he begins, where he ends. It's an astonishing role, it's a Rorschach test, and it's draining. It's like living and dying. In front of an audience. More than any other role I've ever played, because you have to be so committed. You know you expend the physical energy of a man digging a ditch for eight hours and just the stamina required is extraordinary, because at the end you're sort of mad and you have to face your own death. And you have to face very important issues, like suicide. What you think about it, what you think the character thinks about it. So you go through a very painful journey. And one of the things about playing the role is that you're very alone. Nobody in the play likes you, including your girlfriend, Ophelia, including your mother. The only person who sort of likes you is Horatio. And it's very alienating.

I'll tell you a story. On the final preview in Stratford, before we opened, there was a full house, at which some very eminent people were there—Hume Cronyn being one of them and Carol Shelley being another. And I came to the end of "To be or not to be" and suddenly I hear from the audience, a very loud voice saying "Richard, you are a bullshit actor." And I thought, "I'm losing my mind. Or the director is giving me notes."

And then there was this rumble from the audience and I thought, "Oh my God, somebody actually said this. What am I going to do?" And a million things go through your head. One of them is—lights go up and we have him ejected. The second thing is we start all over again, and then it suddenly occurred to me, maybe this person is right. So the only thing to do is to continue and prove them wrong.

So I then went into the "Get thee to a nunnery" scene with my Ophelia, Marti Maraden, who is standing like this by my side shaking with her book. And I threw her around like a frisbee. It was the fastest nunnery scene in the history of

Hamlet, because I'd just spent all this pumped-up adrenaline. Well, I got off and I got a five-minute ovation. So much so that I went all the way down underneath the stage, came back up and they were still applauding for bravery, if for nothing else.

So I get home, and Nicholas Pennell who was alternating with me phoned me up and said, "Richard, I've just heard what happened. This is terrible. What did you do?" And I said, "Well Nicholas, there was only one thing I could do. I took a very long pause and then I said 'if you think I'm a bullshit actor, wait till you see Nicholas Pennell play the part.'"

OUZOUNIAN:
Let's leap ahead a few years to when Peter Ustinov came to Stratford to play King Lear. You were Edmund in that production. What was it like?

MONETTE:
Well, Peter Ustinov was a very big star. It's always interesting working with big stars because you, as an actor, approach them in a different way, involuntarily. But he was an extremely kind man and an extremely funny man, and he was very good to me. I liked him enormously. And it was a thrill having him here, because the audience was just abuzz.

He was also wildly entertaining in rehearsals. I remember one day where we were doing the fifth act of *Lear* and he was asked by the director, Robin Phillips, to sing it. And he started with Monteverdi and ended up with Strauss, singing "Howl, howl, howl, howl!" And going through the whole history of opera at the same time. Well, he was in full swing as he put Cordelia down, and then he suddenly stopped in mid-note and he said, "and I've split my pants." *(laughs)*

Oh, they were great rehearsals. He was asked what he thought about Lear. And he said, "Well, I think Lear is like Franco, the Spanish dictator. You know when Franco lay dying, his daughter came to visit him, and he heard pacing on the tiles outside and he asked, 'Who is there?' And his daughter said, 'It's the Spanish people, Father. They've come to say goodbye.' And Franco said, 'Where are they going?'"

That was Ustinov's whole theory behind Lear: he was the king and he was right and that was it.

OUZOUNIAN:
Over the years, you've worked with every artistic director except Guthrie. How would you characterize them?

MONETTE:
You had more of a cerebral director in Michael Langham. Then you had more of a theatre person in Jean Gascon, who brought all that French vigour, and then Robin Phillips who was a theatre man as well, but in a very different, very reserved style. And then you had John Hirsch who was a moody but brilliant Hungarian, John Neville who was a straightforward man of the theatre, David William who I would characterize as an intellectual, and then myself, an actor who became a director. It's been a fabulous journey, and a great balance has been maintained. I don't think there was any plan in Stratford's board of directors. I think it's just the way it happened.

OUZOUNIAN:
John Neville, an actor who became a director just like you, was the one who first asked you to direct Shakespeare here on the main stage with The Taming of the Shrew. *What was your reaction?*

MONETTE:
I was very, very surprised, honestly, and I said, "Well, I'll have to think about it." You see, I had to come up with a *reason* for doing it because that play also is fraught with political correctness. I thought, "Do I have anything to say? Can I offer anything?" And then I came up with this Fellini concept of the fifties, just pre-pill, set in Italy. And I worked on it for a year. I went through every word. I was thorough because I had to be, because I'd never done it before. I didn't know if I could hold a room of thirty actors.

The actors thought it was a bizarre concept (although the first *Shrew* that Guthrie did here was set in modern dress), but I didn't know whether they would buy it. Well, some did and some didn't. Getting there was not easy. I remember one day John Neville walked into the auditorium all dressed up. I said, "Where are you going?" He said, "Oh, I'm just saying hello and I'm going off to a board meeting." And I said, "Sit down and watch for just ten minutes. We're doing a run-through and they're not acting."

Neville knew what I meant, so he sat there in about the tenth row and the play started and they were brilliant. Everybody rose to the occasion thinking if I'm bad, he won't invite me back next year. And so it really, really worked.

OUZOUNIAN:
After a few years of directing successful productions, you were asked if you would assume the artistic directorship of Stratford. How did it happen?

MONETTE:
Well, they were looking for an artistic director and the then artistic director, David William, asked me to put my name in the hat. And I said, "Oh, I don't want to do that. I don't want that job. I've never run anything. I can't even run my own life." He said, "Just put your name down and you can withdraw later because we need to have a list." So I said okay and I did the first interview.

Now you know when you don't want something, it's like auditioning for a part. If you don't want it, inevitably, you get it. So because I had nothing to lose at the first interview, I said exactly what was on my mind, and all of it was pretty positive. You know I said how great Stratford is, that there was nothing wrong with it, all it needs is a little bit of a paint job now just because we're turning forty-something and you know, we just need to get back into the gym and, you know, with the press and everything because the work has always been good. I mean there's been a, a note of triumph since the beginning. It's really a remarkable theatre, you know, given how many shows have been done here. I told them to look for somebody who is going to maintain the standards of the work that we had been doing.

Months went by, I was interviewed again, and I started to think this would be all wrong. So I wrote the president of the board a letter, which I sent on a Friday night, saying I wished to withdraw my name. On Saturday morning, he arrived at my doorstep in my home and said, "Now if we were to offer this to you, what would you say?" And I said, "When you get to your office on Monday morning, you're going to find a letter saying I'm withdrawing my name." Well, then we had a chat. And then I suddenly thought that I cared about Stratford, that I'd spent my life here. That I believed in it and if that were the case, I would at least bring love to it. And care to the best of my abilities. So I said yes.

OUZOUNIAN:
And what was it like?

MONETTE:
It was very difficult at first. Not many people know how bad things really were. My predecessor, David William, had a very hard time of it because of the GST, the recession, the rise of the mega-musical. The councils were cutting money. No, Stratford was not in a very good financial state and what I tried to do for the first three years is keep the doors open.

Then, slowly, things got better and better. I was able to pay back the debts. We didn't have a deficit, but we owed a lot of money. I mean I was here when we had to borrow money to pay for the heat in the winter to heat the buildings. So it was a very serious time. But then the audiences started to grow and kept on growing and now it's a completely different organization than it used to be. It was very paternalistic at the beginning, and stayed that way for many, many years. Now, it's less so. It's responsible for the livelihood of the town. It brings in $360 million to the town every year. We employ 875 people. Our budget is now $40 million. It's doubled in the time that I've been here. So we've grown. But as we have grown, the audience has grown as well because there's a need. You can always shrink. "Honey, I shrunk the festival!" But right now, there are still people coming. And you do the theatre for people. You don't do it even for yourself as an artist. It begins that way. But your art, theatre, the art of theatre doesn't exist without people. Plays on the shelf are literature. Plays on the stage are theatre. So you need an audience. And they're coming. And that thrills me.

So with this turn of events, I then set about to have a little vision. I started the conservatory for classical training, which will give us artistic stability because many actors began here, fifty years ago and have been with this theatre but they're getting older. And they're going to move on. And so as I said to the board, we need . . . young people to be trained in the classics. This school is going to be the future. And in about three years, the age of the company is going to be approximately thirty, I imagine, years of age. And it's going to be the same age as it was in the very first company. Because they were all young as well. So this is a great thing.

Shakespeare's one of the reasons I became an actor. If not perhaps the only reason. And I know this will sound sentimental, but I'm glad I gave something back. But when you love something this much, and you apply yourself this much, sometimes it works. And this has worked.

OUZOUNIAN:

What would you wish Stratford for the next fifty years?

MONETTE:

I hope the level of excellence never declines. I hope it grows, not necessarily bigger 'cause I think we're about as big as we can get, but I hope it continues in its spirit of excellence that it has had for the last fifty years. I hope the times encourage classical work, you know 'cause Shakespeare goes up and down in fashion. Right now he's up in fashion. All those Hollywood movies. But I don't think he will ever really go out of fashion because people want to commune, especially in an age of computers and telephones, when you're never in a place with other people. You're always on your own. And I think this is one of the experiences that people find here. That they laugh with other people. They cry with other people. And so I hope that there will always be that need. And I hope it has enough money to be able to maintain this excellence. And I hope artists will continue to realize that there's Shakespeare and then there's everything else.

OUZOUNIAN:
When I say "The Stratford Festival" what images come to your mind?

MONETTE:
The stage, the thrust stage. The tent. That spirit of adventure. When I think back on it, it's astonishing that this started here! And that they did Shakespeare because the town was called Stratford and Sir Tyrone Guthrie came over and insisted on building an Elizabethan stage, which altered the way we produce plays.

I think of myself as a young man, coming here. I think of a life spent with Shakespeare, my life. I think of growing up with this audience. They saw me when I was twenty. Now I'm fifty-seven. When I act . . . I've grown up with the audience. I think what a wonderful way to spend a lifetime . . . to explore the human condition by putting on plays for other people and exploring it together, with a genius like Shakespeare. I couldn't have imagined my life being any better professionally. I count my blessings. I was blessed.

Len Cariou as Prospero in the 1982 production of The Tempest.
Photograph by Robert C. Ragsdale.

Len Cariou

Winnipeg-born Len Cariou first joined the Festival in 1962 and remained for four seasons, appearing most notably in *The Rise and Fall of the City of Mahagonny*. After an award-winning career on stage and screen, he returned to the Festival in 1981 for two seasons, appearing as Prospero, Coriolanus, and Petruchio. I spoke with him at the Players' Club in New York City in April 2001, while he was appearing on Broadway in Neil Simon's *The Dinner Party*.

OUZOUNIAN:

Len, how did you first become involved in the Stratford Festival?

CARIOU:

I was in Winnipeg, just starting in the theatre as an actor, with John Hirsch. This is like 1959 or '60. I had never seen any Shakespeare. I'd only read it as we did in school. I'd never acted in any of it. I remember reading it and thinking how on earth do you make this stuff work for an audience today? And then all of a sudden, I was asked to come and be in the company, and I was astounded! *(laughing)* Kate Reid and Doug Rain had done a play with me at the Manitoba Theatre Centre, and they both recommended me to Michael Langham. Sight unseen, Langham sent me a wire asking if I'd like to be a part of the company. I went to John Hirsch and said, "I'm absolutely astounded," and he said, "Well, you've got to go." And then something occurred to me and I asked him, "Did you have anything to do with this?" And he said, "Well, maybe, yeah."

I'll always remember the first day I arrived, going up to the balcony of the theatre, opening the centre doors and looking down on that stage. That was awesome. To see that incredible theatre was breathtaking. I mean I just stood there for about ten minutes. I don't think I moved. Just looked at it. And thought, what is this place? It's like a temple of some kind. And so that summer was a real revelation to me because at the end of it I went back to Winnipeg, to MTC, and I said to John, "I've discovered what I want to do. The classical repertory has just opened the world for me."

OUZOUNIAN:
So there you are, a young guy who'd never even understood Shakespeare, and suddenly you're acting with people like Christopher Plummer. Was it at all intimidating to you?

CARIOU:
A little, but I figured I didn't have a chance in hell if I didn't embrace it. So I spent an awful lot of time that first year sitting in rehearsals. I mean I virtually spent every minute in the theatre, even when they were rehearsing scenes that I wasn't in, I would sit and watch. Just 'cause I needed to know how to make this stuff work.

After I'd been there a few seasons, they were going to do *Henry V* and I went to Michael Langham and said, "I'm Henry." And he said, "Yes you are, but there's a line." And so Douglas Rain played the part, and there was really nothing much for me to do in that season until Jean Gascon asked me to come and be in *The Rise and Fall of the City of Mahagonny*.

OUZOUNIAN:
That was supposedly a very different show than anything they had seen up till then at the Festival: very edgy, bold, sexy, colourful. I mean, it was Kurt Weill, so you knew you weren't getting into a garden party but what was it like to work with Jean Gascon on a show like that?

CARIOU:

He was wonderful. He had that incredible energy as well as a really clear idea of what he thought it should be, and he was always great fun to be with.

OUZOUNIAN:

Some people say that Jean certainly felt clearly what he wanted and thought clearly what he wanted, but had trouble saying clearly what he wanted sometimes.

CARIOU:

Oh, that was always a problem. We always used to bug him about it. "Jean, why don't you talk English at home and not French? You might learn how to make things clearer, you know." But, of course, he couldn't do that. And he would talk to us in his broken English and it would come out very strange sometimes. You'd have to say "Jean, wait a minute. I don't understand what you just said." And that became kind of a catchword among us. "Excuse me, Jean, I don't understand what you just said."

OUZOUNIAN:

Now after that, you went to the Guthrie Theatre in Minneapolis, you went to Broadway, you went all over the place. You didn't return to Stratford for years. But it was John Hirsch who brought you back. Do you recall how he approached you about returning?

CARIOU:

I was doing a film in California, and he called me and asked me whether or not I'd be available to come back to Stratford. And I said, "I'll be there with bells on. Just tell me what you want me to do." And he said, "How about *Coriolanus?*" So I sat down and started to read it. Well, I guess I know why it's not done very often. It's a pretty tough cookie. But John said, "Come on, we've got to do this." And I remember Brian Bedford directed it, and we had a tough time making it work, but in the end, we managed to do a really good production of the play.

OUZOUNIAN:
Your other big show that first season was The Taming of the Shrew. *Did you find it difficult to play Petruchio in a post–women's lib generation?*

CARIOU:
There were some issues that came up. I remember once we were in rehearsal and Sherry Flett was playing Kate. And we came to the speech at the end about "I am ashamed that women are so simple" and she refused to do it. So I said, "Okay, I'll go and have a cigarette and when you decide you want to do it, I'll come back." And I just walked off. Everybody suddenly went "Wait, whoa, whoa!" and Sherry got very apologetic, and I asked, "What is the point of this? Do the speech and then tell me where you stand politically after it's over, because we have a play to do here. Don't waste our time on such nonsense as that," which I thought it was. And I'm certainly not anti-feminist. I think that the feminist movement was long overdue. But it had nothing to do with us doing the play so that was that. Sherry obviously got over it and did the speech beautifully.

OUZOUNIAN:
How did you sense the mood in the Festival, the mood in the company that year?

CARIOU:
John was not the most popular guy in the world because he's a pretty tough cookie. So there were some people who felt "Oh great, there's new blood here and it's going to be terrific" and I think there were probably the same number of people on the other side who had a bad experience working with John or they were just missing Robin Phillips or maybe they didn't even want to be there. But that happens in companies all the time. When we did have success with the season, I think everybody relaxed and then the next year was even better.

Hirsch came up to me one day and said, "I'd like you to play Prospero next year," and you don't say no to that. I thought he was one of the great directors. He was a difficult guy, but he's sorely missed to this day in my opinion. He had a great theatrical sense and he was a very, very intelligent man.

OUZOUNIAN:
Hirsch had been one of your mentors in your early years, but now almost twenty years had gone by. You were certainly different. Was he different as well?

CARIOU:
I think he was a little more mellow . . . if that's a word you could ever use to describe Hirsch. He certainly had an absolute idea of what *The Tempest* should be, and how he saw the story unfolding. And I think some people were a little taken aback by how strong and bold it was. I think everybody was upset about the violent way, for example, that I delivered "Our revels now are ended," but it made great sense to me that he was that upset, and it made the transition at the end of the play, when he buries the book and sets Ariel free, even more poignant for me and for the audience.

OUZOUNIAN:
Many people drew direct links between Hirsch and Prospero: the magician still at the height of his powers but maybe wanting to bury his book, and a great deal of anger and all those other things coming out. Did John ever speak directly to you about his interpretation?

CARIOU:
He was really not one to do that. I think he would insinuate and he would cajole you to do it, but I kept feeling that it had quite a bit to do with him personally. The hell that he had gone through in the revolution, and being betrayed, losing his family, lots of parallels could be drawn.

OUZOUNIAN:
What specifically do you remember about working with Hirsch?

CARIOU:

(smiles) Anybody who ever worked with him would tell you that just about at the dress rehearsal or the first preview, you would hear John snapping his fingers. Snap snap snap snap snap. John and his sense of pace. That lived with me forever . . . still does. I hear it all the time. Whenever I feel something's kind of dragging, I hear snap snap snap snap snap in the back of my head.

OUZOUNIAN:

When you left the Festival after that season, did you and John have a goodbye of any kind?

CARIOU:

Not a real goodbye, because we both thought we would cross paths again. As it turned out, we didn't . . . and then he was gone.

OUZOUNIAN:

What words, images, pop into your mind when I say "The Stratford Festival"?

CARIOU:

The Avon River. Swans. The incredible stage. The bar at the Avon Theatre where we had a lot of good times. Tom Patterson. Michael Langham. And the golf course, the Stratford golf course. I spent a lot of time there . . .

James Blendick as Orgon in the 2000 production of Tartuffe.
Photograph by Cylla von Tiedemann.

James Blendick

James Blendick first appeared at Stratford as Ratcliffe in the 1967 production of *Richard III*. His work over the years has included many great roles such as Falstaff, Claudius, Titus Andronicus, Big Daddy, Orgon, Sir Toby Belch, and Matthew Harrison Brady. In the Fiftieth Anniversary Season, he will be playing Alfred Doolittle in *My Fair Lady* and Gloucester in *King Lear*.
I spoke to him at the Festival Theatre in the fall of 2000.

OUZOUNIAN:
You first came to the Stratford Festival during the extraordinary season of 1967 and were part of two legendary shows that year: Richard III *and* Antony and Cleopatra. *Let's talk first about working with Alan Bates as Richard . . .*

BLENDICK:
I was very excited. Alan was a very hot movie star then, but he also proved to be a charming, wonderful, gentle man. And eventually we became quite close friends throughout the summer. It was a marvellous experience.

Alan and John, at the beginning, were very exciting to watch. Of course, there were differences of opinion. The actor sees a scene one way and the director sees it another. Sometimes little arguments went on. But nothing big. Nothing big at all. Alan was not what you would call an open fighter, you know, where he's just saying "Well I disagree with this" in front of the whole company. Maybe words were spoken, you know, privately about the scenes. I think they didn't necessarily agree totally on the way that John wanted it played. But I think there was compromise throughout.

OUZOUNIAN:
What do you remember of Hirsch's feelings on the play?

BLENDICK:
The concept was very insectlike. We looked like a lot of large bugs. Even Alan, I mean his hair was very stringy and greasy and long, with lot of hairs and feathers sticking out of the body. I was playing Ratcliffe, one of Richard's henchmen, and Hirsch had me shave my head so that I looked like a large beetle, with all this hair and fur sticking out of me. He saw it as these festering insects devouring the kingdom, and placing Richard on the throne—the ultimate bug, so to speak. *(laughing)* But it worked.

OUZOUNIAN:
The same year you're also in Antony and Cleopatra *with Christopher Plummer and Zoe Caldwell, directed by Michael Langham. What comes to mind from that?*

BLENDICK:
I remember Chris came to rehearsals a bit late because he was filming *Oedipus* in the Mediterranean. So Max Helpmann—who was understudying Chris in the show—worked with Zoe initially. When I saw Zoe starting to rehearse, I was just floored by her. I mean she's not a large woman, but the power, and excitement and presence and voice . . . it was just staggering! The talent. And so right from the get-go you thought, "Oh, this is hot!" And then finally Chris arrived. Well, it just got hotter and hotter and hotter.

Chris had just finished shooting this film so he was absolutely brown as a bug, in terms of being tanned. And he was really fit, you know? Well, he came in. I remember his shirt was unbuttoned way down and he had these little loafers on, you know, and designer slacks and he walked in. I remember Zoe sitting in the corner, kind of like a little girl of about fourteen, as he walked by. He didn't even know she was in the corner. He walked up to Langham and said, "Hello, Michael. How are you, darling? Nice to see you" and then Michael said, "Well, why don't we just start right at the top? I want to go right into the first scene." So the two of them come out from centre stage, and it's a scene in which they've, you know, been making out and they're having fun with one another and it's all foreplay in a funny kind of way. They came out and they were just improvising. Well, it was astounding. I mean we were all standing there with our mouths hanging open and they had never done the scene before. The chemistry was fantastic. I'll always remember that.

OUZOUNIAN:
How did you and Plummer get along?

BLENDICK:
Chris was very friendly. I think what Chris basically demands, before he reaches any kind of friendship in the theatre, is that people take their work seriously. He doesn't suffer fools gladly, and he doesn't give them much time. But if you were earnest and honest in what you wanted to do, and . . . you really applied yourself to the show, then you were fine. But you had to be there one hundred percent all the time because he's very demanding of himself. I mean I've heard stories of him, in the earlier years, where he would come in late at night into the theatre, and turn on the lights and work on the stage by himself for hours, going over his role. He's a very hard worker—hard on himself, and I think consequently, hard on other people. But only for the betterment of the show. However, if people are just walking through it and really using him because of his talent or his fame, I think he really doesn't have much time for that.

OUZOUNIAN:
You've been fortunate in having worked with most of Stratford's

artistic directors, and I'd like to ask you about them. Let's start with Langham? What's he like to work for?

BLENDICK:

Wonderful. Precise. But he can be difficult about that precision. You've got to do your homework. I think he's probably one of the best directors I've ever worked with. He's taught me enormous things about the theatre, about *this* theatre, this stage. Things about myself. What to do. What not to do. Baggage that I had to get rid of as an actor, in order to improve myself.

He's another person who worked very hard. I mean he came in and he knew the play backwards. He was very much to me like Alfred Hitchcock apparently was. He did all his homework and that, and they say when he finally got on the set, all the shots were set up and he would just sit there and read the newspaper. Because all the homework was done. They knew what the shot was going to be. They knew what the cuts were going to be. The editing was almost done in his own head, and it was just a matter of shooting it. And that's what Michael was like, and that's why he was so successful with the classics. I mean he's one of the best at them. And with the language as well. I mean he was extraordinary with the language.

OUZOUNIAN:

How would you contrast him to Hirsch?

BLENDICK:

John was more emotional, worked on more of a heart basis, more of a sexual basis. Not that he's not disciplined, but he wanted you to be as real as possible and whatever that took, it didn't matter to him as long as he got that. The reality of it. Whereas Michael was a little more technical. And both schools are valid, of course. What you'd like to do is incorporate both of them into a performance. The technique and also the reality and the compassion and the guts and all of that. But ultimately, the thing that will always hold you in good stead, is having a great sense of technique. Because there are some nights that you just don't feel like doing it, and you still have to muster it up.

OUZOUNIAN:

How would you characterize John Neville as a director to work for?

BLENDICK:

Neville is very much an actor's director. He gives you the freedom to explore that most directors don't. John was a lot more liberal, he left a lot of it up to you. And sometimes that's good. Sometimes that's bad, because if you don't have people that are experienced enough, they can just go right over the edge and really wreck a production. But I must, I must give Neville credit for taking chances, because Langham, by contrast, was very rigid. Not that he wasn't right. But he was very rigid. Sometimes you felt very claustrophobic, and that's not good for an actor, because you keep doing the same thing over and over again. But Neville was good that way. And he knew when to say "No, no, that's enough. Now you're going awry."

OUZOUNIAN:

Next was David William. How would you characterize him?

BLENDICK:

David is from the Michael Langham school. You know, a man who is very informed, very bright, very well read—well read in all fields, and not just the theatre. He's a man of precision. A man with strong ideas. Perhaps, to my thinking, maybe a little too rigid. But it worked for him. Sometimes it didn't work for us. Maybe because we were too flexible. Or wanting too much flexibility in our performances. I don't really know sometimes. But I think of him as a teacher of the Bard, of the classics, of the language. He's another wonderful contributor to the theatre in this country.

OUZOUNIAN:
And finally, Richard Monette. What's it like to work for him?

BLENDICK:
He's a lot of fun. He comes across as a very humorous, open kind of guy, which he is. But there's also a precision about him, as well as a trust that he places upon people. He says, "Now look, I've hired you for this. You can do it, and I don't need to tell you what to do most of the time. You've got to do your homework, and if you really have problems, we'll talk about it." It keeps you on your toes, but the final result of the show is usually entertaining, which it has to be. That's the business that we're in.

I think Richard is a pleasure to work with, and I also think he's been very good for this place because he's sensed how the business is changing. You know, with government cutbacks, we have to rely basically on sponsorship and raising money; he's very good at that. And obviously the audiences are coming and they love what we're doing. And there's some very important work that goes on here. Very important work.

OUZOUNIAN:
What would you wish the Stratford Festival for its next fifty years?

BLENDICK:
That it stick to its mandate and continue to do Shakespeare and the classics. That's what's special about it. And that's why people come. And I hope that stays the same. You don't change Tiffany's.

OUZOUNIAN:
What words come to your mind when I say "The Stratford Festival"?

BLENDICK:
A new beginning. Greatness. Joy. Family.

Kenneth Welsh as Hamlet in the 1969 production of Hamlet.
Photograph by Douglas Spillane.

Kenneth Welsh

Kenneth Welsh came to the Stratford Festival in 1966 and remained there for seven seasons, playing roles such as d'Artagnan in *The Three Musketeers*, Octavius Caesar in *Antony and Cleopatra*, and the title role in *Hamlet*. He then went on to a distinguished career on stage, screen, and television in both America and Canada.
I spoke to him in Toronto in the spring of 2001.

OUZOUNIAN:
What's your first memory of Stratford?

WELSH:
I was a student at the National Theatre School and at that time we used to go to Stratford in the summers and see the plays. So I saw John Colicos play Lear, and Bruno Gerussi as Mark Antony . . . these amazing performances! And I always had this fantasy that something would happen and I would find myself on the Stratford stage as a result of someone in the company not being able to go on for some reason. And they couldn't find anybody. The understudy didn't know the part. This was part of my fantasy. And they would come to me, and I would take over this role and, you know, I'd be famous from then on.

OUZOUNIAN:
When you did get to Stratford, you arrived at the end of the Langham years. What are your memories of him?

WELSH:
Michael I remember as being very fastidious as a director, very

precise and very humorous. He was, in terms of his structuring and blocking of plays, always very precise. It wasn't one step. It was two steps. It wasn't a turn to the left. It was a half a turn. He choreographed his productions so brilliantly in fact, that you fit in, and you felt completely comfortable within the context of Michael's directing. He was also very humorous and kind of fatherly. I would say he was very paternal to a lot of us, the younger actors, many of whom had just come out of the theatre school and were completely new to this, this experience at Stratford.

OUZOUNIAN:
A few years later you became the first person to play Hamlet since Chris Plummer back in 1957. What did you do when you heard?

WELSH:
I think I fainted. You know the routine was that we would be called into the office and we'd be sat down and told which roles we'd be playing. And, of course, everyone's got their ear to the door outside because all of us young actors were kind of thinking, well, I'll get to play Hamlet. Or maybe he will. Or maybe he will, you know 'cause there was this kind of constant competition going on between us all the time. And when I went in there, they said, "We'd like you to play Damis in *Tartuffe*"—which was a revival of what I had played the year before—"and Barnardine in *Measure For Measure*"—which was a nice little cameo role. And then they said, "Oh yes, we'd like you to play Hamlet." *(laughs)* So, I literally fell on the floor in a sort of mock faint, because I didn't know quite else what to do. I was so thrilled, you know. Overcome. I mean it was a kind of secret hope that I would be chosen, you know, and that I would undertake it, and that it would be great fun, you know, and . . . well it was, you know.

John Hirsch planned a production of *Hamlet* that was, I suppose, intended for a student audience mostly. John was very aware of political situations, because he came from so many of them in Europe, so the *Hamlet* that he wanted would be one that spoke directly to the younger generation.

The first time we played it was in Chicago, prior to our season, to a lot of student audiences there. And they responded enthusiastically, wildly, to it. And the play was very quick, fast. You know I came out and I practically tripped over the soliloquies. And the kids lapped it up 'cause they had to keep up to the pace and energy of this. And they could feel themselves right inside it.

But then when we got back on the Stratford stage, which tends to stretch everything out, suddenly you're like in a frying pan, you know, you're kind of like an egg frying a bit. *(laughing)* it lengthened quite a bit, you know. By the time we got to opening night, I believe there wasn't a single critic, except some Americans who actually liked it, or me in particular. There was one critic I think who even failed to mention me. *(laughs)* There was a review of *Hamlet* with no mention of the Hamlet.

You know, but then at the end of the season, at the other bookend of it, when we did all those student matinees, that was the payoff, because that's who John had directed it for. And they just ate it up, because they recognized it. They identified with Hamlet.

OUZOUNIAN:

How did you and John approach it? Did he ever sit down and say to you, "This is my idea of Hamlet"?

WELSH:

No, no. John let the Hamlet emerge out of me, mostly. He built a production around that. I mean he cast it in a certain way. He cast it with a lot of recent graduates from the National Theatre School—myself and Jimmy Blendick and Anne Anglin and Neil Dainard—about ten of us I think, were in that production. John wanted to build up a production based on some of Canada's most recently and intensely trained young actors. And they would interact because they came from the same base of training. I think he allowed that to play out quite a bit. And I think what he was focusing on was the pace of the production, and just kind of taking away the poetry from it, and concentrating more on the story, you know, and letting the politics take care of themselves as they will I think in that play.

OUZOUNIAN:
You mentioned that it got a certain amount of negative response. Do you think it was because it was young and fresh and not what was anticipated?

WELSH:
Absolutely. Some of the reviews actually longed for that poetic reading that they were used to. I felt like a pioneer in a way, because first of all I refused to use any kind of mid-Atlantic dialect, and I spoke in the role as I spoke normally. John wanted us to be who we were. He wanted us to bring ourselves to the roles that we played in Shakespeare. So yeah, it was me out there, this guy from Alberta. *(laughs)* I think actually Nathan Cohen in his review pointed out something about my farmerlike walk, which I took as a direct slap at me being a Westerner.

OUZOUNIAN:
When you look back on it, was there a moment that you loved playing more than any other?

WELSH:
I think it was after all the hard stuff was done *(laughing)* and he comes back from England, and there's suddenly peace on stage. You know, I think John even lit it that way. There was suddenly golden light. And he's there with Horatio and they have this very gentle conversation about life and about death.

He says:

There's a special providence in the fall of a sparrow.
If it be now, 'tis not to come; if it be not to come,
it will be now; if it be not now, yet it will come:
the readiness is all.

That sort of gentleness that comes after all Hamlet's been through. You know you've gone through your night. You've blown all the ammunition you've had. Whether this worked or not, you've done it. You've given all your energy, and now you're given this moment, to contemplate, and speak of something more profound.

OUZOUNIAN:
What was John Hirsch like as a director?

WELSH:
He was a very emotional director. I mean he seemed to have very strong intellectual concepts about plays. But when it all came down to it, John was very visceral. He'd get out in front of the stage and he'd say, "No, don't . . . let's not . . . you don't get it that way. Get closer to her and you know, faster . . . why aren't you doing this with more emotion?" He would direct on the spot as a kind of emotional field general, you know?

We had the same experience when we were doing the TV version of *The Three Musketeers* with John. The CBC was on a sort of slowdown strike. We were trying to get this thing produced, and the day would end at five. And John would have ten minutes. We'd be heading off to our rooms, thinking, okay, we can't do anymore. And John would say, "We have ten minutes more. Come back." "But John, we haven't rehearsed." "Doesn't matter. We will shoot it. I know you can do it. Jimmy, Kenny, you're over there and everybody, take your places. Camera."

He was an improviser, you know. John was at his best when he could feel like he was in the middle of a big grand improvisation. Which I think was what he really wanted out of *Hamlet*, the sense that it was being improvised as we did it, you know? And I have a very sweet memory of John after I'd gotten all these dreadful reviews, he called me up the next morning and said, "Come, let's go for a walk." So we went for a walk, you know, around the field there outside the theatre. And John, he just said, "Don't worry about it. Don't worry about the reviews. Play it the way that we rehearsed it. Because you are a very good Hamlet. I chose you because I wanted you to do it. And you are excellent. Forget about the reviews. They don't matter."

OUZOUNIAN:
If you could make a wish for Stratford's next fifty years, what would it be?

WELSH:
I wish that they maintain an honesty about the exploration of Shakespeare's plays, a simple, emotional directness in the production of them, and that they be done with the same amount of love that they've been done for the last fifty years.

OUZOUNIAN:
If I say to you "The Stratford Festival," what pops into your head?

WELSH:
It was seven of the best years of my life, and I felt like I was in the hands of Shakespeare in so many different ways during those seven years—in comic ways, in tragic ways, in personal ways, and in emotional ways. I'll never forget it.

Alan Bates as Richard, Duke of Gloucester, in the 1967 production of Richard III.
Photograph by Peter Smith.

Alan Bates

Internationally renowned stage and film star Alan Bates came to the Stratford Festival in the 1967 season to play the title role in *Richard III* and Master Ford in *The Merry Wives of Windsor.* I spoke to him in New York, in December 2000, when he was appearing in Yasmina Reza's play, *The Unexpected Man.*

OUZOUNIAN:

The story has it that you were in England filming Far from the Madding Crowd *when you got a telegram, inviting you to come to the Stratford Festival. Is that true?*

BATES:

Absolutely. And I knew it as one of the famous theatres of the world.

You're always surprised when you get an offer. *(laughs)* You're pleased, you know, and this particular offer was terrific, because I was very much in need of it at that time. Although I was theatre trained and theatre experienced, I had gotten lucky in film, and had not been on the stage for two years and that's really quite a long time. Because if you really want to do theatre, if theatre's going to be part of your life, you've got to just keep doing it. You've got to keep everything in shape—your voice, your breath, your confidence, your ability to walk across a stage, you know.

OUZOUNIAN:

When you were first asked to play Richard the Third, what's the thought that went through your mind—terror?

BATES:

Oh yes. Complete terror. I mean it's one of the great parts that you imagined yourself doing one day, but it's always in the future. Then suddenly you're faced with it, and the terror strikes, but it's everything you've always wanted to do, and so you've got to do it.

OUZOUNIAN:

Did you have the shadow of the Olivier movie hanging over you?

BATES:

You can't avoid it. You can't avoid something that is so definite, so positive, so renowned as it was at the time when I did it. Probably people wouldn't be as scared of it now. But back then, it was recent enough. So you think, "How am I going to just avoid that?" And then you think, "Well, I can't consciously avoid it." You see, you can't consciously avoid something, really, anymore than you should consciously go for it. You should let a play happen to you. You should let a part happen to you and let it sort of creep up on you and become yours. But images are hard to shake off.

OUZOUNIAN:

Another difficult image to shake off was the fact that the Festival had opened fourteen years before with the late Sir Alec Guinness playing Richard the Third and you would only be the second person to play it.

BATES:

Yes I knew that *(laughs)*, but you just have to ignore that in your head as much as you possibly can. I mean there isn't a single classical part where you're not treading in a lot of other people's brilliant shoes, so that's a given and you either play these parts or you don't.

OUZOUNIAN:

John Hirsch was your director for Richard III. *How did you get along?*

BATES:

I liked him enormously as soon as we met. We first got together for dinner at The Ginger Man here in New York, talked about the play until the restaurant closed, and then wound up late at night, walking up and down the streets of the West Side practising limps that Richard might have.

I thought he was terrific. He had a dark side to him. He could suddenly go funny on people but it was usually out of a real love of the work, and an appreciation of them. I once saw him do it to a wonderful actress and he really made her very unhappy because he realized how good she actually was. And he just wanted the most out of her.

But he was very very careful with me, because he was guiding me and I was not supremely confident. I had to really come to it very slowly. And I don't know that I was all that ready for it when it opened, although we had sort of terrific houses and we had huge pleasure in it and the basic work on it was very sound. But then, something happened to me that had never happened to me before. Six weeks into it, we were re-reviewed by the *London Free Press*. And this guy said, "Anyone who saw this show on the first night, forget it, because it is now transformed; it is a totally different thing." He meant that we were not quite ready. I said "we"—I mean "me" I suppose. *(laughs)* It's wonderful to include everyone else, isn't it? But six weeks later, obviously I'd found myself, and for the rest of the run, I felt much different. It was so great to have that re-review. It's something that should happen a lot, I think. I believe shows deserve a second viewing when people have relaxed and they've got going and they know what they're doing. There's always a tension you can't get rid of up to the first night, however many previews you have, however rehearsed you are, there's still a tension. You can't get rid of it until you're over that hurdle. Until you've been accepted, or not, talked about, whatever it is.

OUZOUNIAN:

What did Hirsch bring personally to the play?

BATES:

I know he'd suffered a great deal from being a Hungarian Jewish refugee and he'd seen and experienced a lot of horrors and cruelties. And that was very much part of his influence in doing a show, which is about this manipulation, political manipulation, this evil, this corruption, this "We are not safe." Nobody's safe. And I think he brought a lot of his experience to that.

OUZOUNIAN:

Did you believe Richard was truly a villain?

BATES:

I think you have to accept the play for what it really is on its own terms. I don't think you can take other works like Josephine Tey's book *The Daughter of Time* too seriously when you're playing it. She may have been right; perhaps Richard wasn't all that bad. But that's not what Shakespeare wrote. In his play, Richard's the villain. And he may be better at it than everyone else, but that doesn't make him good.

OUZOUNIAN:

Do you recall the way you began the play? The famous "Now is the winter of our discontent . . ."

BATES:

I was just some kind of shadow in the corner, and suddenly, slowly, the lights revealed a figure. And I had a brilliant design by Desmond Heeley sort of like a spider. It was a wonderful costume, with sleeves that were like other arms so that he almost had six limbs, you know. It was kind of spidery and it slowly revealed itself through the speech as I crept closer to the audience.

OUZOUNIAN:

Everyone was interested in the way you would play the wooing scene with Lady Anne because you had a very romantic reputation on screen. Only now you were playing a deformed villain . . . could you still be romantic?

BATES:

I think that's possible. There's nothing impossible about that. I mean you bring a romantic conception to a part, however unlikely a figure you represent. And if you've got some kind of extraordinary magnetism, some kind of a something that will work, all is possible. You know, I think, in this character you reach out to the ultimate. You think, "How can anyone be taken in by this?" But you *can* be taken in by this. You can. It's a one in a million chance. But it can happen, you know. And that's what Richard the Third's got to be. He's got to be just possible.

OUZOUNIAN:

Bill Hutt played Clarence . . .

BATES:

. . . and gave a wonderful performance. He made you see that this man is not a fool. This is just a good man who perhaps doesn't want to see what he actually can see. It gave his scenes a whole new series of emotional resonances. I mean, Bill never does anything that hasn't got six layers to it.

OUZOUNIAN:

The moment in Richard III *that everybody talked about—and still remembers thirty-five years later—was the final scene. You're battling with your Richmond. You find yourself in a position where you could kill him, but instead you took your dagger, tossed it to him, and he killed you.*

BATES:

That was a big decision, and a controversial one, but it was at the heart of the production that John Hirsch set out to do. But I think that Richard knows what he's done. He knows who he is. He plays the game to the nth degree. He's had a great run on this terrible mind of his. But now he realizes that it's over, and it must end. Yet he feels he has to control everything . . . right to the final moment.

OUZOUNIAN:
Your other part that season was in The Merry Wives of Windsor. *What do you remember about playing Master Ford?*

BATES:
(laughs) I remember not being very comfortable in it. And I don't know why. I wish I had. Because some people have actually said they liked it, you know. And I think the problem is that he's a paranoid and jealous man, which I'm not. I found it strange to do that and I wish I hadn't, because it was very successful. Overall, it was a huge success, and yet I don't think I ever quite got into him, never really fulfilled the part. It's a funny thing, you know, but an actor might be executing a part quite well and somehow just not feel in the centre of it. It's quite a subtle thing that perhaps only another actor would appreciate. *(laughs)*

OUZOUNIAN:
Do you recall much about working with David William, who directed?

BATES:
Well, he knew exactly what he wanted to do. He's got great energy and great insight. I love David. David's a wonderful sort of intelligent, funny guy. Sometimes I think he's such an actor, because he loved to do our parts for us *(laughing)*, especially mine, because I don't think he thought I was doing it right.

OUZOUNIAN:
Two of the young actors who were in the company that summer . . .

BATES:
I know what you're going to say. They now run the Canadian theatre. *(laughs)* Oh, I remember Richard Monette and Christopher Newton very well. Very, very well. Yes, playing second- and third- and sometimes even fourth-level parts. There was no ambition seemingly lurking in them at the time, but there was enormous ability, and energy, and love of the theatre. If you had told me then that those two young men

would turn out to be incredibly successful, it wouldn't have surprised me at all.

OUZOUNIAN:
What comes to mind when I say "The Stratford Festival"?

BATES:
A great place to be. A young actor. A wonderful summer.

Hume Cronyn as Shylock in the 1976 production of The Merchant of Venice.
Photograph by Zoë Dominic.

Hume Cronyn

One of the great actors of stage, screen, and television, Hume Cronyn appeared at Stratford on three occasions: in 1969 in the title role of *Hadrian VII*, in 1976 as Bottom in *A Midsummer Night's Dream* and Shylock in *The Merchant of Venice*, and in 1980 as Hector Nations in *Foxfire*.
I spoke to him in Stratford at the Festival Theatre in the summer of 2000.

OUZOUNIAN:
Although you didn't appear personally at the Stratford Festival until well into its existence, you were born down the road in London, Ontario, so did you play any part in the creation of the Festival?

CRONYN:
Tom Patterson contacted me in New York while this was still just an idea and needed some help in trying to reach Larry Olivier. Well, I got hold of him and put Tom in touch with him. Nothing happened there, and Tom approached me and I told him that I thought the whole idea of starting a Shakespearean theatre in Stratford, Ontario, struck me as wildly ambitious, and somewhat impractical. So I backed away from that opportunity. Then, over a period of time I heard that he got Sir Tyrone Guthrie. Now Tony had a relationship with Jessie (Tandy)—they'd done one or two things together in England—and so we came down here for the dedication ceremony. There was a big muddy hole in the ground, and Tony being in charge, there was a rector who was officiating and here we were. Then, the next thing I knew was that he

had Alec Guinness and Irene Worth, and we came to see that production and we were very impressed.

And I remember going to Tony, and said if you ever do this again, will you keep us in mind? And years went by, some years, I don't remember how many, and I got a note from him saying "Doing it again in Minn. This time, will you care to come along and if so, what do you want to play?" So I wrote back and said we're for it. I'd learned my lesson about Stratford and so we helped him open the Guthrie Theatre in Minneapolis, where I played Polonius and Richard the Third and Willy Loman and all sorts of things.

OUZOUNIAN:
But you didn't come to Stratford.

CRONYN:
No, I didn't come here, and I rather resented the fact. Michael Langham was in charge, and he failed to—how shall I put this tactfully?—appreciate Jessica, which was a grave mistake on his part, and nearly ten years went by and I was never invited. And I came only from thirty-five miles away and I felt goddammit, they've got that theatre going and it sounds just wonderful and I'm not part of it!

And then, Jean Gascon finally brought me here in 1969 to play the title role in *Hadrian VII*, which started a year-long North American tour here in Stratford. National tour. And I think I remember that year. Sixty-nine.

OUZOUNIAN:
Did that whet your appetite to come back here again and do something else?

CRONYN:
I don't think the appetite ever left me. It was a place I wanted to be.

OUZOUNIAN:
Robin Phillips finally brought you and Jessica Tandy here in 1976 and

that season you played two very different roles: Shylock in The Merchant of Venice *and Bottom in* A Midsummer Night's Dream.

CRONYN:

You know, it's interesting, as the years went on, everyone always thought of me as a very serious actor, but I began doing a lot of funny roles for George Abbott. I was known as a farceur in shows like *Boy Meets Girl* and *Three Men on a Horse*. So Bottom was kind of a return to those roots. I've always loved playing comedy, and you couldn't have had a better teacher than I did with Mr. Abbott.

In the production we did, the mechanicals were a marvellous group and old Will Shakespeare knew what he was doing, the way he salted them in at significant moments. One can take just so much airy-fairy fantasy, and then one needs to be brought down to earth sometimes with a jolt. And if the jolt's laughter, all the better.

You know, my heart has always belonged to the theatre. When I was sitting here last night watching that wonderful production of *Fiddler on the Roof*, a woman next to me said that she thought she recognized me from the movies and I said, "Madame, I am a stage actor who occasionally lowers himself to appearing in films."

OUZOUNIAN:

You had some experience using the thrust stage when you worked with Guthrie in Minneapolis, so what did it feel like to go out onto the Festival stage?

CRONYN:

Just fine. It presents no real problems for an actor. You learn very quickly and I found it quite painless to perform on a thrust stage. It's exactly the same performance, but you just have to be aware the audience is so close to you.

OUZOUNIAN:

How did you feel about The Merchant of Venice?

CRONYN:

I was rather proud of my work as Shylock, but at the same time I know it was not a very good production. I don't want to slander anybody, but it was not well directed. The Belmont scenes were a catastrophe, at least that was my possibly erroneous impression. But I had a great sense of sympathy for Shylock. I think he's a very sympathetic figure. Yes, he does some appalling things, but if you open the play properly, those people who surround him are really scum. And I don't wonder that when he cries, "Hath not a Jew eyes?" it's from the heart, and very understandable.

OUZOUNIAN:

The next time you came back to Stratford was with a very special project to you and that was Foxfire, *which you co-authored with Susan Cooper.*

CRONYN:

I wrote to Robin saying Susan and I have written this play, what do you think about putting it on? Well, obviously he liked it, because the next thing I know, Jessie and I were back here again. And we had young Brent Carver in the show, his very first season here. I had supper with him last night after seeing his marvellous Tevye, and I wanted to say, "Brent, how were we ever so lucky as to come across you?" I don't remember how he happened to be. I think it must have been Robin who recommended this young actor who could sing, which Brent certainly can. And he always manages to somehow look like an innocent, no matter what's happening around him, which is why he was very good in *Foxfire* because he had an unspoiled quality about him.

OUZOUNIAN:

What was it like to come back and visit Stratford again after more than twenty years?

CRONYN:

I sat in that splendid theatre last night and thought about how Tony Guthrie always felt that if you had that kind of a theatre with the audience wrapped around it, it created more of a sense of communion. And you could all be in the same church together. And Tony was right. The thrust stage gets rid of any artificial division between you and the people watching you. One is playing right in the middle of the audience, which is just how it must have been in Shakespeare's time.

Pamela Brook as Marina in the 1973 production of Pericles.
Photograph by Robert C. Ragsdale.

Pamela Brook

Pamela Brook first came to Stratford in 1970 and remained through 1974, playing roles such as Hero in *Much Ado About Nothing*, Celia in *As You Like It*, and Marina in *Pericles*. She then went on to a career in the American theatre, before returning to Canada as a professor of theatre. I spoke to her in Niagara-on-the-Lake in the spring of 2001.

OUZOUNIAN:

What's your first memory of the Stratford Festival?

BROOK:

When I was a little girl, my parents took me to the first season at Stratford to see *All's Well That Ends Well*. I remember exactly where we sat. It was house right, just above the stage left tunnel, and apparently on the way home that night, I gave a complete review of the production and my parents were very surprised. I was five. And that's my first memory.

Years later, when I was playing at Stratford, I would sometimes look up to those seats and think—I was there and now I'm here.

OUZOUNIAN:

How did you first actually get to Stratford as a performer?

BROOK:

I auditioned for Jean Gascon and I came directly from graduate school at the University of Minnesota to Stratford and I was twenty-three.

OUZOUNIAN:
What was it like to work with Gascon?

BROOK:
When we'd work on Molière together, of course, he'd be in his element. His Gallic fervour, his sense of gesture, his spirit of fun—they all shone through, because he felt comfortable with a French author. When it came to Shakespeare, I felt that he *imbued* what he wanted. You learned to sense it from him. He would say very little to me verbally, but you would intuit what he meant. He communicated a great deal, but not always through language. Yet you knew what he meant. He was a man of enormous heart.

For me, the most profound and delicate and touching time with Jean was rehearsing *Pericles*, which was a pivotal point in my career. Jean and Nicholas Pennell and I would work late at night in the old rehearsal hall upstairs in the Festival Theatre. There was a mystery and poetry about what Jean gave. It was almost as if he already heard "the music of the spheres," the rarest sounds. It was the most emotional that I remember him. Yet again, he didn't say much but he understood that scene where Pericles is reunited with his daughter Marina after so many years of thinking her dead. He understood the sense of the miraculous and of myth and of the mystical, the radiance of it. That's when I saw most into him.

OUZOUNIAN:
Why did playing Marina mean so much to you?

BROOK:
It's a gift of a role. It's all there in the text, if you can meet the state of being it requires. That recognition scene is transcendent and somehow for me, Marina was the right part at the right moment. In retrospect, Jean was doing it towards the end of his regime. It was towards the end of my time at Stratford, so I had had time to mature. And it was the right

play at the right moment, with the right person as Pericles. Nicky Pennell. I adored him.

I was thinking about how we ritualized each performance. If we had had a matinee in the afternoon, Nicky and I always stayed in the theatre until the evening, if it was an evening *Pericles*. And we would just be together. We would have a bite to eat or we would warm up together or sit in each other's dressing rooms. We didn't say very much but we were together. Pericles and Marina don't see each other in the play until the reunion scene near the end. But somehow we needed to be together in order to carry each other through the play in our thoughts. And always after we performed it, we would go out for dinner together, but again we'd be very quiet. We didn't say very much.

One night he came into my dressing room and he seemed a little shaky. He said, "I will never have a daughter but I had you." And that was our relationship. So to be blessed with remarkable parents in my life, and remarkable parents in my theatrical career was quite extraordinary. Because Nicky played my father and Martha Henry played my mother.

OUZOUNIAN:

Is there a moment from that play you remember most vividly?

BROOK:

The moment I hold most dear is the one at which Pericles hears the music of the spheres. And he says, "List my Marina, the music of the spheres." And so I would move into him and he would be looking up and hearing this music and holding me and I suppose the question of that moment is—does Marina really hear the music, or does she hear it through him? The picture in my mind's eye is of the two of us together with whatever falls from above coming to him, and then through to me.

OUZOUNIAN:

Is Stratford a legacy you carry with you for the rest of your life?

BROOK:

To the very end, I think. For me it has affected every chapter of my life since. When I moved to New York where I lived and worked for twelve years, the foundation that Stratford had given me made all the difference in my ability to compete. It was the passion that was always underneath my teaching when I started teaching acting and Shakespeare, and in this chapter of my life, which is about writing and directing and producing, that muse that comes from Shakespeare is part of every day. I don't think I'd understand my life without Shakespeare.

OUZOUNIAN:

What would you like to wish Stratford for the next fifty years?

BROOK:

Hope and courage. I think in Gaelic, hope and courage are one word. They aren't separated. They're one. So I wish them hope and courage. And long life. I'm fiercely proud of Stratford as a Canadian and hopelessly sentimental about my own time there. I hope it lives forever.

OUZOUNIAN:

What do you think of when I say "The Stratford Festival"?

BROOK:

I feel it gave me something for every chapter of my artistic life and my contemplative life. And I thank them.

Berthold Carriere. Photograph by Terry Manzo.

Berthold Carriere

Berthold ("Bert") Carriere joined the Festival in 1974 and has been the heart and soul of its music ever since. He has composed the scores for dozens of shows and musical directed all of the Festival's major musical productions since his arrival, including all of the Brian Macdonald Gilbert and Sullivan operettas, as well as the contemporary musicals that have filled the Festival Theatre since 1986.

I spoke to him outside the Festival Theatre in the summer of 2001.

OUZOUNIAN:

Music has been an important part of the Stratford Festival from the very beginning . . .

CARRIERE:

That's because it's so important for the plays, starting with the trumpet fanfares to announce each performance that Lou Applebaum composed, which have been used all these years. It's a beautiful tradition.

OUZOUNIAN:

Who decided that they would be kind of the calling card of the Festival?

CARRIERE:

That's the kind of thing that Guthrie loved. Pomp, circumstance, tradition. We always have the fanfares and then we have the cannon, to announce to the city that the show has started and there's the famous bell, of course. It's very ceremonial, which would have appealed to Guthrie.

OUZOUNIAN:

Guthrie picked Lou Applebaum to set the musical tone for the Festival, and then years later, Lou picked you as his protégé.

CARRIERE:

I remember Lou taking me under his wings as if he were my mentor. On the first week I arrived here, he said, "Follow me." So I followed him into the theatre. They were rehearsing *King John*, and Peter Dews, who was directing it, said, "Lou, I need something dramatic here" and Lou said, "Whoever's closest to a bass drum, hit it." So the bass drum player hit the bass drum and he said to Dews, "Is this what you were looking for?" And Dews says, "Yes, but it needs something else." So Lou said, "You on the cymbal, roll it" and that was all it took. So it just indicated to me that he had the tricks of the trade and all of a sudden, it sounded so dramatic. It made all the difference. And these are little things that I picked up all the time.

Lou would say, "Come in with me and sit" and decisions were made right there on the spot and he was so fast. You know he didn't even write it down. He just said, "Play that and I'll deal with it later."

OUZOUNIAN:

Did he have any favourite music he wrote for the Festival?

CARRIERE:

I think the very first plays that he did were certainly some of his favourites, for sentimental reasons, but he enjoyed everything he did here and he gave it all great heart.

You know, composing for the theatre is such miniature work. Everything we deal with is five seconds, twelve seconds. He used to have a magic way of putting really interesting musical things in that little space of time. I learned an awful lot about scene changes from him as well, because Lou would write in a way that you could cut everywhere. So if it was too long, he'd say, "Take those two bars of music out and it'll work." And he was right; it *would* always work.

OUZOUNIAN:

Has the size of the orchestra changed much over the years?

CARRIERE:

Well, when I started, we had ten musicians in the loft, which is up over the stage, and five of these people are fanfare players. So you have four brass, one percussion, and the rest of it would be a piano and maybe a clarinet and a flute and a cello. That was it. We didn't have that much choice. Now we can tape, we can multi-track, we can do all kinds of different ways with the technology, you know. So, it's easier this way.

OUZOUNIAN:

Another aspect of music at Stratford is the production of the musicals. There was Gilbert and Sullivan in the early years, and then an assortment of other shows scattered through the decades, but it really became important when Brian Macdonald started his series of Gilbert and Sullivan operettas for John Hirsch with The Mikado.

CARRIERE:

Brian wanted to do something different. So we all had a chance to create our own world around *The Mikado*. And I added some percussive instruments to make it more Japanese and gongs and all that. But then Brian wanted every show to have a different personality. You know, *The Gondoliers* was influenced by *commedia dell'arte*, and *Iolanthe* was inspired by the British music halls, and I tried to echo all those things in the music as well.

Brian also wanted special dance music tailored for his choreography: a tap dance for *Iolanthe*, a tango for *The Pirates of Penzance*, and he always needed it right away. But I like working like that. I like the pressure of having to come up with something immediately.

Of course, some people thought these changes weren't right for Gilbert and Sullivan, but it was all material from the play that we put together. It was like a puzzle and the way that we worked it out was exciting. And what happened on the stage was fabulous.

OUZOUNIAN:

After John Hirsch left, John Neville came and made a very important decision that changed the face of the Festival. He moved the musical down to the main stage. What was your reaction the first time he told you they were going to do that?

CARRIERE:

I got a bit scared because, you know, you're dealing with the loft upstairs. In those days there were all kinds of problems. The sound used to bounce on the walls and come back to me so there was always a half a second delay. And it was difficult to keep together because the performers cannot see the conductor, but you get used to this kind of situation and it became okay after a while.

OUZOUNIAN:

The size of the orchestra obviously had to grow in the loft as well. You said at one point there were ten musicians. What does it sit at now?

CARRIERE:

About twenty-seven, twenty-eight. I know it would be easy to say, well we can cut the orchestra and use three synthesizers. But it's never really the same. I like to hear the score, and the people that come and see the shows expect to hear the score, the way they remember it. I wish I had more strings, but that's always the case.

OUZOUNIAN:

When musicals were first being done here, people sang acoustically. Now virtually every actor wears a body microphone. How do you feel about that?

CARRIERE:

Well, you know, with technology today, people expect this. It would be very hard in the Festival Theatre *not* to be miked, because first of all the orchestra's in a different room. When we first tried it, it sounded like it was coming out of a matchbox, because nothing was amplified. The singers could be heard, but barely. So now everyone wears a microphone for the musicals, but it has to be done with taste.

OUZOUNIAN:

Some young musicians crossed your path over the years who were to become major stars—I'm thinking of Loreena McKennitt.

CARRIERE:

Loreena. She began as one of the "sisters and cousins and aunts" in the chorus of *H.M.S. Pinafore*, then she went on to write some music for the Third Stage, as we called it then, and then recently she composed the score for *The Merchant of Venice*. That's in addition to her performing and recording that's made her such a big star around the world.

I'll always remember her because she was lovely to work with. She has such a great voice, and such a wonderful attitude. I told her at the end of her first season, "I hope you're going to come back next year." And she said, "Well, you know Bert, I'd like to start doing my own thing." And I said, "Good for you. Go and follow your dream and just do it." And there you are.

OUZOUNIAN:

What do you wish Stratford for its next fifty years?

CARRIERE:

I hope for the next fifty years that they'll keep doing musicals, and I hope they keep getting some good Canadian musicals in here, new projects. I hope they keep the idea of music composed specifically for the plays. I just hope the Festival keeps flourishing and remains as important as it is now to everybody.

OUZOUNIAN:

Tell me what words or images come into your mind when I say "The Stratford Festival."

CARRIERE:

A great place to work, great people, great musicians . . . great everything!

Robin Phillips. Photograph by V. Tony Hauser.

Robin Phillips

Robin Phillips was artistic director of Stratford from 1975 through 1980. He brought Maggie Smith, Brian Bedford, and Peter Ustinov to the Festival, and directed some of its most memorable productions, including *Measure For Measure*, *Richard III*, *As You Like It*, *Private Lives*, *King Lear*, and *Virginia*. I spoke to him at his farm near St. Mary's, Ontario, in the summer of 2001.

OUZOUNIAN:

How were you first approached about running the Stratford Festival?

PHILLIPS:

I was running a company in Greenwich and I was phoned by Ron Bryden, who then was a critic in Britain. He had been asked if he could offer any suggestions to go onto a list of people that might benefit from running a large classical complex. And he wondered if I would be interested. And I said, "Yes, I would." And he told me it was Stratford, and that thrilled me, because I had heard about it for years.

OUZOUNIAN:

What was your first impression when you saw it?

PHILLIPS:

Oh God, I was over the moon! I thought—and still do—it was the most extraordinary theatre. I also heard actors speaking Shakespeare in their wonderful Canadian accent, which I thought gave more vitality than I had ever heard Shakespeare have. I think over the years, the British accent has diminished the Shakespearean language, and when Canadian actors are at their best, they speak it better than anyone.

OUZOUNIAN:
What shape did you find the company to be in?

PHILLIPS:
It had extraordinary potential, but was a little creaky in its technique and its artistic view was a bit old-fashioned. The repertoire *(sighs)* was vickery-pokery, Old Vic-ish. It wasn't worthy of the company. It was a very tough time. Jean Gascon was an extraordinary man and an amazing personality with great Gallic flare, but there were a lot of people surrounding him who'd been around for a very long time, who sort of represented—not quite colonialism—but that slightly old-fashioned feeling of the Old Vic of worthy, classical work. I think Jean Gascon was better than the people around him.

OUZOUNIAN:
What was the financial situation like when you took over?

PHILLIPS:
God, when I took over, the Avon Theatre was to be closed. And I had to beg them to let me keep it for one year to see if I could turn it around, which is how the Young Company came into being. I put a Young Company in there and we did what I hoped was a fresh look at Shakespeare. And we had a very successful season and that was it. I was allowed to keep the Avon open.

OUZOUNIAN:
What did you want to show in your first season?

PHILLIPS:
I always have felt that theatre for me is a vocation. I believe that we do it for reasons other than just to entertain. And that if we do it well, we can make a huge difference to people's lives. And I think I wanted to startle them into realizing that Stratford was more than velvet costumes twirling around.

There was an awful lot of spinning that went on. Dear, oh dear! So I wanted to remove spinning and I wanted to have people who wore clothes like we wear clothes, as opposed to costumes. I wanted the audience to stop stretching out their hands from the front row and feeling the costumes and sort of nudging each other and saying, "You could make a nice cocktail dress out of that." Oh, the terrible sort of stuff that used to go on! I wanted people to leave with their blood pumping. The audience used to be so lethargic that you really thought that most of them would just sort of dive into the Avon River and just drift back to Toronto. I guess I was looking for things that would certainly make them sit up and take notice.

OUZOUNIAN:

Your production of Measure For Measure *certainly did that. It was one of Brian Bedford's first shows at Stratford. How did you get him to join the company?*

PHILLIPS:

I went to visit him in his home in upstate New York, and he swears that I changed clothes four times the first day that I was there. Kept going upstairs and changing 'cause I was trying to figure out how I should be dressed to be in the country visiting a major star. I'm sure that's not true, but it's a nice story. I wanted him to come not just because of his theatrical skill, but also because Brian has always had an extraordinary . . . power of thought, which is what I felt we needed in the company.

I wanted to get away from the Stratford shouters. As well as twirling, a lot of shouting went on. So they used to spin a lot and shout a lot and spit a lot, and I wanted to come back and draw people into a more intimate whispered sound. I think that theatre can be much more intimate than we believe, and because we're constantly up against film and television, we ignore that at our peril. I don't think that the flamboyant theatre that spins, spits, and shouts necessarily makes you feel that you're watching a live production. Very often it just seems to me like a lot of spinning-top toys that are as dead as a dodo . . .

Anyway, Brian was a very thoughtful actor so that's why I was after him. I wanted somebody with that sort of thought power, and a particular sort of icy sexiness. I was thrilled he said yes and came. And indeed he was terrific. He was lizardlike in his lechery as Angelo. I thought he was absolutely marvellous and he was a terrific counter to Martha (Henry) playing a porcelain-breasted nun.

OUZOUNIAN:
Martha had been at Stratford for a long time. What made you seize on her and say, "This will be the person I'm going to take on this journey"?

PHILLIPS:
From the first moment I saw her, I latched onto an intimacy that you don't share with everybody. She was very unactressy, very human, very "still waters run deep," sensual, mellifluous, extraordinary. Everything about her excited me. And she proved to be extraordinarily good too at the power of thought, allowing thought to do it. And no spinning.

OUZOUNIAN:
In one scene, after Angelo had left her alone, there was some water on the stage and she plunged her hands in it and then splashed it on her face to cool herself. Where did that all come from?

PHILLIPS:
Well, first of all, there is always water in every production I do. And there is always real flame in every production I do. I like having things that cannot lie, just to remind us that water will always behave as water and flame likewise. So the water was there and available should it be required. What was wonderful was what appeared to be an ice cold scene, a scene of such frigidness, you suddenly realized was immensely hot and that she had to in fact, cool herself down at the end of the scene,

and you thought, "Those nipples are erect. They're not just hiding beneath the veil."

OUZOUNIAN:
Did the success of that production please you?

PHILLIPS:
What really pleased me was the way they all caught on to a new style of telling Shakespearean stories. That was the really thrilling thing. It didn't take us years. It didn't take us seasons. But literally with the very first production, they grabbed something new. That made me believe that it was possible. To do something.

OUZOUNIAN:
Why did it happen so quickly?

PHILLIPS:
I think everybody was hungry, that's all it was really. I think they all knew something extra was needed. They all knew something extra was possible, and it didn't take much of a carrot to get them to start down a new street.

OUZOUNIAN:
The next season brought your next major star, Dame Maggie Smith. How did that come about?

PHILLIPS:
Maggie was on tour with *Private Lives*, and it came to Toronto. I knew that it was quite a tough tour. It was also the middle of winter, so I just sent her a note to say "Welcome to Canada. Hoping you're well and would you like to escape for a weekend?" Her husband called me within two seconds of receiving the note and said, "We would adore to escape for the weekend."

And Barb Ivey , Stratford senator, and at that time Stratford board member, very sweetly lent me her cottage, which is on Lake Huron.

We picked her up at the Royal Alex, Maggie covered in fur,

and drove her through the snow for hours until we got there. And it was perfect. Beautiful white polar bearskin rugs, great log fires. Maggie said, "Bring the snows. I don't want to go back to Toronto. Let's stay here."

The next day we went for a huge walk, and that morning, the very first morning that we were together, I asked her if she would like to come and do Cleopatra and Millimant. And half of the thing about casting is knowing what they want to play, what they *need* to play at a given point in their careers. You have to throw the right bait. She said yes and that was the beginning of a really wonderful relationship. She came to see the Young Company rehearse that weekend. It's been probably the deepest relationship I think I've had in this business. Not one where we have necessarily talked about our work very much but just a very deep understanding of each other and why we do it.

The humour of a Maggie performance was always a miracle to me, something I could marvel at, but never explain. For example, after the first time she meets Orlando in *As You Like It*, she's about to leave the stage and she turns to Celia, who's already exited, and she says, "He calls us back." And she brought the house down with it, because the audience knew that she was lying, and they knew that she didn't know how to tell her friend "I have to go back because I want to have another look at this beautiful guy." So on the spur of the moment, she comes up with this ludicrous and blatant lie, done with guilt, and shame, and betrayal and so many emotions. And yet you had no idea why it was funny. There was nothing clever about the inflection. There was nothing Maggie-ish about the hands. Just breathtaking reality and it was devastatingly funny. Those things became sublime, because one was aware one was in the presence of the sort of acting that is indefinable, the sort of acting that is unreachable as star performers must be—out of reach. Totally understood, crystal and glitteringly clear, but at the same time, you can't define it. You cannot analyze it.

OUZOUNIAN:

Sometimes getting people to do the right performances wasn't as easy as others, and when you worked on Richard III *with Brian Bedford, you were very much trying to keep some of his Bedfordisms down. Do you recall how difficult that got?*

PHILLIPS:

It was quite tense. He was marvellously good in the role, but Brian has a very cheeky little smile that he will sometimes add after a humorous line, in order to sort of wink at the audience. It's what I call British semaphore acting, and it allows you to tell the audience "It's okay, you can laugh at this." And it's very charming and very good and he does it with great skill and I love him for it. But I didn't want him to use it in *Richard III* and I asked that he should never smile. Ever ever ever ever ever ever. And a couple of them crept in. And I said, "Brian you don't have to do it. You can get the laugh without the smile." And he, and he got quite tense. This was in the dressing room after one of the previews and he said, "I don't understand. Why do you find that so objectionable?" Well, I was very tired and so I wasn't my, at my most tactful. I'm not very often at my most tactful, to be honest, but nevertheless . . . I said to him *(sighs)*, "Because it's cheap." And he was so mad, he got into the shower, and he still had his costume on. But he forgave me and he didn't smile. And he was wonderful.

OUZOUNIAN:

You're doing excellent work. There are new strides being made. Audiences are coming. Everything is going well. Why after a period of about five years did you feel it was time to depart from Stratford?

PHILLIPS:

I didn't feel it was time to depart. What I had originally done was to set up a directorate that would allow people to rotate into my chair from time to time. I just found that it was too exhausting. I was having to concentrate one hundred percent every second of the time. You owe it to the authors, the actors, the audiences that you don't shortchange them. So I was exhausted. I was happy to stay. I was desirous to stay. But I had to share the load. I couldn't do it by myself. And there was a feeling from the board of directors that it was either "all of you or none of you." I had to do it all or they didn't want it.

OUZOUNIAN:
What were you feeling when you finally prepared to leave Stratford at the end of the 1980 season?

PHILLIPS:
It was quite tough for me at the end. My father died when I was directing *King Lear*. I had been hemorrhaging for nearly six months and didn't know what was wrong with me. So I had that anxiety as well as the anxiety of my dad's death. And the president of the board came round to the artistic director's house, owned by Stratford, to ask me when I would be moving out. Could I give them a date? And I said, "I still have two productions to open this season." I tell you that just to show you the amount of pressure and confusion that was going on at that time. It is not easy to open *King Lear* at the best of times. But to try and fly back between a technical rehearsal and a dress rehearsal to bury your father and to be absolutely convinced that if you didn't make it into hospital soon, you might be following him, and then to have what seems to be immensely insensitive requests, like "When will you be moving out of the house, so that we can put your replacement in?" It was a difficult time.

OUZOUNIAN:
After a few years, John Neville invited you to return and you directed for him, as well as running the Young Company . . .

PHILLIPS:

Johnny Neville was so kind. It was not easy to come back. I cannot tell you the terror of going back into that building. Part of it was because I thought it would be hostile. Part of it was because I wasn't sure that I would be able to cope because of the emotional upheaval. But he was extraordinary. He came and met me, literally took me by the hand. Took me into the theatre. He couldn't have been more generous or more understanding and the company likewise were very sweet. And it very quickly became fine. But it was a huge thing for me to go back into the building. It's like going back to a home that you no longer own where you were brought up. Now somebody else owns it. It's their house and you go back. It's full of memories.

OUZOUNIAN:

What would you wish Stratford for the next fifty years?

PHILLIPS:

That it be laceratingly honest, and demanding, and truthful.

OUZOUNIAN:

When I say the words "The Stratford Festival" to you, what images pop into your mind?

PHILLIPS:

I see a magical stage, a stage that demands that a person should stand on it and say something. An empty space, a person, and a voice. Language. And thought.

Marti Maraden as Sonya in the 1978 production of Uncle Vanya.
Photograph by Robert C.Ragsdale.

Marti Maraden

Marti Maraden first appeared on the Festival Stage in 1974 as Katharine in *Love's Labour's Lost*. Between then and 1979 she played many roles, including Ophelia in *Hamlet*, Irina in *The Three Sisters*, Miranda in *The Tempest*, and Regan in *King Lear*. She returned in 1990 as a frequent guest director and her productions have included *Macbeth*, *Les Belles Soeurs*, and *The Merchant of Venice*. I spoke to her at the National Arts Centre in Ottawa, where she is currently the artistic director, in October 2001.

OUZOUNIAN:
What is your very first memory of coming to Stratford?

MARADEN:
My first memory of coming to Stratford is not being told how to get there. I came from Vancouver and when they hired me—apart from being told roughly that it was somewhere west of Toronto—I didn't really get any directions. So my initial memory was the terror of figuring out how to get to the first rehearsal. Then I walked out onto the stage and I looked all around at almost twenty-three hundred seats and I thought, I can't do this. I must get on a plane and fly back to Vancouver. There is no way I can do this. It was terrifying. And at the same time it was exhilarating. The stage is surprisingly small when you stand on it. And the space is so vast. And so you feel very vulnerable. You feel as if you were in a hand that's being held out towards an audience. And to think that one could go forth and speak the words of Shakespeare with that amount of vulnerability was really quite awe-inspiring.

OUZOUNIAN:
After your first season at the Festival, Robin Phillips took over as artistic director. What do you remember of him?

MARADEN:
He came in talk to the company, and he sat in a cream-coloured cableknit sweater, kind of hunched over on the edge of the Festival stage, and spoke to us very quietly and calmly and my impression was—right or wrong—of incredible vulnerability at that time. And I expect he was feeling that. You know, being a young man coming over to head a major theatre here with a certain amount of hostility facing him. I had an impression of a person who could inspire people, someone who could make everyone feel valued and important in a production. Sometimes perhaps they were made to feel that they were doing better work than they were actually doing, I expect. But sometimes not. He could recognize real value in people and I think there was always a genuine air of excitement around him.

OUZOUNIAN:
Ironically, one of the most important shows you did in that early period wasn't Robin's. It was The Three Sisters.

MARADEN:
That was my first encounter with John Hirsch and it was one of the greatest experiences I've ever had in the theatre. I think John understood that play from his bones. He told us extraordinary stories from his own past in Hungary, which pertained to the work we were doing, that were so filled with emotion and absurdity. I think he had a wonderful ability to walk that fine line between comedy and despair that exists in Chekhov. Anyone who says his plays are fully dramatic or fully comedic misses the point, because they are both things always. And I think John really really understood that. I think he understood how ridiculous

people can be. And still be somehow pitiable or likeable.

Maggie Smith and Martha Henry played my sisters, and while I can absolutely understand that the idea of three such disparate women coming together as sisters might seem curious or even improbable, in fact, it was marvellous. It was consistently a fabulous experience.

One of my favourite things is that rare instance when you're in a play where people interact well enough together, that you can leave a little bit of anarchy, a little bit of time where you never know quite what will happen, leaving the actors free to do whatever comes to them in the moment—within certain parameters. In the third act of that play, which is a three o'clock in the morning scene where there's been a great fire and everyone is a bit out of their mind, all kinds of confession come forward that nobody wants to hear. All kinds of things get said. All kinds of despair are given into. As Irina, I was in a rocking chair and breaking down at my despair over life as it was and where it wasn't going, and I was allowed to go wherever I chose—to fly sometimes into Martha's arms, sometimes into Maggie's arms, sometimes into no one's arms. And John said, "I'm going to let you do it. Please don't hang from the chandeliers, but go ahead, because something wonderful happens."

OUZOUNIAN:

In the very same season you played Ophelia, but you ran into Robin Phillips's quirk of casting multiple actors in the same role, so you had two Hamlets—Nicholas Pennell and Richard Monette. How did that strike you?

MARADEN:

I was excited by the idea. I was curious to see how it would be done, hoping that my relationship to Hamlet would be different in each case. And in fact, it was very much so. Nicholas was a more reserved, private, ironical Hamlet, more held-in, more mysterious, more kind of frightening to me, I think. Richard was more open. His Hamlet was more openly vulnerable and one of the great differences was doing the nunnery scene, which is the crucial encounter between the two characters. With Nicholas, it became very hurtful and painful on a verbal level. The words were the daggers. The words hurt. With Richard, it was more physical, more violent. He held me, he shook me, he struck me.

OUZOUNIAN:
You began by playing all the great Shakespearean innocents, but a few years later, when Peter Ustinov played Lear, you were the evil Regan instead of the saintly Cordelia. Did this surprise you?

MARADEN:
Far from it. I lobbied for it. I had played so many young women and believe me, I was grateful. They were wonderful roles, but I thought I must grow up. This is getting dangerous for me as an artist, not to take a step forward. And I said, "Please cast me in something where I'm grown up and preferably something unpleasant."

And Robin heard me. He understood. He did. You know, when you get to be well into your thirties and you're still playing sixteen year olds, it's lovely to speak those gorgeous words, but it really is time to start exercising other muscles.

So it made the playing of Regan very interesting. I loved delving into the evil of it. I loved some of the explorations we did with sexuality and the perversity between the sisters and their coveting of Edmund or even Oswald. I think the sickness in the play was very interestingly explored and it was so juicy and delicious for me to have a chance to go down that road, which I can only think that I had quite a wonderful time playing in it.

OUZOUNIAN:
After King Lear, *you left Stratford for over a decade. Is there a reason?*

MARADEN:

There is a reason. I think I've got a wandering spirit. I really do. I just sense a time when I've been somewhere long enough, and that it's time to move on. It's time to scare myself. I think I just needed to shake my own wits.

OUZOUNIAN:

You spent seven seasons at the Shaw Festival during that decade, and then David William brought you back as an actress and a director. How did you enjoy the transition to directing?

MARADEN:

I loved coming to directing. I loved telling the story. It used different parts of my mind, my sense of logic and storytelling, and it's a different act of creation and imagination, so I fell completely in love with it.

OUZOUNIAN:

How would you characterize the Festival today?

MARADEN:

Oh, the Festival has changed significantly over the years. Some of the changes are not for the better, and there are some that are. I actually am quite happy to see those, some of the renovations to the theatre, particularly what I always called the "greedy" seats gone in the main theatre—those ones all the way over on the side where no one could really see. I don't think Tanya Moiseiwitsch ever really quite wanted those seats there from what I've heard.

There's certainly a real vitality in the company. It still has incredible prominence and importance to this country. It's well known abroad. It's one of the theatres people know wherever you go. And it's lovely to know that we have a theatre that reaches out so well.

But it makes me sad that in the past, one could do more obscure shows like *King John*, *Pericles*, or *Love's Labour's Lost* all on the main stage and not worry about whether or not they would sell tickets. For one thing, you know, shows sold very well at that time, in my memory at least. Also there was so much more support. There was so much more government support. The funding was extraordinary. And I don't know what has happened in the erosion over the years. I don't think it's been one administration. I think it's been incremental. People have done what they needed to do over the years. And there have been programming choices—not just in Richard's time, but in years prior—that have reflected the need to make money at the box office. But I would like to think that someday there would be enough funding and support for the theatre, that whoever runs it can say "I will do whatever plays I damn well please. If they're Shakespeare's plays, then people should come and see them."

OUZOUNIAN:
What would you wish Stratford for its second fifty years?

MARADEN:
Courage. Brilliance. Finding the best and most gifted young actors and really helping them to speak the text. Not just with clarity but with passion. To live through the language. To dare. To keep daring.

OUZOUNIAN:
When I say the words "The Stratford Festival" to you, what images come to mind?

MARADEN:
A theatre that is unique, I believe, on the face of the earth. One that still has real magic for me. When I go into the theatre, empty or filled, I feel its power. A guardian of the beauty of language. Of great words, great ideas, of huge canvasses.

Brian Bedford as Elyot Chase in the 1978 production of Private Lives.
Photograph by Zoë Dominic.

Brian Bedford

British-born Brian Bedford is generally regarded as one of the finest actors of classical comedy in the world today. He first came to Stratford for Robin Phillips in the 1975 production of *Measure For Measure*. He is best remembered for his Stratford partnership with Dame Maggie Smith, which included *Private Lives*, *Much Ado About Nothing*, and *The Seagull*. In recent years, his memorable performances have included Shylock, Tartuffe, Bottom, and Benedick. I spoke to him in the Festival Theatre in the summer of 2000.

OUZOUNIAN:

The first time you came to Stratford was for Robin Phillips. How did that come to pass?

BEDFORD:

A mutual friend of ours said Robin Phillips is taking over Stratford and he wants to talk to you about coming there. And I said fine, well have him come up and visit me. Well, my farmhouse in upstate New York is in the middle of nowhere, and he was going to have to stay the night. So Robin arrived with about three very large suitcases and changed several times, but we had a very nice giggly time. He asked me to go and play Malvolio in *Twelfth Night* and Angelo in *Measure For Measure*, and I said yes, because they were two parts that I terribly wanted to play, and I'd always very much wanted to come to Stratford. Little did I know, of course, that I was getting myself into rather a historic situation, because those Robin Philips–Maggie Smith years were pretty heady and I've got so many wonderful memories of them.

OUZOUNIAN:
That production of Measure For Measure *turned out to be the calling card for a whole new style of Shakespearean production.*

BEDFORD:
I thought it was absolutely brilliant, with some of Robin's best work. It was meticulous and the text was fascinatingly investigated . . . and excavated. Robin encouraged us to go down into it.

I'm tremendously grateful to Robin because he encouraged me to become the kind of classical actor that I wanted to be . . . my own kind of classical actor. When I was going to theatre school, we always used to argue over whether John Gielgud or Laurence Olivier was the better actor, all that kind of thing. But the danger is that, if you're not careful, you start copying these people. And so, so you don't give your own performance. That's the big danger as a classical actor, that you're actually giving somebody else's performance. What Robin did was try and get me away from all of that, all my early influences and all the people I was tremendously impressed by, and to get me to appreciate my own uniqueness and to pursue that in classical text.

OUZOUNIAN:
The sexuality that was all over Measure For Measure, *did Robin lay that out to you in advance or did it come from within?*

BEDFORD:
It just evolved. Because luckily, Martha (Henry), and Robin and I, were all on the same page. Of course, the pages changed, as the production evolved. But we stayed on the same page. And so all that, all that sex, was because Angelo and Isabella are two very closeted people with regard to their emotions. And, of course, it's exciting when there's that sexual cauldron underneath this icy exterior.

OUZOUNIAN:
A few years later, when you set out to do Richard III *for Robin, did you find it daunting at all?*

BEDFORD:

I found it difficult to find within myself the capacity to murder all those people. Yet somehow you have to find this, and that was kind of hard for me, but eventually I did manage to find that capacity within myself. But there again, you see, Robin encouraged me to be as dimensional as possible. He didn't want a sort of Olivier, kind of winking at the audience, gleefully revelling in his own villainy kind of thing. He wanted the tragedy of Richard, rather than the entertainment version.

OUZOUNIAN:

What did you and Robin seize on as his tragic flaw, as it were? Where is the key to the tragedy of the character?

BEDFORD:

(patting his back) It's in the physical deformity, and that drives him in every way. He can't stand the injustice of it, and so he goes to war against God.

OUZOUNIAN:

Were you and Robin in total agreement on how to play Richard?

BEDFORD:

There were—how shall we put this?—slight differences of opinion. When we were in previews, Robin came to my dressing room, and used the "c" word—cheap—about some element of my performance. And I was absolutely horrified, and angry and hurt and all the rest of it. And all I could, all I could do was go to the bathroom and turn on the shower. You do the weirdest things under these circumstances. But I just kind of had to put the shower on at full tilt, just to— I don't know why. To drown out his voice or something. I don't know what it was. But we actually have a laugh about that now.

OUZOUNIAN:

That was also the year that you and Dame Maggie Smith started working together. Had you known her or worked with her before here?

BEDFORD:
I've known Maggie for a long, long time. We're exactly the same age, so I guess we met when we were twenty, twenty-one maybe. She was doing a play with Kate Reid, called *Stepmother*, directed by a Canadian called Henry Kaplan. And they were at one of those tryout theatres just outside London. Maggie had a small part in it and I knew Kate at that time, and she asked us back to her rented house in Chelsea. And I remember sitting on the floor in a fairly empty house, with Maggie, and talking about Maggie's virginity.

OUZOUNIAN:
So years later when you came to work with her and she was considerably different and you were considerably different . . .

BEDFORD:
Well, she'd lost her virginity by then. I haven't.

OUZOUNIAN:
Which was the first show you two worked together on?

BEDFORD:
Robin and Maggie and I got together in Los Angeles and did a production of Molnar's play, *The Guardsman*, and that was the first time that we worked together. This was in preparation for the following season at Stratford, where we did the play at the Avon Theatre.

OUZOUNIAN:
Was the chemistry between the two of you instant, or was it something you arrived at after a while?

BEDFORD:
I think it was pretty instant. I was a huge fan of hers for years. You see, we both sort of came into the West End at the same time. We were both promising actors together. And I just absolutely thought and still do think that she's a kind of a genius.

OUZOUNIAN:
How did Robin work with the two of you?

BEDFORD:

Well, he let us go, and then he would subtly rein us in, I think, but . . . we . . . we just had a very jolly time with it. When Robin left, I think we got a bit out of control.

OUZOUNIAN:

The one show that people remember most vividly from the two of you is Private Lives*. How were you both able to capture the wit and charm—as well as the melancholy—of that piece so well?*

BEDFORD:

Well, Maggie and I were sort of those people anyway, you know. Elliot and Amanda can't live together and they can't live without each other. I want to say a love–hate relationship, but the "hate" part is too strong. Perhaps a kind of antipathy. And that wasn't quite the situation with me and Maggie, but something of that existed in real life between the two of us. We loved each other . . . and drove each other a bit nuts at times. And so all that was very valuable and ready-made resources for playing *Private Lives*.

It certainly was the best *Private Lives* that I ever did, and I've done quite a few of them. And I think Maggie thought that it was the best one that she'd done. Because we did it as serious, which does not stop it from being funny.

OUZOUNIAN:

Have you ever wished you could resume the partnership with Maggie Smith again, onstage?

BEDFORD:

Yes. Anytime. Anywhere. Maggie had talked about the two of us doing *Who's Afraid of Virginia Woolf?* but unfortunately it never happened. She is a magical woman and I adored working with her so much—especially with Robin there to guide us.

OUZOUNIAN:

What was it like to work for Robin during those years here?

BEDFORD:

I remember them being very, very exciting years. And that all the entire company ever talked about, was the plays and Robin. It was a completely kind of insulated experience. Robin has that affect on people. He induces fierce loyalty and . . . it was a very, very heady time.

I still benefit from the things that I learned from him. I concocted a one-man Shakespeare show called *The Lunatic, the Lover, and the Poet*, which I've done all over the place, and it was dedicated to John Gielgud and Robin Phillips because those were the two great Shakespearean influences in my life.

OUZOUNIAN:

After Robin, you stayed on with the company and you did some shows for John Hirsch who was a totally different personality. What do you recall about him?

BEDFORD:

I miss him. I recall his insanity. He was a mad Hungarian, who was absolutely crazy about the theatre. And I think John Hirsch is the only person in rehearsal that I've ever screamed at, at the top of my voice. Because I'm not that kind of person. John would get so carried away, you know. He was the most hands-on director you could imagine and he was acting the parts and he was right there in your face. Of course Robin was absolutely the opposite. Robin was sitting back, just thinking. But Hirsch was . . . right in there, with this kind of enthusiasm. He'd get completely carried away with it and he'd get very impatient and I work quite slowly. So we were sort of chalk and cheese a bit. But only just now and again.

But offstage he was very kind to me. I was going through a very difficult period of my life, in my own head, and John was a tremendous help to me.

OUZOUNIAN:

You talked about the mood during Robin. What was the mood like at Stratford with Hirsch?

BEDFORD:

Well, it was a bit weird because Robin was a very tough act to follow. And, of course, there'd been all the problems. John Dexter almost taking over and all that business. And so it was a curious time. But I felt an allegiance to Stratford, and consequently to Hirsch. Throughout all the artistic directors, I've sustained this feeling of allegiance because Stratford has given me so much. I've been so lucky. It's made my life, actually, because it's given me the kind of career that I wanted.

OUZOUNIAN:

After the Hirsch years you were away for a while, and then you came back for several shows with Michael Langham. What is he like to work for?

BEDFORD:

He's a very great man of the theatre. He's one of the few. I mean I think you can count the really consummate men of the theatre, certainly on two hands, possibly one, and Michael is one of them. He has . . . a great facility and a great responsibility for making Shakespeare vibrantly, contemporaneously alive. And that is, that's a great thing.

OUZOUNIAN:

You talked about Phillips being the one who sat back and watched and Hirsch being the one who gets in and messes it up with you. Where does Langham fit in?

BEDFORD:

*(laughs)*He bridges the gap between the two. But all three of those people—Robin, John, and Michael—when they're doing a production, they eat, sleep, breathe that project. And this is why, in their various ways, they were so successful, because it was so important to them. Langham is even more meticulous than Robin in a way. And he's more technical and he can help an actor tremendously. I mean I've seen him reduce a lot of actors to tears, which is not a pretty sight. But those actors,

those crying actors, all said to me eventually, "It was hell, but it was worth it because I learned so much."

OUZOUNIAN:

Critics of Langham, sometimes used the word "cold" about working with him. Did you ever find that?

BEDFORD:

I found him chilly sometimes. Never to me, but to other actors. And he could seem a bit rigid in his commitment to making this text come alive, I think that what is actually determination and enthusiasm and concentration, can sometimes be construed as being a bit chilly, because he's absolutely blinkered. But I think this is his *modus vivendi*. This is the way he works, and I think quite often he sees upsetting people and sort of ruffling their feathers as part of his process. He finds it important that this should happen to an actor, because something else is going to come out the other end.

OUZOUNIAN:

Now you're here in the Richard Monette years . . . yet another very different type of personality.

BEDFORD:

Richard is an old chum. We began as fellow actors twenty-five years ago, and now he's a very close friend. Richard's great quality, as a person and as a director, is his love for other people. I don't think Richard has any ego, which is a very rare thing in this business, especially for an actor and a director. But I don't think he does, and I don't think he's got much vanity. So that working with him is a very pleasant process. He, more than any of the people that I've just mentioned, loves and trusts actors. And that's a wonderful feeling. And so, quite often you'd find in a Richard Monette production, a wonderfully kind of benevolent and generous loving feeling. You can't buy that. And that does cross the footlights, if we have footlights these days. But it gets over to the audience.

OUZOUNIAN:

Do you have one final thought about Stratford?

BEDFORD:

Yes. Of all the artistic directors who've sat on that throne, I think the company's been the happiest with Richard, and that's a wonderful way to feel going into the Fiftieth Anniversary Season.

Maggie Smith as Amanda in the 1978 production of Private Lives.
Photograph by Zoë Dominic.

Maggie Smith

One of the most esteemed and beloved actresses of our time, Dame Maggie Smith came to Stratford in 1976 as Millimant in *The Way of the World* and Cleopatra in *Antony and Cleopatra.* She returned in 1977, 1978, and 1980 to play Rosalind in *As You Like It*, Amanda in *Private Lives*, Beatrice in *Much Ado About Nothing*, and Virginia Woolf in *Virginia*, among others. I spoke to her in London in October 2001.

OUZOUNIAN:
Do you recall how Robin Phillips first talked to you about coming up to Stratford?

SMITH:
I was doing *Private Lives* in Toronto, and in fact, I'd been doing it for, it seemed to me for life. And anyway he asked me to come away for a weekend to Grand Bend, and we did. While we were there, he told me the plays he wanted me to do, and I thought, this is crazy. I can't possibly do the things that he suggested. But I was with my husband (Beverley Cross) and he said, "Of course, you've got to do this." So it was through the combination of Bev's determination and Robin's madness that I wound up in Stratford.

OUZOUNIAN:
It's interesting that Robin didn't play the comedy card with you. He asked you to play Cleopatra.

SMITH:
Well, that's what was so bizarre. Cleopatra really threw me for a loop because I don't think anybody would have thought of

me for that. And I must say, I just thought he was mad. And as I didn't really know him very well, I just thought no he's just gone crazy.

OUZOUNIAN:

When I asked Robin why he had picked that role, he said, "Sometimes when you approach a great actress at a certain point in their career, you have to ask her to play a part she needs *to play, whether or not she knows it."*

SMITH:

(laughs) Well, I think he and Bev were thinking on the same lines. And it is true. And that was really the joy, one of the joys of Stratford for me, was in fact playing a lot of roles, that I don't think I would have been asked to play in England. And I will be forever grateful for that. It was so amazing.

OUZOUNIAN:

Everybody wondered what it would be like to have Maggie Smith come to this small Ontario town. How did you find it?

SMITH:

I found it absolutely marvellous. It was a changing point in my life, as well. And it was just like starting—not just with a clean new page or anything—but with a completely fresh new notebook. It was just like having a wonderful new beginning. It was a really exciting time. And a very liberating time. I felt that it was sort of faraway from places and I therefore felt less inhibited. There comes a time, I think, when you are so aware of the critics and what they're going to say and what they don't want to see you do, that you become rather bound and restricted in so many ways. You can almost write your own notice before you go out there and that is horrid. So it felt like, it felt like just a whole new world and a whole new territory and I thought, people don't know me. They aren't going to say, "Oh God, is she going to come out with these boring mannerisms again?" They're not going to knock me down before I start. And it just . . . it was a great release.

OUZOUNIAN:
What was it like actually working with Robin?

SMITH:
It was extraordinary because he gave one courage in a very, sort of subtle way, I think. And he did everything he could to simplify things. I mean, you take a part like Cleopatra and it's daunting from the start. One of the reasons is—apart from everything else—the most enormous part of it for her is right at the end, and so you spend the entire night in terror. You can't sort of get over it. But Robin eased me into the whole thing very gently. I do remember very clearly before the first performance, we were all in the theatre having notes. And I think he must have given me—it seemed like about fifty, probably more. Nobody else got any notes and I thought—"I just don't believe this!" But I took them all because I liked to get notes. And I think he did it just so that I couldn't think of anything else, so I wasn't going to worry about anything other than the entire arc of the thing. I do remember the rest of the company thinking, "This is peculiar. She can't be that bad? Is she that bad?" Maybe I thought that too, but it was wonderful because I found myself going through the script saying, "Right, I must do that. I must do that. I must do that." So it did stop me from thinking too much and freezing with fright.

I remember sitting watching the opening of the dress rehearsal. And the thrill of the lights coming up and seeing the whole stage just crammed with people, out of a complete blackout. And I thought, "This is one of the most exciting things. I can't wait to get up there." And of course, the theatre itself is such a wonderful space to be in. It feels so generous and yet it feels very intimate. I don't know how it works. But it is a fantastic area to be on. You feel it the moment you get onto that stage.

OUZOUNIAN:

There's a story that after one day of rehearsal for The Three Sisters, *you came to Robin and said about John Hirsch, "Where has this man been all of my life?"*

SMITH:

I know. I thought he was wonderful. Absolutely wonderful. With a great gentleness. He was very like Robin in as much as you had a feeling with him that he knew all about the people you were playing, what made them tick. He managed to guide us so that Chekhov was funny and touching at the same time. He captured the contradiction in our characters so well. One minute they'd be up, one minute they'd be down, and it was funny that they were so miserable. Years later, I'd meet John and always found it so warming to see him again. I miss him greatly actually. It's a great loss.

OUZOUNIAN:

One of the things that people remember most about your years at Stratford was your onstage partnership with Brian Bedford. Why do you think the two of you played so well together?

SMITH:

I just enjoyed working with him so much. And he's such a good actor. I mean you always enjoy working with people who are good and certainly when they're *that* good, it's an added pleasure. This is the Bedford Diamond I'm wearing, I have to tell you. A present from Brian when we finished our stint at Stratford.

When we did *Private Lives*, it was interesting because we'd both done it before, but with other people. So we kind of knew it. In fact, there was no way I *couldn't* have known it, I suppose, as I'd done it for years—it seemed to me. But with Brian, it was sort of like a holiday. It was so easy, no problems at all. I remember sitting on the sofa with him in the second act and I felt we could just stay there all though the play really. We didn't really have to get up. It was lovely. It was great fun. It was a joy.

OUZOUNIAN:
The two of you also did Richard III, *with everybody weeping and wailing a lot . . .*

SMITH:
Not at one performance, though. A lot of people were ill—they all had the flu or some other awful thing that was going around. So all . . . the understudies came in and lots of parts moved up. We got . . . we did a quick run-through, well as much of it as we could before the curtain. And Brian was in this fight scene towards the end when all hell had broken loose. He couldn't remember who was supposed to be who. You know how confusing all those names are anyway, well now there were different people playing the parts. Well, it was too much for Brian. He suddenly stopped in the middle of the stage and cried out, "Who's Surrey now?" because he just couldn't think. And he had no idea that he had said anything so funny. I just remember screaming with laughter, because he couldn't cope.

OUZOUNIAN:
The production of As You Like It *where you played Rosalind was absolutely magical. How did Robin help you create that atmosphere?*

SMITH:
It think it's because it was so incredibly *English.* I mean, Robin comes from where I live now in Sussex, and it actually felt as though you were there. That wonderful oak tree in the middle of the stage, and the whole atmosphere that he created. You're right, it did feel magical, because Robin charmed and cajoled and eased us into it. It's also such a joyous play, too. And I think everybody enjoyed being in it. And I remember feeling less alarmed about doing that than almost anything I've ever done. We did some previews before the opening, and I was up to my old tricks. I was all over the place and kind of rushing around. But then I suddenly remember feeling "You don't need to do all this stuff." And I just felt very very calm. And again that was Robin.

OUZOUNIAN:
Had the two of you evolved a personal shorthand working together?

SMITH:
Oh, I think so. I could go by what he meant just by looking at me towards the end, you know? Robin used to say a wonderful thing—it's never "*How* do I do this?" it's "*Why* do I do this?" And it's something I still think about to this very day. And it's very true. It isn't how do you do the scene, it's why. And that sure as hell clarifies a lot of things. So you can be calmer in that way.

OUZOUNIAN:
What about shifting gears totally, to the Scottish play? Lady Mac . . .

SMITH:
(interrupting) Oh, don't say it! Gruoch is her first name, isn't it? Well, the thing I remember most about it is what happened on my first entrance on the first night. Robin was always very keen on people coming on in the blackout. So you'd go groping around looking for these sort of luminous things on the floor which were meant to tell you where to be. Anyway I remember doing that. I think "Thank God, I've hit it!" And then the light came up and I had to undo this letter, one of those long scroll things that you undo. Which I did. And I realized when I'd done it, that it was upside down. *(laughs)* I remember thinking, "You could get a big laugh if you turned it round the right way," but it's not that sort of play. So that was how it started. And then we got through it somehow.

OUZOUNIAN:
Edna O'Brien's Virginia *gave you the chance to portray Virginia Woolf. What was that like?*

SMITH:
It was very interesting to work on, but oh God, it was difficult. It was difficult. There's something very harrowing in the fact that it *was* fact. It wasn't fiction. It wasn't a play. You couldn't

sort of chuck it away with your makeup at night. You were stuck with her rather, and it just haunts you. It doesn't go away. I found it a very disturbing thing. My father came to see it. He said, "Oh boy, Margaret. I don't want to sit through that again. I don't want to go through that." He was really distressed by it. I haven't done that often, played a real person. *The Lady in the Van* was real. And that was sort of distressing in the same sort of way, because you can't say "It's just a play." It's a life. It's somebody's existence. Very much of *Virginia* was her own words, you know. It was her. So it was very strange.

OUZOUNIAN:
When you look back on all the parts and all the time you spent at Stratford, are there moments from them that stick out in your mind most vividly after all these years?

SMITH:
I think the whole thing. The whole mass of work. And the fact that it was all in this extraordinarily little place. I mean there were so many things that come into your mind. It's sort of like a very, very fast film because there were so many people, so many different plays. But what I remember most is the atmosphere of it. The kind of seriousness and the dedication that everybody had. That all the actors were so serious, so intent on making it work . . . and you felt that throughout the theatre. You felt that everybody in the wardrobe was the same. In every department, you felt they were all really striving to make this extraordinary theatre in this extraordinary place function and be a wonderful thing for everybody to come and see.

A wonderful thing happened when my boys were very young there. They used to go around the carparks and see how many different licence plates there were. And they would rush backstage and say to me, "They're from Florida. They're from Maryland." And they'd have all these different lists. You'd think, "This is terrific. People are coming from all over. To this sort of strange place in the middle of a park." It was just great.

OUZOUNIAN:

Do you have any wishes for Stratford for the next fifty years?

SMITH:

Oh, I just hope so that it goes on and on and on and on and on.

OUZOUNIAN:

When I say the words "The Stratford Festival" to you, are there any images that come to mind?

SMITH:

First of all, I'd think of that stage. That's the thing I would remember most. And snow. The magic of snow.

Andrea Martin as the Old Lady in the 1978 production of Candide.
Photograph by Robert C. Ragsdale.

Andrea Martin

Andrea Martin was only at Stratford for the 1978 season, where she played Sybil in *Private Lives* and The Old Lady in *Candide*, a part she later recreated in New York for Hal Prince. The Tony Award–winning actress is best known for her long involvement with SCTV, and she is currently starring on Broadway as Aunt Eller in *Oklahoma!* I spoke to her in Los Angeles in February 2001.

OUZOUNIAN:

Andrea, what was the first thing you ever remember hearing about the Stratford Festival?

MARTIN:

I guess "good acting" and "British." Those were the three words. I just moved to Toronto and then got involved in a lot of musicals and I don't think I'd ever actually been to Stratford until I was asked to do it.

Somebody phoned me and asked me to do *Candide*, and a few days later they tossed in Sybil in *Private Lives* as well.

OUZOUNIAN:

Had you ever seen Private Lives*?*

MARTIN:

No, I hadn't ever seen it, nor had I ever seen Maggie Smith or Brian Bedford or Nicholas Pennell and I didn't know who Robin Phillips was, so oh boy this is a very promising beginning. This works.

I don't think I was so terribly intimidated by who I was

going to perform with, because, to be honest with you, I think I was a little cocky, because I was quite successful in "Second City" and in those days you know "Second City" was kind of the be all and end all in theatre in Toronto, and SCTV was just starting that summer as well, so my plate was kind of full.

I accepted the challenge and I was bragging to everyone that I was going to do a classical play and a musical, and then the first day of rehearsal we did a read-through and I met everybody and I was thinking, "Gee, I think I'm a little fish out of water, but I'll be okay because I'm funny." And I remember the first line I did, I think it was *(British accent)* "Elly, Elly dear, do come out. The boat's are looking so . . ." And Robin Phillips who was the director said, "No, I wouldn't do it in an English accent." And then from that moment on I knew I was really in trouble. Big trouble.

OUZOUNIAN:

But one of the things you are noted for in all of your characterizations is how you always found the right voice, the right accent for somebody . . .

MARTIN:

Yeah, but when you're performing with Maggie Smith and Brian Bedford and Nicholas Pennell and Robin Phillips and they're all English and you know I'm a girl from Portland, Maine, who's done some sketch accents, and all of a sudden I'm trying to do an English one, and I really didn't know how to be a person underneath the accent, really. I was just kind of mimicking voices I had heard. Well, it was obvious it was so fraudulent, you know. So there went all my steam.

I didn't know very much about acting, to be honest with you. I really knew how to be funny. I knew how to get a laugh. But I didn't really know how to inhabit a role. I had had no training at all. I'd never done a straight play before and to be on a stage with Maggie Smith and Brian Bedford, in a part which didn't have that much foundation, and to hold my own every night, I mean it's extraordinary that I got through it. And the other part of this puzzle when I look back is that Robin Phillips was not there for half of it. He got very sick in the middle of it and Brian and Maggie essentially had to direct me. So it was really something.

OUZOUNIAN:
Before Robin had to go away, do you recall anything he might have said about the play or the part to you? Any advice he tried to give you?

MARTIN:
Yes, I do remember. He said, "Just be yourself." And you know, my whole struggle all my life has been, how can I be myself and feel comfortable with that? Can I really be onstage as myself, without an accent, without a wig, without glasses, and feel that I'm enough? And he said that, I wasn't able to incorporate it 'cause I didn't really know how to do that. Now when I look back, I think that would have been everything really, because certainly Maggie and Brian and Nicholas were themselves. That's why I think they're such wonderful actors, because with Maggie and Brian, you really get a sense of who they are in everything they do.

Here's what I remember most about that whole experience: standing in the wings when Maggie and Brian were on, watching in awe, in awe that every night they would break up in the same places, that weren't written in the play, and do it with such finesse you believed it was for the first time.

OUZOUNIAN:
It was a longish run, wasn't it? For the whole summer? What were those months like for you?

MARTIN:
They were really hard. Oh my God. They were so hard. And you know I don't think Maggie was really happy with me in the part, and I didn't have Robin there to be a cheerleader.

Although I remember him as being supportive and kind and I think that he— there was an essence about me that he really liked or he never would've given me that part. I'm so sorry that I was not able to have a relationship with him and learn from him, to be honest with you. But they were long dark, dark months I remember. Yeah, they were something! But listen, I did it and now I would love to do something like that again. Now with the experience I have had since then, I would love to do something on the Stratford stage where I could use some skills that I've developed as an actress over the years.

OUZOUNIAN:
What about the other show that year, Candide?

MARTIN:
Well, that was really fun, 'cause you know I was comfortable and secure in musical comedies and I loved how Brian Macdonald challenged me with a dance and I thought I grew a lot in that play.

The character of The Little Old Lady is a great part, because you get to come in just at the point when everyone's tired of everyone they'd been seeing again, and you zap them up, and you've got a great number and I remember being on that big stage in the round, and saying, "Baby I've arrived. Yes!"

OUZOUNIAN:
Having been parachuted in from outside the Stratford world, did you feel any kind of resentment from the company towards you?

MARTIN:
I never felt resentment, no. But I didn't ever really feel a part of it all. I felt kind of like the way you might feel on a sitcom as a special guest star or something. You know, you're happy for the work and it's good pay and a nice part, but you never really, can't really fit in. It just isn't a perfect fit you know. And that's what I felt like.

OUZOUNIAN:
Give me some quick word pictures of people from that summer. Robin Phillips?

MARTIN:
Stimulating. Enthusiastic. Smiling. Focused. Creative. Impassioned. Scarf. Handsome. Twinkle in his eyes.

OUZOUNIAN:
What about Brian Bedford?

MARTIN:
Sharp. Shrewd. Mischievous. Sly. Dry. Noel Coward. Wordsmith. Skillful.

OUZOUNIAN:
Maggie Smith?

MARTIN:
Demanding. Distant. Detached. Brilliant. Kind of guarded and so wonderful. So frightened underneath, yet so brilliant.

OUZOUNIAN:
As it goes into its next fifty years, what would you like to wish for the Stratford Festival?

MARTIN:
Oh gosh, a Starbucks?

OUZOUNIAN:
And what words come to mind when I say "The Stratford Festival" to you?

MARTIN:
Trumpets and swans and beautiful stages and great restaurants and Shakespeare and history and the people who keep those words alive. I just have great admiration for that. Great admiration.

Brent Carver as Hamlet in the 1986 production of Hamlet.
Photograph by Robert C.Ragsdale.

Brent Carver

Brent Carver first came to the Festival in 1980 in *The Beggar's Opera, Long Day's Journey into Night*, and *Foxfire*. His memorable performances over the years have alternated between musicals *(The Pirates of Penzance, Cabaret, Fiddler on the Roof)* and dramas *(Hamlet, Elizabeth Rex)*. He returned to the Festival in the Fiftieth Anniversary Season to appear in *Shadows* by Timothy Findley. I spoke to him in Toronto during the summer of 2001.

OUZOUNIAN:
It was Robin Phillips who brought you to Stratford. How did the two of you get together?

CARVER:
It was his first season and I saw *Measure For Measure* at the Festival Theatre with Brian Bedford and Martha Henry and Bill Hutt and Richard Monette and I was absolutely stunned. And I thought, well this is it. This is where I want to be. I want whatever is happening here because it is so vibrant and so immediate and so sensual and exciting and . . . it was sort of breathtaking. Then we met and we had a conversation, and it took me five years to finally join the company, but it was worth the wait.

We started rehearsing *The Beggar's Opera* upstairs in the Avon Theatre bar, the lounge up there. And for almost the first month, we touched on the play a little, but it was really like a master class with Robin running all sorts of extraordinary exercises and the kind of laughter that you just, you can't believe. We just laughed and laughed and laughed. And it was a high time in my life and my experience at Stratford, that very first month. And it sort of set for me the tone of what Stratford could mean. And what exploration was about and what examining text was about and really finding out what the humour of the heart was about as well.

OUZOUNIAN:

During that first season you also wound up working some pretty heavy hitters like Hume Cronyn and Jessica Tandy as well . . .

CARVER:

Robin approached me about doing the play that Hume and Susan Cooper had written called *Foxfire*, because they hadn't cast the son, Dillard. Well, I can somewhat play the guitar and it was very much a musical play filled with this great sort of Appalachian country music and folk country. And so I, fortunately, took on that part and we began rehearsing in June. Working with Hume and Jessica was certainly a little nerve-racking, but I just thought well, there was something about the mountains that these people were about and that I felt quite connected to, and so that calmed me down.

OUZOUNIAN:

Was there anything from your own growing up in Cranbrook, B.C., that might have triggered those feelings?

CARVER:

Yes, I think it all really had something to do with the terrain, the mountains where I'm from and that kind of country. Possibly the relationship to the earth. Annie Nations, Jessica Tandy's part, she tried to teach her son what it was to be part of this land and what it was to fulfill rituals and to believe in a kind of higher power.

I'll never forget Jessica. We'd have scenes of flashbacks where she had met her husband for the first time at a dance. And she was just— well, it was like she was sixteen years old again. It was like she was Juliet with a beautiful sweet knowing laugh. She was so radiant. She was luminescent.

I remember Sunday nights. We rehearsed a lot in the church basement after the Sunday matinee. And it was so warm, literally warm, that you could feel the heat of those mountains. I just always felt inspired when I was in those rehearsals.

OUZOUNIAN:
You've talked about Jessica. What was Hume like?

CARVER:
Well, Hume had co-written *Foxfire* with Susan Cooper, and he was playing my father, too, who was a real stickler for rules and things like that, but I think we still had a very good time. I really respected him. He felt so sure and clear. He has a real instinct that's very sharp. Really sharp.

OUZOUNIAN:
You also worked with Robin on Long Day's Journey into Night *that season. Do you recall any particular moment from it?*

CARVER:
I remember our first day onstage and we were doing the last act. I recall the real precision of rehearsing that final act. And it, I guess it's because of the work that we had done before, it all seemed to come together like a card game. Things just dropped into place. And when I asked Robin how that could happen, he said that it really has to do with the text being a guideline. So that there's an opening up of yourself and the story that you're illuminating. You always have to ask what the text is really about and what the thought is *behind* that extraordinary text as well. That whole season was so illuminating for me . . .

OUZOUNIAN:
John Hirsch brought you back a few years later to appear in The Pirates of Penzance.

CARVER:
When I was approached to play the Pirate King I thought that would be really quite a wonderful summer to have in Stratford. Brian Macdonald was directing it and we had really a kind of liberating time, a great time. He choreographed a wonderful tango in near the end of the piece that wasn't in the actual show.

OUZOUNIAN:
When I interviewed Brian, he talked about how he realized watching a run-through one day that there was a chunk missing, he felt, for the Pirate King . . .

CARVER:
Right. The character wasn't completed, he needed to go somewhere in the play. So one day, Brian turned to our musical director, Bert Carriere, and said, "Play me some tango music."

OUZOUNIAN:
And you just cooked it up in the rehearsal hall . . .?

CARVER:
We really worked at it, and it was exciting. It involved me and a whip and a dancer named Wendy Abbott. We just really went at it and discovered all sorts of things about this Pirate King and in the end, of course, she actually gets the upper hand. That was a true entertainment experience and it was quite joyous, with a great company—Jeffrey Hyslop and Doug Chamberlain—just all sorts of wonderful people.

OUZOUNIAN:
The next year John Neville took over and asked you to play Hamlet. Was that intimidating?

CARVER:
At first, certainly it was intimidating. But the most extraordinary thing about *Hamlet*, or one of the many extraordinary things about *Hamlet*, is that each time you approach a soliloquy or a scene, you have the great good fortune of being in Shakespeare's

hands and you are guided all the time. Yes, before every performance, there's a kind of terror and a kind of excitement about speaking that text, about thinking that text. But when you meet it head-on, there's nothing like it. Nothing like it. Heart-on actually. When you meet it heart-on. *(laughing)*

At times when you're playing it, you find that the text almost slips away from you, and it's like you're trying to find hooks to hang onto. But because the piece is so extraordinarily written and it describes the human soul so implicitly, in the end you will always bash through to the truth. Of course it's extraordinarily intimidating but exhilarating as well and before each performance you always feel—oh my goodness, we're really starting over, aren't we? Each time. Each time we're really starting again. But that's the joy of it. You know, you just feel better after finding yourself in that text.

OUZOUNIAN:

You never get through playing Hamlet do you?

CARVER:

No, I don't think so. You know, Hamlet accuses Rosencrantz and Guildenstern of trying to pluck out the heart of his mystery, but anyone who plays Hamlet knows that we can't pluck out the heart of his mystery. We can only look into our own mystery and be so fortunate as to wonder and explore with the gift that Shakespeare's given us.

OUZOUNIAN:

The next year you appeared in Mother Courage and Her Children *with your close friend, the late Susan Wright. What was that like?*

CARVER:

I think of Susan still, pulling that wagon around the stage. I think that she had a really special time playing the part. She was magnificent in the role, and at moments just stunning.

Susan, as an actress, had a kind of steely luminosity, but the steel was a very valuable kind of alloy. She had a slyness but a real openness as well. I don't know, the text seemed to kind of glow when she spoke.

OUZOUNIAN:
What was her secret?

CARVER:
Well, I think Susan's secret was that she had none. Just completely open. Her laughter and her pain were both open-hearted and when she and a text met, then secrets were revealed and treasures came forth.

OUZOUNIAN:
After a bit of an absence you came back to Stratford to play Tevye in Fiddler on the Roof. *You're not typecasting for the role, so how did it happen?*

CARVER:
I know it seems strange, but Susan Schulman, who was directing *Fiddler*, had seen me in *Kiss of the Spider Woman* and *Parade* and she just asked me if I would be interested in the part.

I went, "Well . . ." and I could feel heat, from somewhere, everywhere. I just kind of got very hot and at first I said no. But then I read the script again of *Fiddler* and I came to one line where he says to his wife, "It's a new world." And there was something about that, and I suddenly thought, "That really excites me," a man who was ready to change with the world and change with the times, which we are asked to do every day of our lives, which the Stratford Festival is doing all the time.

OUZOUNIAN:
Tevye spends much of the play pulling his dairy cart. Did you think back to Mother Courage *and Susan Wright pulling her cart?*

CARVER:
Absolutely. I thought of the scene where she looked at me and said, "This is to you and to all the world." I felt that Tevye in

his open-heartedness had that as well, pulling his cart and whatever's in that world, he knows well.

Stratford is about that. It's about going from one generation to the other, carrying the message of the great works of literature. And with each new generation the discovery is fresh each time.

OUZOUNIAN:
What would you wish Stratford for the next fifty years?

CARVER:
Well, fifty more years, for sure. Definitely, at least fifty years. And I wish inspiration for those next fifty years. To be inspired.

OUZOUNIAN:
What images come to mind when I say "The Stratford Festival"?

CARVER:
I think of wonderful rehearsal times with snow up to the front windows. Finding your path to the rehearsal hall through the snow. A special time. And a kind of peace.

Peter Ustinov as King Lear in the 1980 production of King Lear.
Photograph by Robert C. Ragsdale.

Peter Ustinov

The award-winning international star of stage and screen, Sir Peter Ustinov, came to Stratford at Robin Phillips's invitation to star in *King Lear* in 1979 and returned to revive it the following season. I spoke to him in Toronto in the spring of 2001, when he was filming *The Salem Witch Trials.*

OUZOUNIAN:

Why do you think Robin Phillips asked you to play King Lear?

USTINOV:

Well, I've always let it be known that it's the only Shakespeare play I really had an ambition to play because I thought I had a hook on it which others perhaps didn't have since I've always played old men all my life. I wondered, in fact, during the rehearsals whether I wasn't, even then, too old for the role, because you have to carry Cordelia. And I always remember John Gielgud's admonition to a man who was going to play Lear and asked for any advice and Gielgud answered, "Choose a light Cordelia." Well, I think he was absolutely right. *(laughs)*

But I thought I was too old until one day I was having lunch at that extraordinary Church Restaurant, and I knocked a tumbler of water to the floor . . . and caught it before it had landed. By a sort of tennis reflex. And I thought to myself, "My God, if you can do that, you can play Lear!" Gave me more courage than any amount of rehearsals, even with Robin Phillips in charge. And I must say they were extraordinary rehearsals because they took you right back to a state of mind when you were a student. And I always welcomed that because—it must be the Russian in me—I have a great nostalgia for actors who haven't changed since their student days, and who really have a sense of integrity, which is usually obviously missing in the theatre today.

OUZOUNIAN:
Did you know much about Stratford when you were asked to go there?

USTINOV:
I knew very little, except that it was this sort of isolated community—the idea of which I loved—because you were dedicated to nothing but the job in hand. We didn't have cellphones in those days so there was no chance of being interrupted in the middle of rehearsals by Bach's *Toccata and Fugue*, played on a xylophone.

But I must tell you that I was very, very nervous about this whole thing. I'm usually never nervous, but I saw this mountain in front of me, this endless road. You start out "Attend the lords of France and Burgundy . . . God, what's his name? Oh yes . . . Gloucester," and you reach Camp One. And there are four thousand to follow. *(laughs)* Well, gradually the engine warms up and then you have some wonderful people like Bill Hutt helping you along.

Well, eventually you die and you think, "This is the most wonderful moment. I hope the audience doesn't see how relieved I am." And you fall to the floor. From then on, until the end of the play, everybody starts talking terribly slowly in deference to your recent death. And you lie there saying, "For God's sake, get a move on. I'm dead. There isn't anything to discuss now." And while you're doing it, a terrible itch manifests itself on your left ankle. And you think of all sorts of things. It's the worst time of the evening. It's got nothing to do with nerves about lines, it's lying there dead knowing you daren't move because you will destroy the illusion for thousands of people. *(laughing)* So you lie there doing the multiplication tables in your head. No, it doesn't work. The itch continues and then the next night you die slightly differently. You throw the cloak over your leg as you fall. You think, "Now if it happens again, under the great coat I can surreptitiously move and they won't notice that." The trouble is, the itch doesn't reappear on your ankle. As you lie there, it reappears in your nostril. Now what can you do? You can't throw the coat over your face, you'll suffocate, because at the speed they're talking, there's no chance of you being alive by the end of the evening. *(laughing)* And those are the worst moments with Lear.

OUZOUNIAN:

You said one of the reasons you wanted to play Lear was that you thought you had a special fix on it. What do you think that was, in addition to the fact that you played old so much of your life?

USTINOV:

I understand Lear in the sense that he's mad as a hatter at the beginning. You can't be much madder than him dividing his kingdom into various things and deciding real estate problems and wanting gratitude from people that aren't willing to give it. I mean all sorts of nutty sides to his nature. And . . . and then under the pressure of the moor and all sorts of other terrible physical trials, he gradually becomes sane. He begins to remember everybody. And then what I think is touching, is that at the end of the play, he is too tired to pretend anymore but it is still less of a strain to pretend to be mad than to pretend to be sane. And although he's completely sane at the end, he really doesn't care anymore.

OUZOUNIAN:

Phillips set the play in the late Victorian period. Did you agree with that?

USTINOV:

Yes, I did. I think it was the best thing because, if he's wearing a dirty shift on the moor, he's merely changing from a clean shift to a dirty shift. And that doesn't explain anything. But here, of course, when he's at the end, taken prisoner and taken to France briefly, being a king of that period where they were all cousins to each other and all exchanging uniforms and things, it's a very moving moment in our version when he suddenly looks at his own sleeve and says, "Am I in France?" It's the first glimmer of sanity. He's recognized the uniform because he obviously knows all the medals and uniforms by heart. "Why are you not wearing the golden fleece the right way up? On the second row." I'm sure he was that sort of cantankerous individual.

OUZOUNIAN:

You spoke about Bill Hutt, who played the Fool. How about your Edmund, Richard Monette . . . what do you remember of him?

USTINOV:

I remember him as being a very quicksilver, vital sort of person with eyes which I hesitate to describe as shifty, but they just went darting from left to right. He was extremely good at his part, very friendly, and he had a nice Mazda motorcar I remember which I rather envied. But apart from that I know that he's gained in eminence now and runs the whole Festival. Good for him.

OUZOUNIAN:

How would you describe Robin's approach in rehearsal?

USTINOV:

Robin's aim was to try to stimulate you by a series of surprises. To stimulate you into showing something that you were not really prepared to offer, but might be very valuable in the long run and there he was absolutely right, I think. Sometimes his demands were very surprising. "Now all run around the block and come back and do it again." What if I don't feel like running around the block? *(laughs)* Nowadays it would be technically very difficult for me. I'd be back in four hours. The rest of the cast would have gotten to the end of *King Lear* by the time I got back.

But he believed in a certain kind of shock tactic, and once you were prepared to allow yourself to be taken by surprise, which anybody should be in the theatre, it was very salutary. Because I've always maintained that there are very good actors who give you precisely what they rehearsed. And then there are better actors who bother to give the impression on the fiftieth performance that it's the first time they've done it. And that to my mind, is all-important. You've got to take yourself by surprise. And even some other acting.

OUZOUNIAN:

You went back and played Lear again the next year. How was that experience?

USTINOV:

It wasn't quite the same thing. The first year I was tremendously inspired by all Robin had done and all we'd managed to achieve together. The second year it was a little bit, I must say, more like sessions of a guru, which weren't absolutely as productive because they were much more planned. They were much more settled in a kind of groove, and your loyalties were called into question and things like that, which normally one shouldn't have to.

OUZOUNIAN:

When you think about the production, are there moments that come to mind?

USTINOV:

I think of the scene in which eventually I broke into tears and was led off by Bill Hutt. "O fool, I shall go mad!" That was a high point in the pathos. Hutt was so wonderful as the Fool. To have an actor in that part who had himself played Lear several times was incredibly valuable to me.

OUZOUNIAN:
All in all, do you feel that the experience of playing Lear turned out well?

USTINOV:
At the time, it gave me infinite satisfaction and when I remember it now, it gives me an enormous feeling of pleasure.

OUZOUNIAN:
Would you ever want to play Lear again?

USTINOV:
No. Now I'm really too old. I would drop the tumbler, it would splinter on the floor and I'd say, "Well, we need another glass here."

OUZOUNIAN:
What would you like to wish Stratford for its next fifty years?

USTINOV:
To continue rediscovering a youth which has not terribly much to do with its past.

OUZOUNIAN:
When I say "The Stratford Festival," what do you think of?

USTINOV:
A lovely sabbatical, in which you are asked to accomplish some very serious work, in ideal surroundings.

Stephen Ouimette as Hamlet in the 1994 production of Hamlet.
Photograph by Cylla von Tiedemann.

Stephen Ouimette

Stephen Ouimette first came to the Festival as a young actor in 1979. He joined and left the company several times during the eighties, returning as a leading man in the nineties to play roles like Hamlet, Richard the Third, and Mozart. After a brief absence, he returned for the Fiftieth Anniversary Season to make his directorial debut with *The Threepenny Opera*.
I spoke with him at the CBC Broadcast Centre in the spring of 2001.

OUZOUNIAN:
Stephen, what's the first time you ever remember hearing about the Stratford Festival?

OUIMETTE:
I was in grade nine in St. Thomas, Ontario, and there was a school trip to go to see a play at Stratford. I'd never even seen a play before. I mean a professional play or an amateur production of anything. And my grandmother gave me the money. I think it was twenty-five dollars for the bus trip and lunch and the whole deal and we went and saw *A Midsummer Night's Dream*. It was John Hirsch's production, so it must have been 1968, and it sounds corny, but it changed my life because I was sort of headed on— I don't know what kind of track I was on. Probably would have ended up being a juvenile delinquent or something and suddenly this play started, and I just sort of sat there absolutely transfixed and I think that's where sort of a seed got planted that I might like to do this.

OUZOUNIAN:
It only took ten years for you to wind up in the company. How did

you actually make that leap from kid in the audience to actor on the stage in ten years?

OUIMETTE:

Well, when I got out of theatre school, I auditioned for William Hutt's Young Company at the Grand Theatre in London. And while I was there, I did a show with Peter Moss, who was also directing at the Festival and he must have liked me, because the next year I was there myself.

OUZOUNIAN:

Do you recall your first actual performance on the festival stage?

OUIMETTE:

It was playing Falstaff's Page in *Henry IV, Parts 1 & 2*, and I remember that I was still doing a show at the Grand and so they'd all been rehearsing for a month and I had to come a month late. Well, by this time they were out of the rehearsal hall and on the stage. So my first day at work there was walking onto that stage, which I only sort of dreamed about since high school and I just couldn't cope. It was way too much to take in. I mean if I'd been sane, I would have said, "Could we just stop for ten minutes, and let me absorb—it's just too much to take in."

OUZOUNIAN:

What about the first time you faced an audience on that stage? People always talk about that, the embrace of two thousand people around you.

OUIMETTE:

It's what takes the sting and the scariness away. It's because they're sort of wrapped around you. It's not intimidating at all. It's actually quite nice. It's actually a lot of fun being out there.

OUZOUNIAN:

Over the next decade you would come to the Festival for a while, and then go away again. But when you were finally brought back in the Monette years as one of the leading actors, did you think back to what it had been like twelve years ago when you had been just starting out?

OUIMETTE:

Oh absolutely. Absolutely. And it affects how you behave, because I really do believe you have to be a company member. You just can't come in and do your own thing and not be a part of it all. I remember when I was younger how Nicholas Pennell was always giving classes and workshops, just being so kind and generous with his own knowledge, and that always left a big impression on me in terms of giving something back, because I feel you should. You know it's sort of your duty.

OUZOUNIAN:

During these years at Stratford you were doing all these outrageous comic roles, and it seems like you take to them so naturally but you paint yourself as quite a shy boy. Where did the confidence to play that bold over-the-top comedy come from?

OUIMETTE:

I guess everybody's a contradiction. I *was* painfully shy, but somehow when you put the mask on and you've got something to hide behind, all kinds of things are possible. And I love doing that stuff. It gives you a high that's just unequalled.

OUZOUNIAN:

Richard Monette is known for having a great fondness for that kind of broad, very physical comedy. When you two worked together, did he fling things at you and you ran with them or did you bring things and he elaborated? How did it work?

OUIMETTE:

It was, I guess, a bit of both. I mean, I'd sort of start something or he'd ask me to try something and then we'd just build on it from there. I mean he's got a great sense of timing and a real love of jokes and gags and, boy, when he's hot, he can just go and go and go. In fact, sometimes you have to say, okay, that's enough now. You know, cut the fifteen cakes going across. We don't really need it. But, but at least he'll try it, just loving it and laughing the whole time so you know, I think . . . I think Richard's a bit like a kid on the playground.

OUZOUNIAN:
How did you finally come to play Hamlet at the Stratford Festival?

OUIMETTE:
Well, I guess you could say it was a present from Richard. Way back in 1980, when Robin Phillips was leaving, I was slated to play Hamlet the next year on the Festival stage, as part of the season that Peter Moss, Urjo Kareda, Martha Henry, and Pam Brighton—"the Gang of Four"—had planned. And then it didn't happen. They were all fired and I wasn't even asked back to the company. Richard had been in the company at the time and knew everything that had gone down, so years later when he was in charge, he said, "I think now it's time that you played Hamlet." So it was really a gift.

OUZOUNIAN:
And when he first uttered the sentence, "I want you to play Hamlet," what was your reaction?

OUIMETTE:
Oh, terror of course! *(laughing)* And then completely mixed emotions. I mean, I wanted to do it, but I was also extremely cautious because it had a history for me. I mean, everybody thinks they want to play Hamlet, but maybe some people shouldn't play Hamlet and I thought maybe I'm one of those. Maybe I'm the eternal footman and I should just keep my mouth shut.

OUZOUNIAN:
Did you collaborate much with your director on it in the preparation of the play?

OUIMETTE:
Richard was very clear in terms of wanting a very pared-down production, not a lot of sets, not a lot of costumes. Which was fine with me. And I always made him talk in rehearsal. He doesn't like to talk in rehearsal but you have to with that play. I had a lot of questions.

OUZOUNIAN:

Did the two of you ever say what the play is about, in the twenty-five words-or-less answer? You know Laurence Olivier said it's about a man who could not make up his mind. What was it to you and Richard?

OUIMETTE:

Well, I think we felt the same way, that it was about a man who couldn't make up his mind but it's also just a really fantastic murder mystery.

I mean it is really quite an extraordinary journey in terms of finding out who the killer is.

OUZOUNIAN:

When people think about Hamlet, one of the things that stands out for them is the soliloquies. How did you sit down and approach them?

OUIMETTE:

I'd known for a year before that I was going to do it, so I went on a vacation and sat with the script on the beach and just sort of worked and worked and worked and worked in really nice surroundings. But I don't think I really made any decisions until we got into rehearsal. Then I made my choices as we went along. *(laughs)* I think I'm still making some of them. Take "To be or not to be." I keep discovering new things about that speech. I was reading it the other day and thinking, oh God, yeah, now I get that! I understand what that one little phrase means. You know. It's amazing how much you miss. I mean, I guess that's why people say they play the part five and six times and still didn't feel they got it right.

OUZOUNIAN:

You've gotten to play some of the real monster roles—Hamlet, Richard the Third—things like that. Are they more satisfying for you or do they have their downside as well?

OUIMETTE:

I think they do have their downside. They're workhorse parts.

You know, you just never, ever stop. And the key with doing any of those parts is who you've got with you, because ultimately, it's just scenes with other people, interactions with other human beings and the better the cast you have, the better you'll be. You can't make it in your mind that I'm playing this part or that part. It's just another part in that play. Maybe it happens to be the title role, and maybe you have more lines than anybody else, but it's just a story, because even the guy who's just bringing the wine in thinks that play's about him. I think you've got to look at it like that or suddenly it becomes too big a mountain and you can't possibly climb it.

OUZOUNIAN:

Is that where Stratford has an advantage, because you are working with a company of actors?

OUIMETTE:

Absolutely. You become close-knit and you get a shorthand so you can cut to the chase, and it makes your work much richer. But there's a downside as well, because it's so intense that after a few years you get burnt out and you actually have to have a little sabbatical from there and go off and do something else. Work with new people, learn some more things. And then go back and bring that knowledge with you.

OUZOUNIAN:

If you had a wish for the Stratford Festival for their next fifty years, a present you could give them, what would it be?

OUIMETTE:

I think the big thing is the gift of an audience, always hoping that there will be people who want to see those plays. New audiences as well as old. Because, even at those student matinees full of unruly kids which can be so hard to do, I keep thinking that somewhere out there in the dark was me, you know? So there's got to be one of those in every, in every performance, so hopefully they'll rise to the surface and support the theatre.

OUZOUNIAN:

If I say "The Stratford Festival," what do you think of?

OUIMETTE:

Passion. Power. Literature. Dreams. Thrill. Work. Sweat. Tears. Shakespeare.

Brian Macdonald C.C. Photographer unknown.

Brian Macdonald C.C.

One of Canada's most respected choreographers, Brian Macdonald's work was first seen at Stratford when his production of *My Fur Lady* played the Avon Theatre in 1957. Over the years, he choreographed numerous shows, but he is best remembered for the series of Gilbert and Sullivan operettas he staged, beginning with his 1982 version of *The Mikado*. I spoke to him at his home in Stratford in the summer of 2001.

OUZOUNIAN:
Brian, how did you ever first get involved with musicals at Stratford?

MACDONALD:
I had come here one summer and talked to John Hirsch, who was a pal of mine from the Manitoba Theatre Centre days, when we were both in Winnipeg. He was the only man who would laugh at my funny ballets with the Royal Winnipeg Ballet. And I told him I'd like to do something here and he phoned me later and said, "How about doing *The Mikado*?"

OUZOUNIAN:
Had you ever done a Gilbert and Sullivan?

MACDONALD:
No. Actually I had never seen one. It was all brand new territory for me. I had some catching up to do in that sense because I was not aware of all the D'Oyly Carte traditions, but I went at the text, and the music I knew. I mean those catchy tunes, everybody in the world knows them. I just dived in.

OUZOUNIAN:
You frequently attributed the success of The Mikado *to the great*

relationship you have with your designer, Susan Benson. Where did all of those wonderful Oriental images come from?

MACDONALD:

We had talked about a number of things. We were looking for a central image and she came up with lily pads and all kinds of ideas, Japanese gardens, and so on and we slowly discarded things until we got to a more abstract working platform, with just the fan that moved at the back and then later on a moon that came in. Very, very simple things. Susan is quite a rigorous designer in terms of letting ideas go if they're too decorative. She wants something that really speaks of the piece all the time. Well, that was fine but it also made it up to me to be very inventive and keep things moving and block very carefully and make sure that all the production numbers worked. Richard, I believe that a good musical really rises or falls on production numbers. They're your anchors. Yes, there's comedy. Yes, there's text. Yes, there's narrative. There's all those other things. But if your big numbers don't work, that's what you must head for right away.

OUZOUNIAN:

In Gilbert and Sullivan, they usually don't present you with production numbers in the traditional musical sense, but yet you managed to make them happen. How do you do that?

MACDONALD:

Bert Carriere, the musical director, was wonderful about rearranging bits of the music for me while staying very faithful to the score actually. Sullivan didn't write many codas. He drank champagne and ate oysters while he composed and when he'd finished the tune he'd say—"Finito, that's it!" Or else he'd add eight bars and he'd write on top of it—"all dance." *(laughs)* So I used that as an excuse to put in more colour and movement and swiftness. I didn't want anybody standing around. Everybody had to be there for a purpose.

OUZOUNIAN:

One of the things that was most memorable about your Gilbert and Sullivans was that the material got full vocal value and was sung beautifully but yet it was also danced and acted and moved in a style much freer than typical productions. How did you get everyone to do everything?

MACDONALD:

Well, I come from a choreographic side of the theatre, and I had assistants who were ready to keep people in lines where they had to be, or do asymmetrical movements. I suppose as a choreographer, you're very much in control of where the audience, where their focus is, what they are seeing at that moment. Not just what they are hearing textually, but where have you taken the eye?

OUZOUNIAN:

One of the things people remember most about the Gilbert and Sullivan operettas that you did is the political humour, how Gilbert's topical references were very much updated to the moment about Canadian politics. What gave you that impulse?

MACDONALD:

Gilbert himself was very much up to date. You know a lot of his references that seem oblique today if we . . . because they have no meaning . . . gave me the licence to satirize the way he satirized. Remember Sullivan was knighted by Queen Victoria long before Gilbert was, because she was not amused at some of Mr. Gilbert's jokes about royalty and the navy and so on. But Gilbert was very much of his time, and I thought that the pieces would reflect that, and that any additional jokes didn't detract. I was very careful that we were not, if you'll pardon the expression, smart-assed. That wouldn't work. We had to be funny within the context of the narrative.

OUZOUNIAN:

The Mikado *was such a huge success that obviously you had to continue the pattern.*

MACDONALD:

The next was *The Gondoliers*, which Susan and I treated in a different way. Susan came up with the idea of spectators. We liked the idea that in this Venice there were spectators watching the show, so we invented *commedia dell'arte* characters who would set the scene and poke their noses in and look at things at odd moments. And that led to little finger puppets and that led to the bigger dummies we used in the Cachucha number.

OUZOUNIAN:

That's one of the sequences people still talk about. Suddenly the stage seemed to be filled with three times the people that were there before. How did that happen?

MACDONALD:

Well, it was tough actually. A simple concept—two dummies attached to each dancer—but it was a hard number to do, in the sense that when we first got the dummies they were very heavy. And Susan later lightened them and found different ways to make them easier to handle. But we moved along and got some very funny things happening.

OUZOUNIAN:

The next Gilbert and Sullivan operetta you tackled, Iolanthe, *is not one of the most popular and it's also one of the most political, but you had one of the best strokes of casting ever in getting Maureen Forrester to do it. How did you get her?*

MACDONALD:

We're old pals from Montreal and we've known each other for a long, long time, Maureen and I, so I took her to a smart lunch at a hotel in New York and said, "Would you like to play the Queen of the Fairies?" And she said, "Well, do I get to have jokes?" And I said, "Yes, you have lots of jokes. And I'll make sure Susan Benson gives you a beautiful costume." She said, "Sure, I'm in." Just like that.

Susan found a sketch of the Prince of Wales looking at music hall girls, so we thought to make the fairies slightly music hall and that kind of thing. We based it on that and on Victorian children's books where you open them and little castles pop up and that sort of thing. We had all sorts of scenery that popped up out of a giant box we brought onstage.

The trickiest part of the piece is that in the finale, all the British Peers suddenly sprout wings from the backs of their robes. And I thought well, that's not going to work, that's going to be the biggest dead gag in the world. But you know, I was completely wrong: the audience went mad over it. The wardrobe department managed to make these robes with pop-up wings in the back so that the guys could turn their backs, pull a little string, and out popped these wings and it had a logic from what we'd done before with the scenery.

We performed it in repertory with the first two shows—*Mikado* and *Gondoliers*—so the team was getting stronger and stronger because they were doing these things regularly: singing a lot, dancing a lot, being funny a lot.

OUZOUNIAN:

So that there was a house style developing?

MACDONALD:

Absolutely, and then next came *The Pirates of Penzance*, and I was fortunate enough to have Jeff Hyslop as Frederick and Brent Carver as the Pirate King. I knew Jeff would be good because he's an excellent singer, and Brent—well, I knew he could give me a zany Pirate King. I didn't want to go to what Kevin Kline had done on Broadway. I wanted a Pirate King who was perhaps not the brightest man in the world. And so I suggested to Brent that maybe he whips his crew from time to time. And Brent said, laughing, "Oh, do I get to whip people?"

Ultimately, the production was true to the original, except I felt there was something lacking near the end where there's a battle between the pirates and the police. It's a set-up which is never taken advantage of. And I thought, no, we're going to have a little Agnes DeMille dream ballet in here. *(laughing)* And we had a chorus girl in the show, Wendy Abbott, who played her character as a straight-laced spinster, with little funny glasses on and so on. And Brent was this wild Pirate King and so one day I said, "Why don't you two come together in this dream ballet and start to get off on each other?" And we went into rehearsal with Bert Carriere, who's marvellous at improvising on the piano and I'd say, "I think I need another thirty-two bars of tango here, and maybe a change of key" and he would accommodate me. And we just started playing at that, the whip and the straight-laced girl who throws her glasses off, and it got funnier and funnier and we were falling off the floor laughing, and suddenly it occurred to all of us at the same time, that it had to end with the girl in charge, because the Pirate King was going to enjoy being whipped. And it happens very quickly and it's just as nonsensical as Gilbert and Sullivan were. Their pieces are not about ideas; they're about situations, about conundrums. So as long as you approached them with that idea in mind, you can do practically anything because you've remained faithful to the spirit of the piece.

OUZOUNIAN:

All of these Gilbert and Sullivan productions were done while John Hirsch was the artistic director at Stratford. Then, after a short hiatus, you returned to do a series of modern musicals: Cabaret, Guys and Dolls, Carousel, Gypsy, The Music Man. *The musical became more and more important to Stratford, financially as well as artistically. Do you think that was a good thing or a bad thing?*

MACDONALD:

Well, I have very strong thoughts about that. The musical, as long as it's done well, belongs on the Stratford stage. If it's not done well, or if the artistic director cannot assemble a proper team of people that he or she knows is going to be quality, then it shouldn't be on that stage. Because we are with one of the great dramatists the world has ever known on that stage and the actors take it very seriously. So, therefore, you must take the musical very seriously. Every aspect—the visual, the narrative, the dialogue, the musical aspects—have all got to be enormously respected. I feel that . . . it's sometimes regarded as the money maker. So, that's wonderful. Why not? As long as it's well done.

OUZOUNIAN:
What would you wish for the Stratford Festival for its next fifty years?

MACDONALD:
Survival, I guess, in the economic rough seas of the theatre. And television and digital this and digital that. I have very strong feelings that when a youngster today looks at, let's say television, they know instinctively that it's edited. They see a commercial for McDonald's with a close-up of the hamburger and then a longer shot on the cook and then a longer shot on the parking lot, etc. But when they go to the theatre, they know that person is really portraying that character. They know that lady is really singing from beginning to end because in the theatre, it's your eye that does the editing. So the theatre is an extraordinarily important place for performers to be and for audiences to be. And I think that's becoming more and more apparent to young people. They go for an experience. You park the car. The lights come down and there you are. You're in a place that has a beginning, and a middle, and an end. You can't get up and go to the kitchen and have a beer. So it has a whole difference series of attributes. And that's one of Stratford's strengths.

OUZOUNIAN:
When I say "The Stratford Festival" to you, what comes to mind?

MACDONALD:
Gratitude. Gratitude for having great insights to the theatre laid out before me in such a beautiful way.

Loreena McKennitt. Scene from the 1984 production of The Two Gentlemen of Verona *with foreground l r: William Dunlop as Thurio, Laurence Russo as First Outlaw and Loreena McKennitt as Musician. Photograph by David Cooper.*

Loreena McKennitt

Loreena McKennitt first came to Stratford in 1981 in the Chorus of *H.M.S. Pinafore*. She appeared the next year as Ceres in *The Tempest* and wrote the music for *Blake* and *The Two Gentlemen of Verona* in the subsequent two seasons. After that, she embarked on a career that made her an incredible popular and esteemed musician, with a worldwide reputation. She returned to Stratford in 2001 to compose the music for *The Merchant of Venice*. I spoke to her in the Festival Theatre in the winter of 2001.

OUZOUNIAN:

You first came to Stratford in the Chorus of H.M.S. Pinafore. *Were you a sister, or a cousin, or an aunt?*

McKENNITT:

I think I was an aunt, actually. *(laughing)* That was a very exciting time for me, to actually become a part of the Stratford Festival. The production was tremendously successful, and that whole season was like summer camp. We became a real family, that company. There were all kinds of celebrations: we had birthday parties, we had talent nights, we had basketball games. And it was also really quite thrilling to be part of such a professional company and be introduced to the discipline that comes with the theatre: the production discipline, the rehearsal discipline, the performance discipline. I hadn't been involved in a production prior to that, to that degree. And so it was quite exciting to be exposed to that aspect of things as well.

OUZOUNIAN:

That first year you were only in the musical, but the next season you came back in some dramatic roles, and got to understudy several major parts . . .

McKENNITT:

Yes, like Raina in *Arms and the Man* and Portia in *Julius Caesar.* I know John Hirsch had invited me over to the company, primarily to sing the part of Ceres in *The Tempest*, but he was, I think, curious to see what other acting capabilities I might have. But to my mind, I certainly didn't have the training or background for theatre and my focus was primarily on music.

OUZOUNIAN:

This was the point in your life when you were starting to expand and discover all the things you could do. Was the challenge of working in drama something that you then kept with you and used?

McKENNITT:

Oh, definitely. And I think being woven into the mystery and the excitement of the theatre was something I absorbed and certainly went on to incorporate in my earlier recordings. I love every time I come into Festival Theatre, for example, and I hear the bell go off. I love the ritual of the theatre, and there were aspects of that which I kept and wove into my work as I went on to be a solo artist in my own right.

OUZOUNIAN:

What did you learn from working with John Hirsch on The Tempest*?*

McKENNITT:

I became aware of the degree of insight and understanding necessary for a director to work with a range of people with a range of skills to bring forth an idea and a concept and a sensibility to an audience.

OUZOUNIAN:

The next year, with the production of Blake*, the Festival started to draw on your composing skills. How did you get involved with that project?*

McKENNITT:

It was Douglas Campbell who really championed my

involvement, because he knew of my interest in period music. And Douglas was always keen to develop talent, so he sensed an opportunity for me here, and saw that I was able to seize it. My contribution was a very modest one. It was a one-man play on William Blake and I merely composed and recorded music for that production, so I wasn't involved in playing at night, every night.

OUZOUNIAN:
Did you go to the original Blake texts for inspiration?

McKENNITT:
Yes, they inspired me a great deal. And it's something that I continue to do: to draw upon poetry, or sometimes Shakespeare. I personally find it quite exciting to work off another medium, whether it's the printed word or working in film. I've scored some music in the past for some productions out of the National Film Board and it's been really quite a wonderful springboard to work off another medium, off the imagery of the language, whether it's Shakespeare or Tennyson.

OUZOUNIAN:
The next year you composed music for The Two Gentlemen of Verona, *which doesn't seem like a typical project for you.*

McKENNITT:
Leon Rubin, the director, was presented with some options for people who might work with him on the music for this project, and he had heard some of my work and so he was intrigued to work with me. He also liked the fact that I play a number of instruments, and he saw this as a kind of street version of the play, with me, not only as someone who could write music, but who could also be onstage, playing this mitt full of instruments, and being this kind of character off in the corner dressed in costume, as part of the whole theatrical experience. So I think that that afforded him an alternative that fit in with his vision.

OUZOUNIAN:

During the years you spent here, did you start to become aware of the background of the Festival?

McKENNITT:

I really got interested in the history and the vision out of which this enterprise was born. The people who had that vision. The nuts and bolts that were involved in building it. And how to transform a dream into an actual reality. One day I saw a notice on the bulletin board for a place called "Annaghmakerrig," which has been Tyrone Guthrie's home in Ireland, and was now set up as an artists' retreat. I started going there to do research and writing, and I remember going into the library of this Irish retreat, opening up the drawers of the bureau, and there were all these photos from Stratford in Canada. *(laughing)* None of them were really organized or archived or anything. The whole house was as if Guthrie and his wife, Judy, had just walked out of the premises, but I could still feel their presence. This fortified the relationship I was already developing with Ireland and Irish music.

I wish I could have been there to witness Guthrie at work, because as I read about his directing around the world to raise money for his jam factory in the village of Newbliss, it's something that I relate to. I'm always trying to juggle various interests outside of my musical career, and you always wonder how to reconcile all these interests, and how to serve them best. And it was quite fascinating.

OUZOUNIAN:

You seem to be dedicated to supporting the town of Stratford, in the same way that Guthrie did with Newbliss.

McKENNITT:

Perhaps in some ways I am, but studying his situation has made me mindful of the pitfalls you can run into. *(laughing)* I'm not making jam, like he did. I'm not trying to make marmalade out of a country that doesn't produce oranges. *(laughing)* But like Guthrie, I have many curiosities and many interests and I'm trying to reconcile them. So yes, maybe there are some parallels. *(laughs)*

OUZOUNIAN:

Now that you're an artist of the world and you could live anywhere you want, why do you still choose Stratford?

McKENNITT:

It's a wonderful mixture of constituencies. I mean there certainly is the theatrical community and all the businesses that are spun off as a result of the theatre. But there's an agricultural dimension. There's the automotive factories and many other facets of the city. And I appreciate the sum of all those parts. I think there's a real grounding in living here, there's a reality to it. When you go to the bank, you go to the post office, you go to the grocery store, people know your name. And there's a kind of intimacy.

OUZOUNIAN:

The Festival finally succeeding in getting you back to compose the music for The Merchant of Venice. *Is there something about the project that seemed particularly apt to you?*

McKENNITT:

Over the past decade, I've been following the path of the Celts and researching their origins. They certainly passed through Italy, as contemporaries of the Etruscans, and there's lots of evidence of the Celts having been in Italy. And so as a result of that, even though there's not an overtly Celtic dimension in *The Merchant of Venice*, my research has caused me to be acquainted with those times and instruments and cultures.

I've also been particularly interested in those Celtic people that would have been in Asia Minor, and who they would have rubbed up against. And I'm quite keen to bring more of those Eastern influences into the music of the play. Venice was quite a melting pot at that time. You have Arragon coming from Spain and you have the Prince of Morocco and Shylock, of course, from another culture as well. You have all of these cultures together so it makes for an exciting mix.

OUZOUNIAN:
In the future, do you see your path crossing Stratford, hopefully more frequently?

McKENNITT:
Of course, when it seems mutually appropriate. Even in the period of time that I have been formally away from the theatre, there has been an ongoing collaboration with the theatre or assistance from the resources of the theatre. For example, when we have set up tours, we often have set up our rehearsals at the Avon Theatre and drawn upon the crew. We recorded a video on the Festival stage. And even though I've been away formally from this environment, I have felt very grateful for the camaraderie that has continued to be extended to me by the Festival. And I think that's a distinctive feature of being in the theatrical community. It does become a surrogate family. And there is that aspect that I've grown to appreciate as the years go on.

I guess our lives are not really roads. They're more rivers and they wind and we don't know where they're taking us. I often think of how I auditioned for *H.M.S. Pinafore*, and wonder if the river of my life would have gone the same way if I hadn't done that. It was a real turning point in my career and I know it's had a major bearing on what I've done and how I've done it, for sure.

OUZOUNIAN:
What are your wishes for the next fifty years of Stratford?

McKENNITT:
I hope that as a community it can continue to build on the

diversity of constituencies that are found within it, because I think it's an exceptional blend of people and demographics with a lot of mutually beneficial factors, and I think that there's still room for that to be enhanced.

OUZOUNIAN:
What words come to mind when I say "The Stratford Festival"?

McKENNITT:
Dramatic. Mystical. Eccentric. Unpredictable. Provocative and challenging.

Colm Feore as Hamlet in the 1991 production of Hamlet.
Photograph by Tom Skudra.

Colm Feore

Colm Feore made his Stratford debut in 1981 and over the next decade became one of the Festival's leading actors, starring in *Hamlet*, *Richard III*, *Othello*, *Cyrano de Bergerac*, *The Taming of the Shrew*, among many others. After that, he embarked on an award-winning TV and film career including *32 Short Films About Glenn Gould* and the title role in the recent mini-series, *Trudeau*. He returned to the Festival in 2002 to appear as Henry Higgins in *My Fair Lady*. I spoke to him in Stratford in the summer of 2001.

OUZOUNIAN:
What's your first memory of the Stratford Festival?

FEORE:
My first memory is of coming here under the wing of a favourite teacher, who was devoted to the theatre and brought myself and a handful of others and said, "See, this is what I was talking about." And I think I saw John Hirsch's *The Three Sisters* and was carried away.

OUZOUNIAN:
When you came here as an actor, it was during the Hirsch years. What do you remember from that period?

FEORE:
I was originally asked to play the Page in *The Taming of the Shrew* who dresses up as a woman and Hirsch got on the phone and he said, "You will be in drag the whole show. It will be very funny." But in the end, of course, it didn't work out that way and I ended up playing Tranio, a part I was neither prepared for, nor understood, witnessed by the fact that Hirsch came to

me on the opening night and said, "Well, what are you doing? You are supposed to be funny." Well, nobody had told me Tranio was meant to be funny. I thought he's supposed to be a man of grace and style. So I played it straight. I was wrong. *(laughs)*

OUZOUNIAN:
In retrospect, do you think this on-the-job training was a good thing?

FEORE:
Well, I have to be honest with you. Everything I have, Shakespeare gave me. And I got it from Shakespeare by being allowed to stay here long enough through thick and thin. John Hirsch, God rest his soul, believed in me when I was simply really bad. I mean I was most happy as the Officer in *The Comedy of Errors*, a part with no lines but a very nice outfit. The rest of it was a mystery to me. I'd spent three years at the National Theatre School but it hadn't sunk in.

OUZOUNIAN:
What did you learn from Hirsch?

FEORE:
What I liked about John particularly, I mean apart from his intelligence and obvious zeal for the theatre, was that there was no time wasted being indulgent. I mean he may have got things catastrophically wrong at times. Richard Monette today is hugely successful and he's making money hand over fist. John Hirsch did nothing but lose money. By the bucket load. I mean millions of dollars. But we all felt that that was worthy. That was really worthwhile. We did some pretty darn good art there and that was worth the $3-million deficit. What he had, most principally, was a passion for communicating in that space, communicating Shakespeare vigorously in a contemporary way. He believed that if you could not see the streets of San Salvador in *King Lear*, then you should get the fuck out of the theatre. And I thought, that's it. That's right.

That's why this makes absolute sense. That's why it can be reinvented and rejuvenated and if anything fails along this line, it is most likely us. Shakespeare hasn't failed. It's our failure of the imagination.

OUZOUNIAN:

You got passion from Hirsch, and then you went to work for Michael Langham in the Young Company. What did you learn from him?

FEORE:

Precision. And intelligent application of that precision. And the rediscovery of style. We were regimented to a degree that is generally frowned upon, because it doesn't allow artists to be fully expressive. Well, I had nothing to express. I was simply putty in their hands. I was cursed with an ability to speak reasonably clearly and a body on which clothes hung reasonably effectively. Which created the illusion, quite conclusively, that I knew what I was doing. And it took some time for people to ascertain, that I really didn't. I mean I was trying to make it up as I went along.

But when I got to the Young Company, Langham looked at me, and he said, "Hmm. You will play one part: Claudio in *Much Ado About Nothing*." And at first, I thought, "Well, this isn't really very good. I mean I've given up playing in all kinds of grand parts on the main stage in a big theatre to come to this little place and play just one." But that one was particularly instructive because finally, I was playing a young man. Something I actually understood without any training at all. I didn't understand it very well, but at least I had a glimmer of it.

And I had an absolutely galvanic moment doing my one part in *Much Ado About Nothing* just before the scene where Claudio goes on to reject his bride, Hero, at their wedding. John Franklyn-Robbins, who would become a mentor of sorts, was playing Don Pedro. And there was suddenly a moment at the Tom Patterson stage. We're waiting in these little curtained wings for me to go on and reject her. And the light went on and I suddenly turned to John and I said, "I can't do this. I'm really sorry. There's been a colossal mistake. I don't know what I was thinking. Please tell Michael I'm really sorry. I'm going home now. I don't know why, I simply can't do this." And he grabbed me by the scruff of the neck and he said, "Ah, that's the way you're supposed to feel." And he pushed me on. And of course I went tumbling on like some sort of *commedia* trouper, found myself there, and went, "What the hell do I do now?" Which was precisely the moment Shakespeare intended for this guy to feel. Suddenly there was a little lightbulb that went off and I understood what Michael was about. I understood what the play was about. I understood at least what my part in it was about. And then it all kind of started to tumble together.

OUZOUNIAN:

After a year with the Young Company, you wound up on the Festival stage again playing your first big lead: Romeo in Romeo and Juliet. *What was that like?*

FEORE:

Well, it was terrifying but it was extraordinary. I remember after the first run of the first act, I simply passed out. I didn't actually faint but I lay down on a table, heaving. I mean ahhh, this is hard! This Shakespeare stuff is really not for kids. And it was then that I got a glimmer of an understanding about the stamina required to do this stuff properly. And then more and more and more. I got stronger and stronger and stronger. I thought, oh this is fun. This is— I mean if there's a runner's high, then there's a Shakespeare big show high. And it comes from throwing yourself at these parts with abandon and if you can come out on the other end of it, you've really learned something.

OUZOUNIAN:

By 1986, you were playing roles like Iachimo in Cymbeline *and*

Leontes in The Winter's Tale. *Had your work process changed by then?*

FEORE:

You know I used to get terribly embarrassed because I didn't really know what was going on. I would see very smart people around the place carrying dictionaries and concordances and lexicons. Really big word books around the building. What the hell's going on here? They know something. They seem more confident, more able. So I found some books and I started to learn and I thought well, I'm really getting a handle on this. This is really making my acting different.

Then on the first day of rehearsals for *The Winter's Tale*, I ran into Susan Wright. She had been astonishing. She was playing Paulina and she came on and excoriated me about the death of my wife and my son and how I'd been a monster. And it was magnificent. It was electrifying, as Susan very often was. So I said, "But I must buy you a drink. Let's go and have a drink, You're just amazing." And so we sat down at the old Jester's Arms. I said, "You know, you just overwhelmed me with the way you used the scansion in that speech of yours." She said, "What?" And I kept going, "And the way you used the masculine and feminine verse endings was extraordinary." She looked at me and said, "Really? I'll have another drink. Tell me more about this."

Suddenly I thought, "Wait a minute. All of these books and all of this stuff, this is nothing on the native intuitive response to Shakespeare's play." I remember that Susan would never write a director's note down. She would just listen. And she would take it in, she'd go hmmm. And instantly had reassessed and re-evaluated what she'd done with the note. If the note stuck, it stuck. And it was instantly adjusted. If it was crap, it was instantly discarded. And that was just it. I thought, "Oh, there's more to this than meets the eye. There's no amount of book learning that's going to do this." Now I'm not suggesting for a moment that Susan was merely a native genius of these things. She worked very hard and she knew what she was doing. But she had a soul. She had a heart that came to these things that was undeniable in its power. And I thought, "Feore, without that, you're nothing." So that was part of my education as well.

OUZOUNIAN:
The next director to cross your path was Robin Phillips . . .

FEORE:
People had told me, when you work with Robin Phillips he's going to change your life. Change my life. He's not going to change my life. I mean his shows are wonderful. They're always elegant. They're always stylish. I need some elegance. I need some style. I'd be delighted to work for him. And I've always had a very nice time with Robin. Because he's so smart. He's so on top. He's so kind of, you know, watching. Looking straight through. And I think well, there's no hiding here. I'm going to have to come up with something or I'm screwed. But I remember doubting him once. And I never did it again.

I was playing Iachimo in *Cymbeline*. I was going to come out of a box at the base of the bed, in which lay Martha Burns, damn near naked. And I say "damn near" because this is a very subtle Phillipsian kind of point. Naked is not interesting. Damn near naked is really interesting. And he wanted me to get out and slink around. And I stole everything from David Carradine I could possibly use. I mean Kwai Chang Caine slipped out of the box. And I said, "I should be in black with a toque and all that." Robin said, "No, no, you'll be in riding boots, jodhpurs, and an emerald green velvet sweatshirt." I said, "What are you talking about? That's ludicrous. I'll be in black. I'll be in sweats. I'll look like a burglar." "No, you'll be in riding boots." I said, "Now Robin,

I've got this idea." "Trust me." Well, I did it his way and it was the answer to a maiden's wet dream. I came out of this box with a radio microphone and slightly unshaven, green sweatshirt, heavy big boots, slithering around. The microphone was so you could hear the breathing and the sound of my beard against the silk on the crotch of Martha Burns's nightie. You could hear a pin drop. There wasn't a dry seat in the house. It was extraordinary.

And suddenly the lightbulb goes off again. This guy knows something about layers of understanding, so just do what he says. And trust it. What Robin gave me, was a real sense of elegance. It's the finesse of just so much and no more. Trust that. Trust that you are in good hands.

OUZOUNIAN:

Over the next few years you played giant roles like Petruchio, Iago, Richard the Third. What was it like to be constantly performing on that scale?

FEORE:

I cannot pretend that playing big parts doesn't make a huge difference. If you have a big canvas, you have a chance to throw a lot more paint up. You can stand farther back and you can get a better look. And it was an awful lot of fun to put yourself into them in ways that I thought would speak to people like me. That would be contemporary. Why reinvent the wheel? Because it doesn't know it's a wheel. It's like a computer. My Apple computer wakes up when you turn on the power and tells itself that it's a computer, and it has to tell itself it's a computer every time. Once it gets powered up and is booted or whatever they call that, it works wonderfully, and each generation works better than the last. But they still have to spend that little moment going "Wait a minute. Wait a minute. What am I?" And I thought, "Well that's kind of what we do. We can say, wait, this is who we are." You'll never find it better expressed than in Shakespeare, and I've been very fortunate to have a good crack at playing a lot of it.

OUZOUNIAN:
What about the biggest one of all—Hamlet?

FEORE:
I was thirty-two when David William asked me. And I thought, well, this is kind of biblical. I'll be thirty-three. It's a chance to re-evaluate everything. And I made a kind of closet deal with myself that if I failed to go the distance with it, then I would retire. I would simply stop because I knew, or I felt I knew that this way madness lay. I would become disappointed, bitter, or rather, say, more disappointed and more bitter. Not about what hadn't happened to me. I'd been extremely blessed. But you know, the grass is always greener. You always think, oh, there must be something else out there. Why am I not celebrated? I mean, there was always some kind of problem. And the most important one was self-examination and self-discovery. The commitment to explore and use yourself fully for the paying public.

I knew that I could get away with not going into it deeply. You could just hold the skull, dress in black, say what you know and get off. It works for all kinds of people. And Hamlet is a wonderful part in that way. That if you, if you say most of the lines in the order in which they come, and remain standing until you're supposed to fall down, it will be called an interpretation. So I thought, what will mine be? It will have to be at least honest. I don't mind if it's bad. But if it's honest, I'll continue. If it's dishonest, I'll stop. And so with that I undertook to do Hamlet. And I must say, it was, it was the Top of the Pops for parts that repay your investment. I always felt there was something to learn. I was never finished. I'm still not finished. I still think about Hamlet.

I think the reason it's so successful over the ages, is that everybody can see themselves in Hamlet somewhere. So man, woman, dog, monkey, goat, everybody goes, "Oh yes, I recognize that moment." And from that moment of recognition, from that moment of understanding, personal understanding, we develop a relationship with the play and we go backwards and forwards and figure out, "Oh yes, so Hamlet there must be this and this is me." And so I did it as fully as I could do it at that time. And I felt I hadn't shirked. David William directed it and he would not let me shirk it.

I don't know that the production was, you know, successful, good, bad or indifferent, it really didn't matter to me. I simply didn't care. The journey that I was on was: will I be a better actor? And I discovered something that was very interesting. Everybody who comes backstage and tries to tell, to give you what it is you think you need, will be by definition inadequate. Their response to what you've done will not measure up to your need for them to respond to what you've done. As a consequence, you've got to go home and figure out yourself. And the only person who came and responded I thought appropriately, I married. My wife, Donna, came backstage and simply stood at the door and said absolutely nothing. And I thought, "She gets it." I don't know if she got it. I don't know what she got. She ended up with me.

OUZOUNIAN:

Olivier said his Hamlet was the story of a man who could not make up his mind. What was your Hamlet?

FEORE:

I will steal David William's line. I think it's the story of a man who was born without eyelashes. He has to look, he has to see. And in seeing, he's cosmically disappointed, in a Beckett kind of sense.

OUZOUNIAN:
What would you wish Stratford for the next fifty years?

FEORE:
I would wish Stratford in the next fifty years, a growing, a swelling audience of interested people, willing to come. Demanding, rigorous standards for classical theatre. Believing wholeheartedly that through the classics and a firm understanding of them, the truth is revealed. I think that will make for a better society. I think it will make for a healthy theatre.

OUZOUNIAN:
When I say "The Stratford Festival," what words, images come to you?

FEORE:
I see a very small, brown chain-beaten piece of wood, built with a few different sides, on which over twenty years ago, after a long night at the bar, I would come in—break in essentially—take a broadsword from the shelf, turn on one work light, drag it on to the centre, and say everything I could remember from *Henry V*. That's what I remember, yeah. That's what I think of here.

And if I could make a movie of Stratford, I would want a camera to come out of the sky, come in over the Canadian flag, and I'd want an animation that would twist off the top, really quickly, and we'd come swirling down on a full performance of Alec Guinness's *Richard III*, and say, "What the hell was that about?" This is where it starts. Boom. And then take it backstage and follow through fifty years.

Eric McCormack as Baron Tusenbach in the 1989 production of The Three Sisters.
Photograph by Robert C. Ragsdale.

Eric McCormack

Eric McCormack came to Stratford in 1985 in *King Lear* and *Measure For Measure*. He remained with the company through 1989 and his most notable roles included Tusenbach in *The Three Sisters* and Demetrius in *A Midsummer Night's Dream* (which I directed him in). Since leaving Stratford, he has become a successful TV star, best known as Will Truman on the top-rated NBC comedy series, *Will and Grace*. I spoke to him in Los Angeles on the set of *Will and Grace* in February 2001.

OUZOUNIAN:
Eric, can you remember the first time you ever went to the Stratford Festival?

McCORMACK:
Yeah, and a really ironic thing happened in light of what I do for a living these days. We were driving into town on a student trip. I was probably in ninth grade and we were almost at the Festival Theatre when we passed FAG Ball Bearings right there on Main Street and one of the guys said, "Hey, McCormack, is that where you work?" And I said, even in ninth grade, "No, but if you wait a few minutes I'll show you where I'm going to work." And so a self-fulfilling prophecy, I guess.

OUZOUNIAN:
Why did you want to go there?

McCORMACK:
I very much dreamed locally. For all of my watching sitcoms and you know dreaming of winning Oscars, I never thought that as soon as I was of age I'd head to New York or head to L.A. I always thought, "I want to work at the Stratford Festival."

OUZOUNIAN:
How did you actually wind up there?

McCORMACK:
I was in my third year at Ryerson and we all did our auditions for the apprenticeship program. It was the last year of John Hirsch. And the auditions were at the Tarragon Theatre and I went, very nervous and very excited. I had the lines in my brain and I wanted to make a great first impression, I wanted to walk in and blow him away. Well, I go to the men's room first and I'm at the urinal and he walks in. So the first time I ever see John Hirsch, it was not the most prestigious way to begin. I just sort of went "Hi." He said, "Hello." And then I had to go and audition for him. You'd think that would break the ice but it didn't. It made the ice thicker.

I was doing the Bastard's soliloquy from *King John* and I get to that part where I say:

That broker, that still breaks the pate of faith,
That daily break-vow . . .

And he says, "What does that mean?" and I say, "It means he does it every goddamn day." And there was this silence in the room and I'm staring at John Hirsch and he's staring at me. And I've just sworn at him and he went, good, thank you, that's fine. And I was dismissed. And I'd only gotten through eight lines. And I thought that's it, I'll never, I'll never work in the country again. I just yelled at John Hirsch. But, of course, that's all he wanted was for me to yell at him and stop being such a theatre school phony. And when I got the job and made that connection, it was one of those, those key moments in your life when you realize you should cut the crap and try to find some truth.

OUZOUNIAN:
So what did you do when you got there?

McCORMACK:
My apprenticeship started with Michael Bogdonov's *Measure*

For Measure, which was modern dress and as I would soon find out, I was expected to be in full drag. You see everything was leading me to *Will and Grace* eventually.

So whereas I was expecting to show up and immediately hold a spear and wear a helmet, instead I was in wig and heels and singing songs.

You see, I was actually part of the show that began before eight o'clock. There was a bar on stage, and we would bring people up from the audience with the lights still on and get them dancing as if it were a club. And the first time my parents had ever come to the Stratford Festival, I got my father onstage and myself in full leather drag and danced and he led.

OUZOUNIAN:

The next year, John Neville took over the Festival. How did you get along with him?

McCORMACK:

Neville looked after me in those years, in ways that I sort of almost took for granted. He didn't give me a Hamlet or a Romeo. He brought me along so slowly to the point where, by the time I got to know him well, I would go to him and say, "I'm hungry." He'd go, "Relax, relax, it will all be there."

I think he recognized, as I have certainly in hindsight, that too much too soon wouldn't have worked for me. I wasn't ready to be Colm Feore, to jump into it that early. I needed that whole five years that I was there, to be a kind of apprenticeship, a kind of training ground and not my great bust-out. By the time I did my shows in the fifth season, even those were not leads. I did, I never had my big lead. The biggest roles I had were the Baron in *The Three Sisters* for Neville and Demetrius in *A Midsummer Night's Dream*, which I did for you.

OUZOUNIAN:

Why do you think your contemporaries like Colm Feore and Geraint Wyn Davies were ready to star and you weren't?

McCORMACK:

I've thought about this a lot over the years because it's finally happening to me, and I think, "Why did it take me so long?" I think it's because Davies and Feore had something I lacked at the time: a *chutzpah*, a confidence, a kind of a leading man "this is who I am, get me now while I'm hot" kind of arrogance that I didn't have. I was way too Canadian, I was way too Scarborough, too suburban. I just didn't have the balls to say, "Damn it, here I am, get me while I'm young and hungry or you'll regret it." I never thought that way. And I think that kind of showed. I think I always, I always had a little extra weight on me. Chubbier in the face . . . I just . . . everything in my mind said you're not a leading man, you're a character man. And I guess I kept making that happen and it was why Neville put me in those roles.

I just thought all good things come to those who wait. I'd think, "I'm going to be a nice guy about this." Well, you know, nice guys may finish first but it takes a long time for them to finish.

OUZOUNIAN:

Who made the strongest impression on you during those years?

McCORMACK:

Susie. Susan Wright. She would give you the shirt off her back in a performance, but she was also real. There was a great real, down to earth side of her. I don't remember ever seeing her hit a false note. Maybe I was a little too in awe of her. But I loved her spirit.

And I loved her kind of "I know it's Shakespeare but let's not get too arty with it" attitude. You know, I always said that if my mother can't understand it, then we're doing something wrong, which is something that David William disagreed with me on. He took offence at that. But I said, "Man there's got to be a way to make this hit people, I mean every time, not just the occasional production where somebody wore roller skates."

OUZOUNIAN:

David William took over after John Neville left and let you go from the company.

McCORMACK:

Yeah. He said, "I don't like the way you play lovers. It's like a sitcom: too modern, too American, too funny." I guess he was right, because look at what I'm doing today . . . *(laughs)*

OUZOUNIAN:

Would you ever want to go back to perform at Stratford again?

McCORMACK:

It's a romantic fantasy of mine, but right now it would be very impractical because of those long seasons. They're a godsend when you're a young actor, but now it just wouldn't work out.

I'm not even sure what I would play. I hate the competitive nature of classical theatre. You know: "Oh, I saw McCormack's Hamlet and it wasn't as good as so and so's Hamlet."

I don't think I ever really wanted to play Hamlet. I don't need the pressure. I don't need that form of judgment. If I ever went back to Stratford again, I think it would be for something brand new, or something rarely done.

OUZOUNIAN:

What would you like to wish Stratford for its next fifty years?

McCORMACK:

More challenge, challenge for themselves and for the audience. Keep trying to be new and fresh, because the one thing it must never become is a museum.

OUZOUNIAN:

What do you think of when I say "The Stratford Festival"?

McCORMACK:

My twenties. Growing from a boy to man. Great friendships. My starting point. Where my career began.

John Neville. Photograph by Michael Cooper.

John Neville

After a distinguished career in the British theatre, John Neville came to Canada in 1972 and served successfully as the artistic director of the Citadel and Neptune theatres. He came to Stratford in 1983 to play Don Armado in Michael Langham's *Love's Labour's Lost* and stayed on to run the Young Company. He was artistic director of the Festival from 1986 to 1989 and his productions included *Hamlet*, *Mother Courage and Her Children*, and *The Three Sisters*. I spoke to him in Toronto in the fall of 2000.

OUZOUNIAN:
How did you first come to the Stratford Festival?

NEVILLE:
Michael Langham was running the Young Company in the early 1980s, and he invited me to join them as a senior actor to help the training part of it, and from then on I guess I was almost permanently at Stratford pretty well.

OUZOUNIAN:
Had you known Langham before this?

NEVILLE:
(laughing) Oh yes, absolutely! I've known him for fifty-odd years, I guess. He gave my beloved wife and I the afternoon off to get married, at the Birmingham Repertory Company. But just the afternoon, mind you, because we were back onstage that night, together.

OUZOUNIAN:
The Festival was being run by John Hirsch at that point. How did you remember the mood or the atmosphere of the place when you came there?

NEVILLE:

It was not good. It was gloomy. And that remained, throughout. It was not a good atmosphere.

OUZOUNIAN:

What do you think were the reasons for this gloom?

NEVILLE:

I guess John himself, who was a strange man—talented, of course—but he wasn't a gregarious man in that way, and he certainly wasn't kind to the community, which was in a terrible state when I took over.

OUZOUNIAN:

Were you aware of the serious financial trouble the Festival was in during those years?

NEVILLE:

I became aware of it when I was asked to become the next artistic director.

OUZOUNIAN:

How were you first approached about taking over the Festival?

NEVILLE:

I was sounded out by the board. John was going to leave, they were looking for someone, and I became a candidate. And soon as I became a really serious candidate, that was when John Hirsch started campaigning against me. Actively. He approached every member of the board to say that I was a bad choice.

OUZOUNIAN:

Why do you think he felt that way?

NEVILLE:

I guess he didn't like me. He thought I would be a director who preferred the sort of play where the leading actor comes in through French windows and says "Would you like a drink?" just because I came from England. Notwithstanding the fact that I had spent six years at the Old Vic doing nothing at all except Shakespeare.

OUZOUNIAN:
Despite all this politics, you were finally offered the job. Did you have any conditions about accepting it?

NEVILLE:
Yes. I said I'll do the job for $20,000 less than Hirsch did it. And then when they gave me the contract I said, "Now take another ten off."

OUZOUNIAN:
Why did you do that?

NEVILLE:
Because we had a $4.5-million deficit. And we had to get rid of it. It was essential that we got rid of it. As I explained to the board, we were paying $900,000 a year on that debt and I could do four plays for that.

OUZOUNIAN:
*And yet, with all that financial pressure, you programmed some of Shakespeare's most obscure plays—*Pericles, Cymbeline, Henry VIII. *Why did you do that?*

NEVILLE:
I felt very strongly that we should nail the flag firmly at the masthead. And so we did, as you know; we did difficult unknown plays.

And the audience came back, which I was very relieved about, but I was determined. As I said at the time, the popular comedies had been done over and over again. Let's put out plays that have not been done. And it worked, fortunately, it worked. But it was . . . a rough crossing really.

OUZOUNIAN:
You also moved the musical into the Festival Theatre. Why did you do that?

NEVILLE:
I did that because it had 2,200 seats. And if you fill them, it will certainly help to get rid of the deficit. And it did. Yes, I did

put the musical onto the main stage and was severely criticized for it. Very, very severely. I ignored the criticism because I knew that if we did them well, it would make money.

OUZOUNIAN:
You also brought Robin Phillips back to lead the Young Company.

NEVILLE:
He did that for two years and did fine work. They all did fine work. And that was a very important thing for me. You know when I took the job, I told the board, "You could save $600,000 a year by getting rid of the Young Company, but if you do, I walk." But it stayed for a while, yes. And the work was good and very complete, in that they would do classes while they were rehearsing—dance and swordplay and speech and diction and text—and the classes would continue when their two plays went on in repertory. It was a wonderful thing. But after I left, the fact is that the Young Company was killed. And I think that was wrong.

OUZOUNIAN:
After four seasons, you decided to leave the Festival. Why?

NEVILLE:
I was tired. I worked very hard running the Stratford Festival because I did run it. I was hands on. I chose the plays and I chose the plays for a company. I didn't choose them for a star. I chose them for a company. My company stayed the same pretty well throughout and I thought, "I think I can do that play because I've got the cast for it."

So I ran it and I would go in at seven-thirty in the morning and I would know the names of all the cleaners, cleaning the main auditorium. And every day—every day—I would go through the big wardrobe where they were making things, and spoke to everyone, asked them what they were doing, and so I ran it in the way that I think it should be run. And that's tiring. That's like sixteen hours a day, seven days a week, pretty well. So I was tired. But, in a way, looking back on it now, I perhaps wish I had stayed another couple of seasons.

OUZOUNIAN:
Was the deficit totally eliminated during your years there?

NEVILLE:
Oh absolutely! We had money in the bank. I used to say to my friend, Gary Thomas, the general manager, "Hide some of this money. Hide it! Put it in another account."

OUZOUNIAN:
So, in four years, doing the kind of programming you really believed in, you still got rid of a $4.5-million deficit. How?

NEVILLE:
Part of it was putting the musical on the main stage, but quite honestly, I also upped the quality of the program. There's no question about that. I had a permanent company and at the time, I never once said I'd done a great job. I said continually, "I have a great team." And that means the actors, technicians, everyone, management. I had a great team, and that's how we did it.

OUZOUNIAN:
Looking back on the years you spent at Stratford, is there anything you would have done differently?

NEVILLE:
No, I don't think so. I did what I had to do. And I'm not sure that I would change anything, really.

OUZOUNIAN:
What kind of a future do you see for Stratford?

NEVILLE:
Obviously, it's drawing people in. It's going to be secure. Whether one will be able to say there's great art going on there, is another matter. That's a matter of opinion. But it looks like they'll be secure for quite a while.

OUZOUNIAN:
When you think of the Stratford Festival, what words come to mind?

NEVILLE:
"Miracle" I think is the word that comes to mind. The miracle of Tom Patterson, and Tony Guthrie and William Shakespeare.

Lucy Peacock as Rosalind in the 1990 production of As You Like It.
Photograph by David Cooper.

Lucy Peacock

Lucy Peacock first came to Stratford in 1984 as a member of the Young Company. By 1986, she was playing Ophelia in *Hamlet* and she has remained one of the company's leading ladies ever since, known for roles such as Rosalind, Portia, and Titania. She will appear as Helena in the Fiftieth Anniversary production of *All's Well That Ends Well*. I spoke to her in the Festival Theatre in the winter of 2001.

OUZOUNIAN:

Lucy, what led you to the Stratford Festival?

PEACOCK:

I was at the National Theatre School as a student, and Stratford called me in my graduating year, asking me to come as an apprentice. And I said, "Well, I'd really like to come into the Young Company, if you don't mind." *(laughing)* And they said they'd call me back. I was on tour in Saskatchewan with the Globe Theatre School company, getting my requisite Equity card and all that sort of thing, which a lot of us did back then, paying my dues, doing the school tour. And I got a call from Stratford saying, "John Hirsch is in the area doing a cross-country audition tour and would you be willing to talk to him?" So I met John Hirsch for the first time in a hotel lobby in Saskatoon. And we sat there and didn't even take off our coats, but I told him in very enthusiastic terms about my performance as Scrabble the Dog, for the five year olds and how wonderful it all was. I must have made an impression, because they invited me into the Young Company, and it was unbelievable!

OUZOUNIAN:

After just one season with the Young Company, John Neville comes along, and the next thing you know you're at the Avon Theatre playing Ophelia to Brent Carver's Hamlet. What was that like?

PEACOCK:

It was really nerve-racking for me at the time, because it was a pretty major role for me to be playing out of the Young Company, but John had great confidence in me. I had never even met Brent before but he was thrilling, absolutely thrilling. I watched every performance. And he was never the same. He was always right on the edge and sometimes it was fabulous and sometimes it sort of would miss the mark, but then he'd get it back. I remember learning so much from that. And feeling so unable to do that at the time. I thought, you know, I had to be very safe. I had to have everything in its pocket and it's taken me years to feel that kind of freedom.

OUZOUNIAN:

Playing Ophelia would be enough in the opening week of the Stratford season for most young actresses, but on Friday night of the same week, the actress playing Anne Boleyn in Henry VIII *got her foot caught in the hem of her gown at the last preview, fell on the stage, and broke her ankle.*

PEACOCK:

Oh, I'll never forget that! Because in those days, Stratford didn't do understudy rehearsals until after the opening week. So I had never had a rehearsal. I had sort of vaguely kept an ear out. And sort of knew that I was having to work up to that in ten days or so that I'd have to have it under my belt, you know, and then we'd rehearse it and all that sort of thing. But at three o'clock in the afternoon on the day of the opening, Brian Rintoul, the director, said, "We're going to have a rehearsal now because Lucy has to go tonight as Anne

Boleyn." I remember standing up and my face got all red, and then I had to get squished into this costume because Camille Mitchell who was playing the part was so much smaller than I was, and everybody was racing around, and then, just before I walked onstage, I remember saying, "Okay, Lucy, you know the words. Now just say them as slowly as you can." Because I knew that if I went in the other direction, my head was going to fly off my neck.

So I walked out and I saw a sea of black and white, black and white, black and white, black and white, all the tuxedos and the black evening gowns and all that stuff. And away I went. What that did teach me—and I sometimes tell students this—is that sometimes, if you just clear your mind, then Shakespeare does all the work for you. Just having free energy, and putting it straight into the text, can work.

OUZOUNIAN:
Over the next few years you played an amazing assortment of roles—Nora, Cassandra, Helena . . .

PEACOCK:
I was learning as I flew. And Neville was very good to me . . . John . . . because he didn't just shove me out there and hope for the best. He was taking great care to put me in the right play at the right time, so that I could learn and grow and mature, and get all that experience under my belt.

OUZOUNIAN:
What was John Neville like to work with as a director?

PEACOCK:
He was great. People used to mock me a little bit because he would turn to people—if I was in a show that he was directing—and he would say, "This is where Lucy comes in and tries to save the show," because I always brought too much energy I thought. I was there to pick up the pace and grab the show by its neck and shake it into life. John cured me of that.

I know he was very fond of me and I know he loved watching me learn new things. At rehearsals, there was no sitting around the table. He never was keen on that. He wanted you up on your feet and getting going and he felt that you couldn't find out what's going on unless you're walking around. He taught me a lot.

OUZOUNIAN:
You also seem to get along well with Richard Monette. What's he like to work for?

PEACOCK:
He's a madman. But fun, really fun. I find he's game for anything, as long as you come along with some stuff, you know, tricks you can pull out of your hat. He's willing to look at them, and that's how, I think, he works best—if you throw something out, then he's the one that can take it further, or have that director's eye that will say, "Yeah, that's great but what if we add this and this and this and . . ."

(laughs) Once in a while you need to just do that full-blown theatrical stuff, and I enjoy it.

OUZOUNIAN:
There are some criticisms that Monette's work is too *theatrical at times.*

PEACOCK:
I think that Richard is supremely talented and that his critics are a bit mean-spirited sometimes about him. And unless they've met him and talked to him, they wouldn't understand his passion for this place and for the theatre that he does . . . his passion for Shakespeare. They don't know how bright he is and how committed he is and how he actually may *be* committed one day (*laughs*), but it'll be this that drives him to it. It's his life.

OUZOUNIAN:
What would you wish the Stratford Festival for its next fifty years?

PEACOCK:
I would wish that it could be more on the world stage. If I won a billion dollars, I'd take that money and use it to get Stratford's productions out there to be seen in other parts of the world. That's what I would do for sure.

OUZOUNIAN:
What images come to mind when I say "The Stratford Festival"?

PEACOCK:
Shakespeare. Summer. Friends and love and bar time and dressing-room mates, and that stage out there. That wonderful stage.

David William. Photograph by Michael Cooper.

David William

David William first came to the Stratford Festival in 1966 to direct *Twelfth Night*. Over the years he directed many successful shows, including *Romeo and Juliet* and *The Winter's Tale*. He was artistic director of the Festival from 1990 through 1993, and his productions then included *Hamlet* and *The Bacchae*.
I spoke to him in the Festival Theatre in the winter of 2001.

OUZOUNIAN:
What do you recall from your first time working at Stratford?

WILLIAM:
I can remember the first moment I stood on the stage and that was very moving. I knew Guthrie, of course, and I'd worked with him in England so that added a sort of element of affection and nostalgia.

And I remember some of the actors I was fortunate enough to work with—Martha Henry and Bill Hutt, to name just two—people who were very experienced in handling Shakespeare and making the dialogue sound like human beings talking, instead of people reciting—so that reality seemed quite accessible.

OUZOUNIAN:
You directed Bill Hutt as King Lear during this period. What was your working relationship like with him?

WILLIAM:
I only found one thing worrying about rehearsing with him: he

never seemed to learn the lines—he was like Gladys Cooper in that respect—and eventually I expressed concern about this and he said, "Oh, don't worry, it'll be all right." And lo and behold, at the first dress rehearsal, he was so fluent that there was none of that interval period whereby actors start to stumble a bit over the lines. For thirty days he'd have the book in his hand and then suddenly the book was out of his hand and he was as fluent as can be and a consummate performance with it. So obviously the homework he did at home was spectacular. The *Lear* went extremely well, and Bill was very fine in it. Very fine.

OUZOUNIAN:

When you returned a few years later, Robin Phillips was artistic director. Did you find the whole mood of the festival different under his regime?

WILLIAM:

Oh yes, very different. I mean Robin's signature was very strong, very strong indeed. I think when he got Maggie Smith here and the Cronyns, then the whole example within the company strengthened enormously. And I think visually he brought a lot of very enlightened work here.

But he did, of course, enormously expand the season. Far more plays were done than ever before, and I'm not yet convinced that's on the whole a good thing. It stretches the butter rather thin on the bread.

OUZOUNIAN:

It was also during those years that sold-out audiences and big box office became a given for the Festival. How do you feel about that?

WILLIAM:

It's impossible to deny that, since that time, the concept of marketing in the theatre has moved very much centre stage. And clearly with triumphant results. I believe the Festival is doing better now financially than it's ever done before. But I think it can be dangerous because with marketing you have to express yourself a certain amount in slogans, and if you think too much in slogans, the process tends to be irreversible, with a result that the kind of depth of thought and feeling that you bring to a play gets a bit mortgaged. I'm not saying that happens all the time, but I think it is a tendency and not just here. I mean it's just as true in England in the companies that aspire to sell classical work, which, for whatever reason, is not as easily assimilable as it used to be to a large audience.

In Stratford, for example, the main brunt of the revenue is now borne by the musicals. Well, this inevitably generates a different kind of audience. But what does Dr. Johnson say?

The drama's laws, the dramas patrons give,
For we who live to please must please to live.

OUZOUNIAN:

You came back again near the end of the Hirsch years. How do you think Hirsch perceived his time here?

WILLIAM:

I think John was dissatisfied with the acting level of the company as a whole, but he always had been and I don't think that's a bad thing. His cultural background was very rich. He was Jewish. He was Hungarian and then he was Canadian, so he had a very marvellous mix of sources of imagination. And he'd been very exploratory about the whole history of the theatre. So he knew a great deal about the possibilities of acting. So he was always dissatisfied and became quite famous for the complaints of John, about his own work, and indeed—I may say—about everybody else's. But he was a very fine director and when I was artistic director of the National Theatre of Israel, I invited him there to do a production of *The Seagull* and the actors adored him, because his temperament, which could be a bit scratchy here, was totally assimilated there. I mean he screamed at people, but that's what they did all day long anyhow, even when they were asking each other the time, and so he fit right in.

OUZOUNIAN:
In John Neville's first season, you directed a production of The Winter's Tale *that is still thought of fondly . . .*

WILLIAM:
I, too, remember it with enormous affection . . . enormous affection. It's long been one of my favourite plays and John and I got a very good cast together. It was the last Shakespeare I think that Susan Wright did. And wonderful she was to work with.

I set the play just a few years before the Industrial Revolution at a time when there was a kind of feeling about nature, before the town became more important than the country. I shared all these ideas with the company who were enormously receptive. And we had just about the right amount of time in rehearsal.

I can remember watching one school matinee and seeing a mackintosh over somebody's head at the emotional statue scene at the end of play, and I thought, "Oh God, are they playing some kind of jape?" But when it was over, the mackintosh came off the head and it was a boy of about seventeen who'd been weeping. So moved had he been by this play about which he could have known nothing. Shakespeare had taken possession. And that, of course, is the best kind of tribute one could hope for.

OUZOUNIAN:
This production was the first time Colm Feore played one of the mature Shakespearean leads. What was the process like?

WILLIAM:
To begin with, Colm, as I recall, was very shy of the part, and very shy of being a leading man. He sat at the back for the first reading and was slow to—as it were—commit himself to being a leading man. But after a couple of weeks, he's a proper actor

and he grew into the part wonderfully and rose to all the challenges. I thought he gave a mighty performance and was profoundly moving.

OUZOUNIAN:

You also spoke about how effective Susan Wright was as Paulina. What qualities made her so special?

WILLIAM:

A blazing honesty, great emotional power, total availability to anything I had to offer, generosity with her colleagues. She was an ideal member of a company like this. She's terribly missed.

OUZOUNIAN:

It was around this time that you were asked to lead the Stratford Festival yourself. What was your reaction?

WILLIAM:

Astonishment to begin with, and then I was very honoured to be offered the job. But it's an incredibly demanding position. You're always running to stand still, really. Its demands are so intense. They were especially so at that time, when we were in a recession, and audiences were well below what they had been . . . even the musicals didn't do as well as they had done before!

OUZOUNIAN:

What was the first thing you felt needed to be done with the festival?

WILLIAM:

I thought the repertoire should be expanded. I thought that one should do and see writers one had never seen here before, because where else is one going to see them in Canada? Racine, Pirandello, the Greeks, Dostoevsky. I still think that was one of the decisions I made which was a right one. And I wish there was more of that now, but, of course, these plays are rarities and therefore they are box office risks. So I can see that there's every good reason why it's difficult to do them.

At the same time, I became very conscious of what seemed

to me the principal problem with doing Shakespeare nowadays, which is knowing who the audience is, that you're doing these plays to and for. We had been through the time when—let us say—certain academic hoodlums took over the academic establishment and in the name of post-modernism or structuralism or deconstruction, gradually dismantled the idea of Shakespeare's sovereignty. In other words, the text was no longer what it said it was. It was what you or I made of it. And fairly quickly, this filtered down into theatrical practice with the result that one got, started to get, productions that were what the director fancied was the play that Shakespeare *ought* to have written, or that he or she would have *liked* him to have written, as opposed to a really strenuous reading of the play.

OUZOUNIAN:
You have very much always adhered to the line that we must believe in the integrity of the text. Did that make you seem, to the outside world, stuffy, old-fashioned?

WILLIAM:
I think so, yes, certainly. But so what? I mean this will pass as all things pass. And I think also, one must be quite honest, it is possible to do Shakespeare in a way that is apparently faithful to the text, and be terribly boring, which simply means that one's imagination has not been quickened sufficiently by what is in the text, or you haven't ignited the actors sufficiently, or perhaps they just weren't up to it.

OUZOUNIAN:
When you look back on your years as artistic director, how would you characterize them?

WILLIAM:
Adventurous in terms of expanding the repertoire, frustrated economically by the recession.

OUZOUNIAN:
If you could offer a wish to the Stratford Festival for its next fifty years, what would it be?

WILLIAM:
Fiery imaginations.

OUZOUNIAN:
What do you think of when I say "The Stratford Festival"?

WILLIAM:
A wonderful invention on the part of our theatrical giant, Tyrone Guthrie, who wanted to create this theatre in England but had to come to Canada to get it built. And I think that the fact that we're sitting here talking now is a tribute to the vitality and virility of that vision, which hopefully will simply expand in a way he would have wished for the next fifty years, at least.

Antoni Cimolino as Romeo in the 1992 production of Romeo and Juliet.
Photograph by David Cooper.

Antoni Cimolino

Antoni Cimolino is now the Executive Director of the Stratford Festival, but he first came there as an actor in 1988, playing a variety of roles that culminated in Romeo opposite Megan Follows' Juliet in 1992. He then developed as a director and his productions to date have included *Filumenia, The Night of the Iguana*, and *Twelfth Night*. He spoke to me on the stage of the Festival Theatre in September 2001.

OUZOUNIAN:

What's the first thing you ever remember about the Stratford Festival?

CIMOLINO:

I came here when I was a high school kid and the first thing I remember about the Stratford Festival was how smart I felt as I left. I felt that the room became so small, this huge room—I was seated way up there in the gods, in the section that we've taken out now, and looking down are all these people, and as the play started, I got all the jokes. All the stuff that seemed impenetrable in a classroom, I totally understood and I wasn't alone. We all totally understood—we became the actor on the stage, so I left feeling taller, more alive than I'd ever felt in my life.

OUZOUNIAN:

What was the play?

CIMOLINO:

It was Michael Langham's *Love's Labour's Lost*, and it just electrified me. It was terrific.

OUZOUNIAN:
Did you decide at that point you wanted to work here one day?

CIMOLINO:
I went home afterward and told my father that I was going to become an actor and he said, "You're going to be an artist" and the way he said "artist" it was like pimp and car thief all rolled into one. But, yes, it changed my life. I felt that here was something worth dedicating your life to, and I didn't specifically intend to ever work here, but I think it's what I really wanted in my heart.

OUZOUNIAN:
When you finally got to work here, what did it feel like?

CIMOLINO:
When you come here, and you're beside all these giants, you know, breathing is the measure of success. I mean just simply being able to get through and stay alive, let alone learn and grow. But every part of it was exciting. There were so many things to do here. And so it was exhilarating. And it was a bit scary because this was the big leagues.

OUZOUNIAN:
What was it like the first time you stepped out onto the stage you're sitting on now?

CIMOLINO:
Well, I wear glasses now and I wore glasses then, but I took the glasses off to act on this stage for the first part of the summer. And at a certain point that summer, I got contact lenses. And was terrified to realize there were people out there. I mean completely surrounded. I don't know where I thought they were but it's a very intimate stage. You work out here and you can see people quite closely. And there's something wonderful about that. All the artifice of having to project and throw a performance out across the great divide that you do on a proscenium stage is gone here. You just simply exist. And that's great.

OUZOUNIAN:
You began during the John Neville years. What were they like?

CIMOLINO:
There was obviously a sense of rebuilding that was going on, and by that I mean financial as well as artistic. We had the sense that there were some very exciting things going on artistically but also, you know, we had full houses. And everybody marvelled at that in the late eighties because there had been this long period when editorials were being written about, you know, "Will the Stratford Festival survive?" But that sense of doom was being lifted during John's tenure.

OUZOUNIAN:
During this same period you also encountered someone who would prove to be very important in your life—Richard Monette. Do you recall the first time you ran into him?

CIMOLINO:
In the year that I came here, he was directing *The Taming of the Shrew*, and there was a palpable sense of electricity connected with it. I mean being around Richard Monette is like being in a circus: there's never a dull moment, you know? So there was this great explosive experience happening and we were all aware of it: his complete manic dedication to the cause of theatre.

OUZOUNIAN:
After John Neville came David William. What's the difference between the two men?

CIMOLINO:
I would say that John is very much an actor/manager and had a sense of building a company, and a sense of communion with the actor. He was a man who supported the company. He defended the company. And he had a sense of theatre as being something with depth but also entertainment. David was much more of a detail person. And much more cerebral. You'd

learn so much from David in a rehearsal. Like you might show up not knowing what a dactyl was but, boy, you'd leave knowing. So he built a strong team of actors. He built the bench strength of the company and had great care for detail.

OUZOUNIAN:
During those years, you'd been gradually working your way up, playing increasingly bigger and bigger parts and then finally they tell you you're going to be Romeo. What did you like doing the best about playing the part?

CIMOLINO:
The ball scene where I meet Juliet, all those rhyming couplets. I felt very at home in that. I felt that was something that I understood, because I thought Megan Follows was terrific as Juliet, and because the language was accessible to me and there was music. . . . I felt there was a magic that came over the audience that worked.

OUZOUNIAN:
What is it like when you have to deliver speeches and lines that you know school kids have studied and parodied and made fun of forever? Do they stick in your throat?

CIMOLINO:
No, not at all. It's so magic, that part. And the kids go right along with it, you know? They cry at the end. You can hear them crying at the end. And even though they want to make fun of it, it's their life. Like as soon as Romeo and Juliet connect, and things begin to fall apart, you can feel the attention being paid by the students. It's their lives that they're seeing in front of them.

OUZOUNIAN:
Shortly after that, you went to the other side of the footlights, assisting Richard Monette, then directing on your own, and now you're the Executive Director of the entire Festival. Does that make you happy?

CIMOLINO:

It does. I believe very deeply in this place and a great discovery for me was how many different people lend their talents to this place. And getting to watch them work and support them in their work and plan for the long term and make for positive change here. That's a huge gift and a very, very creative role to play.

OUZOUNIAN:

Where do you feel Stratford is exactly now at this point in time?

CIMOLINO:

I feel the festival has made great strides in the last decade, in terms of its physical infrastructure, its operations, and it has begun to make some important artistic strides with the creation of the conservatory, the start of a new play development program—all those initiatives that Richard started. The Festival has the resources, the talents, to create great work, and it frequently does.

OUZOUNIAN:

What would you say to the people who claim that the Stratford Festival has been . . . has become obsessed with money and success?

CIMOLINO:

Well, I'd say pick up a paper anytime in the last fifty years and you'll find heavy criticism of the Festival. It's been uninterrupted. When the idea of the Festival first came up there were critics. And each successive artistic director has gotten beat up for one reason or another. I take that as a measure of the importance of the institution. That it's to be criticized. And the criticism's good for us. It makes us work harder, reach higher, and run faster.

OUZOUNIAN:

Where are you trying to reach and run to?

CIMOLINO:

I think one of the things we're discovering right now is that we will have a challenge in the longer term, and I'm talking much longer term now, of making Shakespeare accessible to new generations. Even in the fifty years since our creation, Shakespeare has become much more an old art form. Not because it doesn't speak to us, but because it's taught much less in schools. Our language has changed and the change has been accelerated by the Internet, by television. Education for me has become one of the most important areas that we have to explore. We have to find ways of continuing to make ourselves understood. Simply maintaining the quality that has been passed down to us won't be good enough, we have to grow.

OUZOUNIAN:

If you have a picture of the one kind of audience member you'd like to see come to Stratford, who isn't coming yet, who would it be?

CIMOLINO:

I would like to see more and more children keep coming. I think there's a natural time in our lives when we have a young family, or we're just trying to build a career that it's hard to get to the theatre. But if we had been brought to the theatre when we were young, if somebody who is important to us, our mother, our father, an aunt, takes us to the theatre and says it's important to them, then we'll come back. We'll come back to the theatre in time. So it's really critical that we get the kids in here. That it's not made to be seen as somebody else's thing.

OUZOUNIAN:

What would you wish Stratford for its second fifty years?

CIMOLINO:

I wish Stratford could find a way of making its presence felt far beyond the catchment area. I'd like to think that there are kids in Medicine Hat who actually get to experience and see our plays. And realize how important that we are to them. So I would like to see us do more touring. I'd like to see us get out and go beyond the immediate area and bring that experience much farther out.

OUZOUNIAN:
When I say the words "The Stratford Festival" to you, what images come to mind?

CIMOLINO:
My life. My life. My life.

Megan Follows as Juliet in the 1992 production of Romeo and Juliet.
Photograph by David Cooper.

Megan Follows

The daughter of Stratford Festival veterans Ted Follows and Dawn Greenhalgh, Megan Follows became an international star in the TV version of *Anne of Green Gables*. She joined the Festival in 1992 to play Juliet in *Romeo and Juliet*, and returned in 1995 as Constance in *Amadeus*. I spoke to her in Los Angeles in February 2001.

OUZOUNIAN:

What's your very first memory of the Stratford Festival in any way, shape, or form?

FOLLOWS:

Well, actually I'll have to sort of do it vicariously because my mom (Dawn Greenhalgh) reminded me that she was pregnant with me, when she was at Stratford doing a production of *Antony and Cleopatra*, so my first time on the Stratford stage would have been in my mother's womb. And at one performance, her morning sickness came upon her in the evening, and she had to rush off the stage to throw up, which she did in one of those tunnels that they call the "voms," appropriately enough. So everybody who had to subsequently come off through that exit slid through my mother's throw up. So that's my first experience of the Stratford Festival.

OUZOUNIAN:

Do you recall going there the first time yourself?

FOLLOWS:

My first memory was seeing Maggie Smith in *As You Like It*, and I remember how magical it was, almost like a religious experience—the, the whole tradition of seeing a play at Stratford. When I was a child, my parents were involved in the Festival, and I spent many a summer in that town, swimming at the pool and going to the quarry, and being around the actors who would come and visit my parents at their house.

OUZOUNIAN:
Did you want to be there?

FOLLOWS:
Oh absolutely. It was so much a part of my parents' life, so much of who they were . . . how important working was. And the sort of reverence and respect that a theatre like that commands.

I remember one day when I was working on *Romeo and Juliet*, I was coming from backstage onto the Festival stage, and Richard Monette who was directing it said to me, "Wait a minute, whoa whoa stop! You must savour this moment. You are walking onto the Stratford stage for the first time."

So I slowed down as I came out from under the balcony and onto the stage, and in that moment I saw just how beautiful that theatre is. How extraordinary that stage is. It's a cocoonlike, a womblike feeling as you're surrounded by that dark wood and the empty seats . . . oh, it really had power to it, especially for someone who'd grown up in the theatre, whose parents were in the theatre. It was really a very defining moment.

OUZOUNIAN:
What brought you to that moment?

FOLLOWS:
Richard Monette asked me to play Juliet and I was terrified. What an extraordinary opportunity, what a gift! I knew it was because of my success with *Anne of Green Gables* that I was asked to go. I had done some theatre before, but not very much, and I had never done Shakespeare and that was certainly daunting. But I was hungry for that experience.

I loved playing Juliet. I loved her whole journey, the way that young woman had to take her destiny in her hands and make a choice, when the stakes are life and death. It was absolutely thrilling to play that part. And thrilling to be on that stage.

OUZOUNIAN:

What did that feel like the first time you were on that stage with an audience around you?

FOLLOWS:

All I could think of is my heart pounding, the reverberation of my heart pounding through my ears. And then I remembered something Helen Burns had said to me. She told me to think of every head that you sort of vaguely see out in the audience as cells in my brain. As individual cells in my own brain. So when communing with them, you're really with yourself, and they're a part of you and it's going out of yourself into them. It was a bigger than life feeling, I mean, it's addictive. What can I say? *(laughs)* It's an absolute rush in the best sense of the word.

OUZOUNIAN:

How did Richard Monette approach the part with you?

FOLLOWS:

I remember having an incredible amount of fun with Richard. He really took me under his wing, and he was very gentle with me and very caring. He knew that I needed a lot of attention, specifically because I didn't know what I was doing with regard to the classical word.

OUZOUNIAN:

How did you get along with Antoni Cimolino, your Romeo?

FOLLOWS:

He was very kind to me and very sweet to me as well. I remember that he had the most beautiful blue eyes, and that black curly hair. And when he was in his costume, I remember he had a lovely pair of buns in those tight tights. And it was perfect.

OUZOUNIAN:
What do you do when you're playing what's probably the most famous love scene in history, the one on the balcony?

FOLLOWS:
The language is so beautiful. It's so beyond what most of us are ever lucky enough to utter out of our own mouths, so to have this extraordinary map, basically, through which these two young lovers dance—the level of the artistry of that language is so enormous that you can never be complacent. You're always trying to reach for it and I think that in itself is sort of a wonderful analogy for the love that they're feeling. That it's just so much, it's so much greater than both of them in a sense. That there's just sort of this pureness to it.

Michael Langham later taught me that there's no subtext in Shakespeare really. You're saying your thoughts as you're feeling them. That's the sheer sort of joy of speaking that language: for every thought that you have, he's actually given you the words to express it.

OUZOUNIAN:
A few years after playing, you came back to Stratford as Mozart's wife, Constance, in Amadeus. *What was that like?*

FOLLOWS:
That was a completely different experience. I think I was the only woman who actually speaks in *Amadeus*. It's a very male play. It was a very male experience. I loved working with Stephen Ouimette. I loved his insanity. I loved his playfulness. And I was so excited to work with Brian Bedford, someone of that stature who brings so much of his own power onto the stage.

And wearing Desmond Heeley's costumes was an absolute thrill. Those costumes transported me back into that time, the decadence of them, their sheer weight, the way they moved, and crawling on the floor in them—we had a glass floor, I remember, that was mirrored—was beautiful. The sheer theatricality of it all—that's what I remember.

OUZOUNIAN:
You've said that you would like to go back to Stratford again. What attracts you to it so much?

FOLLOWS:
I think there's something fascinating about the isolationism of the place, because for the nine months that you're there, your only purpose is really to serve the plays you're in. It's very all-consuming and really kind of comes down to that moment of the lights darkening and then coming up, and putting on that show and transporting you to another world.

That's what I think is really extraordinary about it: all these people—the craftsmen and technicians as well as the actors—who've dedicated their lives to really bringing another world to life. When you actually stand on that stage, it all comes down to you in that moment. But up to that point, you've had a whole structure of people around you, supporting you, literally dressing you, clothing you, beading you, wigging you, teaching you how to stand and speak. But it all comes down to that one moment when you're on the stage. It's magical.

OUZOUNIAN:
What would you wish Stratford for its next fifty years?

FOLLOWS:
I would wish it a continued growing audience. I would wish it people to come, appreciate, learn, and enjoy all the riches that it has to offer.

OUZOUNIAN:
When I say "The Stratford Festival," what do you think of?

FOLLOWS:
Ken's french fries . . . the rehearsal room with blankets of snow swirling outside, while I'm in a cocoon, hoping to emerge in the end as a butterfly to go on a journey with the audience. Shared storytelling.

Cynthia Dale as Guenevere in the 1997 production of Camelot.
Photograph by Cylla von Tiedemann.

Cynthia Dale

Cynthia Dale first came to Stratford in 1983 in the Chorus of *The Gondoliers* and *The Mikado*. After a decade in which she became a TV star on shows like *Street Legal*, she returned to star in *Camelot*, *Man of La Mancha*, *The Miracle Worker*, *The Sound of Music*, and the Fiftieth Anniversary production of *My Fair Lady*.

I spoke to her at the CBC Broadcast Centre in February 2001.

OUZOUNIAN:

Cynthia, what's the first time you remember hearing about the Stratford Festival?

DALE:

It would have been probably from my elder sister, Jennifer. And my mom, because they were dragging me off to some production. I would have been maybe nine or ten. I don't remember what the first production was that I saw there. But I know that on a yearly basis we went. And then I guess the next time I remember it sort of resonating as an important place was when my sister got asked to join the company, and what a big deal that was at the time in the house and in the family. And I remember listening to her talk about that stage and all the people she was going to be working with: Maggie Smith and Brian Bedford . . . the Robin Phillips era. So those are my first major recollections of Stratford.

OUZOUNIAN:

Did you ever think you were going to wind up there?

DALE:
Never. I would never in a million years have imagined I would have ended up there. Mainly because I was a musical theatre kid. You know, I was the singer and dancer. And they didn't do big lavish musicals like I thought I wanted to do at Stratford at the time. Thank goodness things have changed. *(laughing)*

OUZOUNIAN:
Years before you came back as a star to Stratford, you started out as a chorus girl.

DALE:
I was a chorus girl, yes. Now let the truth be told. It was in *The Gondoliers* and *The Mikado*. And, of course, you probably would have missed me because I was one of the tall ones in *The Mikado* so needless to say I was in the back row. I wasn't allowed to be in the front row because I wasn't cute enough or small enough or something.

OUZOUNIAN:
Let's move ahead quite a bit in time. You've become a television star, and Richard Monette calls you up, asks you to come back to Stratford. This time as the leading lady of Camelot. *Now what kind of a sensation is this?*

DALE:
Oh, I wanted to get down on the ground and just kiss his feet. I was so honoured and grateful and moved that he had even thought of me. And I had always been a huge Arthurian legend fan and the thought of going to the Stratford Festival to do a show that I'd always loved, it was just a joy.

OUZOUNIAN:
Obviously things went well, because you came back the next season to play two leading roles: Aldonza in Man of La Mancha *and Annie Sullivan in* The Miracle Worker. *Now that's a pretty heavy load. Did you know going in what that would be like?*

DALE:

No, I didn't. Richard had spoken to me about it and had said, "Are you sure you're ready to do this? Do you really want to do this?" So I had been warned, but I'm a workhorse and I wanted to do it. Plus I loved both the parts. What was particularly exhausting about that season though, was the hate of Aldonza. It was very hard to play someone with that much bile and hate and anger in them for nine months. To do a six-week run of that wouldn't have been so difficult. But to have that much hate around you and in you for nine months, and to not be able to let up on that, was really, really hard. That's why playing Annie Sullivan at the same time was a blessing, just a blessing.

OUZOUNIAN:

How did you find working at Stratford in the Richard Monette years?

DALE:

Joyous. It's a joy to work there with Richard. He worked me very hard, and at the same time, he took care of me. And he taught me about that stage, and I will be forever grateful for that. He taught me where the sweet spot was and he taught me about how to have the power and the peace of standing on that stage. I don't know if I always found it and I'm sure I didn't find it in every performance, but he taught me what to strive for.

OUZOUNIAN:

Is there something special about that stage?

DALE:

Oh, there's something magnificent about that stage. I have never ever in my professional life been happier than I was on that stage. Nothing I have ever done has matched my time there. There is no finer place to stand and perform. I think it's a mix of the architecture of the theatre—that you have the audience so much around you and so close to you—and I think it's also the ghosts, and the history, and the magic that has been left there by every single performer. And every single audience member who's had a wonderful time in that theatre.

OUZOUNIAN:

You mentioned a "sweet spot" that Monette showed you on the stage. Where exactly is it?

DALE:

It's in the centre but it's up, and it's literally right below the dome. You're right below where the point of the theatre meets it to the top, and it's not right in the middle of the stage. It's a little further up than where you'd expect. And also the first year I was there, they had just brought in the theatre a bit so they really weren't looking at the back of your ear when you were playing on the stage. You know, the audience was just a little bit further in. And it rings. There's an incredible ring to the sounds you make on that stage. It's gorgeous.

OUZOUNIAN:

Now, you've had a wonderful time at Stratford and Stratford has done very well. But there are people who criticize Monette for having gone too commercial . . .

DALE:

God forbid someone should want to make money in the theatre!

OUZOUNIAN:

They say that he hires too many TV stars and does too many musicals. You're a TV star who's been in lots of his musicals. How do you feel about that?

DALE:

Lucky. *(laughs)* I feel lucky, you know, even though there's going to be people who bitch and complain about it all the time. Sure he does musicals, but they make money. They make money so some of the shows that are more experimental get done. And thank God somebody can program the theatre so that it makes money, because that will keep it alive and well.

OUZOUNIAN:

When I say "The Stratford Festival" to you, what words come to mind?

DALE:

Magnificence. Clear. Joyous. Hard. Lavish.

OUZOUNIAN:

And if you have a hope and a dream for the future of the Festival, what is it?

DALE:

I hope they continue to dream big, and they make the performers dream big. That they continue a Young Company. And continue teaching young performers. And that they continue to hire me *(laughs)* for the hundredth anniversary.

Paul Gross as Hamlet in the 2000 production of Hamlet.
Photograph by Cylla von Tiedemann.

Paul Gross

Paul Gross appeared at Stratford as Hamlet in 2000. By that time, the actor-writer-director was already an international star because of his role on the cult TV series *Due South*. Since Stratford, he has written, directed, and starred in *Men With Brooms*, one of the most commercially successful films in Canadian history.
I spoke to him in Toronto in the spring of 2001.

OUZOUNIAN:

What's your first memory of the Stratford Festival?

GROSS:

I was eleven or twelve, and I knew nothing about it. I'd seen very little theatre I think, actually. And we went to see Bill Hutt as King Lear. So that was the very first time. It was pretty impressive, and it stuck with me. I have this powerful overwhelming general feeling about the whole *event* of going to Stratford. The drive. The parking. The grounds. The trumpets. Going into the theatre and it becoming dark and this thing materializing on the stage.

I even have a spear from it. At some point there was a war staged in the black. You could hear this clanking of spikes and swords and things. And the head of some spear came off and landed in the aisle quite near me so I ran down and grabbed it. And I still have it.

Every time I walk into that place, there's a magical kind of grandeur and intimacy combined at the same time with something that is really truly mysterious. And I've never felt that in any other theatre I've been in the world. It's an extraordinary place to walk into for the first time.

OUZOUNIAN:
You were around Stratford and intimately involved with people there for almost two decades before you ever worked there.

GROSS:
Yeah, I know. It wasn't particularly intentional. I just don't think anyone there really wanted me to ever act. *(laughs)* But somewhere in the back of my head I thought, "I'll probably act here at some point."

OUZOUNIAN:
How did the offer to play Hamlet come to you?

GROSS:
Richard Monette called out of the blue and asked me. At first I thought he was sort of joking, because—this may sound odd—it's not a part that I ever particularly wanted to do. Partly because when I was younger, I never quite understood the play at all. Or I never connected to it. I used to feel "Why doesn't Hamlet get on with it and get going?" It's just that I had no real contact to it. Partly I suppose because I'd seen *Hamlets* that just didn't grab me. Then I saw a production that Robin Phillips directed in Edmonton with Joe Ziegler as Hamlet, and my wife, Martha Burns, was playing Ophelia, and for the first time I thought, "This really is quite a good play." *(laughing)* Yeah, I know that seems really silly in hindsight. But it's one thing to appreciate it intellectually—which I did, because it's a pretty indisputably extraordinary piece of writing—but to actually get the sense of its real life, well, I hadn't, up until that production.

But still, following that, I never thought I'd end up playing it, so when Richard called it was really quite a surprise. And I said, "Well, you know, you've got to give me a little bit of time to think about this. It's a long commitment for me and I just have to read it again." He said, "You've got to be kidding me. You don't have to read *Hamlet*, just play it." *(laughs)* And then we had a few more conversations about it and he said, "You know, this is very peculiar, Paul, trying to convince someone of the merits of playing *Hamlet* at the best classical repertory theatre in North America." I said, "You have to understand, Richard, I said I'm not sure whether I can actually pull it off." So then I talked with Joe Ziegler. I said, "Do you think I can actually play this?" He said, "Yeah." I said, "Well, do you want to direct it." He said, "Do you think I can actually direct it?" I said, "Yeah." And he finally said, "All right, let's do it then."

OUZOUNIAN:

Once you finally agreed to do it, is there a moment in the play or a part of the play you thought of doing first?

GROSS:

Well, I'm extraordinarily shallow, so it was the sword fight. Get to the duel, I'll be fine. *(laughs)* I had almost a year before we started, and at first I watched other versions of it, and read a ton of academic theories and other people's musings about the part, and descriptions of other performances and I gradually realized that none of this is any use when it actually comes to playing it.

OUZOUNIAN:

What made you decide to set the play in the Regency period?

GROSS:

Largely just to keep it as simple as possible. It's also a good cut for men, that period. And I had seen *The Matrix*, and really liked the clothes in that. *(laughs)* But I had, I mean, it is something I feel about any kind of presentation: it has to operate on as deep a level as you can possibly get to, but on a certain shallow level of things it also has to look good. We discussed setting it in the Elizabethan period. I just thought, "Pumpkin pants are kind of goofy-looking" and we wanted to get rid of anything that would act as a barrier to the audience's immediate connection to the heart of the play.

OUZOUNIAN:

As you started to get closer to rehearsing it, did you have a big picture in mind or did you just decide to go in and discover it a scene at a time?

GROSS:

A scene at a time. It's such a strange play to work on. Joe and I would have these conversations about how all this domestic drama sits inside this basket of war. And that the play only becomes as grand and huge and far-reaching as it is because of that. That it's offset against the possibility of the kingdom being lost to a foreign army. And I have seen productions in which they've cut all that and I think they lack resonance and they become much, much smaller. And Shakespeare's not a fool—as anybody discovers when you're working on this stuff—and everything is there for a very specific reason.

After having spent two years on it and eighty performances on it, the play remains ultimately completely enigmatic and mysterious to me. It feels slightly like a hologram of life in general. You can pull out any one thing and somehow everything is in that one scene and it's as though there is no actual centre to Hamlet. It is everything and nothing all at the same time.

OUZOUNIAN:

One of the fascinating things you did was to deliver the first soliloquy blazing with emotion. Where did that come from?

GROSS:

It just popped out one day in rehearsal. It wasn't particularly conscious initially. We sort of talked about it and Joe said, "Boy, that's big right off the top." And I said, "Yeah, but it feels kind of right" and when I started to look at it, it made sense.

If you look on the soliloquies as a reflection of the interior state of Hamlet, he gradually becomes much more organized. The interior thoughts become more structured, till you finally get to the last one, "How all occasions do inform against me," which is practically one long sentence with subclauses, and it's very perfectly put together. The first one—"Oh that this too too solid flesh would melt"—is extraordinarily broken up. He can't quite complete sentences and it started to make sense to me from a dramatic point of view.

Playing Hamlet is a truly weird experience, because you cannot control it. Most other roles, you can sort of steer them a little bit. This thing takes off on you—or at least it did for me. I remember doing the first run-through, thinking, "I'll just put my foot in emotionally and see where it goes." Well, it grabs ahold of you, starts flinging you around the room and kicking you in the head, and it stomps on you and then walks away. We got to the end and Joe said, "How's it feel?" I said, "You can't control any of this, can you?" He says, "No. You just stand on top of it and you just hope to God you don't fall off." A lot of people have said that you don't really play Hamlet. It plays you. And I think that's very true.

OUZOUNIAN:

Every Hamlet I've talked to says that there was one point when the chill of fear overcame them and they said, "I am playing the greatest role ever written. I don't know what I'm doing. I'm scared." Did you go through that?

GROSS:

Yeah, every morning. *(laughs)* Actually, through rehearsals I was fine. And then we got onto the stage. And I'd never, I'd never set foot on that stage. Ever. I felt so woefully inadequate. I phoned Joe and said, "I've got to quit." And he said, "Why don't you at least try doing it in front of one audience?" "All right," I said. "I'll try one but then I'm packing my truck and I'm driving out of this place. Never coming back." Well, we had that first audience and it was fine. And that I attribute to the theatre. It's amazing when bodies are in there, because it's so close, you feel that you can reach out and touch them, and it's rather like doing it in your kitchen all of a sudden. It becomes small and very immediate. And because of that, I finally understood something I hadn't understood at all about the play through rehearsals, and it's that soliloquies are dialogue and the other side of that conversation is the audience.

OUZOUNIAN:
What became your favourite part of playing Hamlet?

GROSS:
Oh, it changed every night. There would be something new every performance. I think it was Olivier who said that you could do it every night for a hundred years and still find stuff in it. I actually would look forward to every scene. They were always exciting.

OUZOUNIAN:
Is there a place in the play that still deeply puzzles you?

GROSS:
I think the nunnery scene will always remain mysterious to me. It's such a peculiar scene. It has almost zero structure. It's almost like he wrote it to be an improvisational scene. It has that quality in the writing because it doesn't ever anchor itself anywhere. It also seems to be the most nihilistic of all his writing. He's saying, essentially, "No more people. No more marriages. No more human beings. We should not recreate ourselves." But as soon as I would start to lean that way, to play it, the scene would shift to somewhere else, and I would think well maybe that's not it. I never really understood it. I think it always played fairly well, or it felt wonderful to do, but I don't really get it *(laughs)* except at some strange deep level.

OUZOUNIAN:

What do you wish Stratford for the next fifty years?

GROSS:

The first thing is they need a map of the underworld, the backstage at that Festival Theatre, because I'm sure there are skeletons in there of people who just got lost, and couldn't find their way out. That's one. What I'd also love to see is Stratford to mount increasingly more new works that tour. I think that this theatre could be the most important in the world, or certainly one of the top five. And it needs to start to get itself out. And bring others in. It's in such good shape now financially that it's ready to take the next step and conquer the globe.

OUZOUNIAN:

When I say "The Stratford Festival," what words come into your mind?

GROSS:

Complicated. Fun. Grand. Enriching. Mystifying. The highlight of my career.

Maggie Blake as Anne Frank in the 2000 production of The Diary of Anne Frank.
Photograph by Cylla von Tiedemann.

Maggie Blake

Maggie Blake is the youngest person I interviewed. She made her Stratford debut at the age of seven in *Julius Caesar*, and later returned to play the title role in *The Diary of Anne Frank*.

I spoke to her at the CBC Broadcast Centre in the spring of 2001, on a day off from filming a role in *The Salem Witch Trials*. It also happened to be her eighteenth birthday.

OUZOUNIAN:

Maggie, what's the first thing you remember hearing about the Stratford Festival?

BLAKE:

I never really heard anything about the Stratford Festival because I grew up in Stratford. My dad, Chris, was an actor there. And I certainly heard a lot of stories about his old acting days. And my mom, Colleen, was a producer there the first time I started acting there. So, I didn't really hear about it. Lived it. I grew up backstage with the Stratford Festival.

OUZOUNIAN:

Did you still think the place was kind of special?

BLAKE:

I thought it was magical. You know I used to get my mom to take me backstage where all the actors were. They were all adults and they were still playing. I thought it was so amazing and I really wanted to be a part of it.

OUZOUNIAN:

So what's the first time you got onto the stage? How did that happen?

BLAKE:

Richard Monette was directing a production of *Julius Caesar* in 1990, and Butch Blake—no relation to me—but a wonderful man, was playing the soothsayer, and they wanted him to be blind. So they wanted a little girl to lead him around, and my mom said, "Let my daughter audition." And I *did* audition. No nepotism or anything but I went into the rehearsal hall and led my mom and she pretended to be blind. Richard Monette was there and he said, "Okay, you've got the job." And I was so excited. I went and called all my friends and it was thrilling for me.

OUZOUNIAN:

Was it as thrilling to actually step on that stage?

BLAKE:

Oh yeah, definitely. And you know I was very proud of it. Very proud that I was there. I was still quite young. I was seven years old. And I . . . it just started to grow in me. You know, just the atmosphere of being there and even though I didn't fully understand what all the work was, I started to appreciate it.

OUZOUNIAN:

You came back to Stratford in 1999 as a member of the company, right, with genuine roles? How did that happen?

BLAKE:

Well, I continued acting after I was seven and went on to do plays at the Grand Theatre in London and the Manitoba Theatre Centre in Winnipeg. And I worked a lot with Martha Henry. She was doing a production of *Richard III* at Stratford, and she wanted me to play Queen Isabella, Richard's young wife. Historically, she was seven when Richard married her. So Martha wanted a younger girl to play it, and so I got to do that. And then they needed another witch in *Macbeth*, so I got to do that too. Two Shakespeares.

OUZOUNIAN:

Did you ever feel at any point you were maybe over your head?

BLAKE:

No, I don't think so. I mean . . . Stratford is a wonderful place to work and it's very nurturing. I had Martha Henry as my director, Geordie Johnson as my husband. I also had a lot of voice classes, and time working on text. Oh, I learned a lot from it. And that's where my appreciation of Shakespeare grew.

OUZOUNIAN:

Now in the other play you did that year, Macbeth, *you were one of the three witches. Why was an attractive young girl playing one of the witches?*

BLAKE:

I think to show that evil isn't always in big scary people—it can be in anyone. And our witches were all under thirty. My witch was actually quite happy, to show that you don't judge a book by its cover. You know, I could play this young witch and be happy and cheerful, but underneath there's something in me that you know is quite awful.

OUZOUNIAN:

Now, that production was largely regarded as one of the least successful productions in Stratford's history. It got terrible reviews. But did you ever feel that you were in anything less than a wonderful show?

BLAKE:

I don't think so. No, because we worked our hardest on it. And you know that's the great thing about doing Shakespeare. It doesn't matter if it gets bad reviews or good reviews, you can still do extraordinary things with it and people keep on seeing it because even though you've seen one *Macbeth*, you haven't seen them all. There are different interpretations. Directors are always trying new things with it. Our *Macbeth* was set post-apocalyptic. Some things worked. Some things didn't. But we tried it. And showed the world that *Macbeth* can be done in different ways. And you know we had a lot of students who came to it, who saw it, and said for the first time they understood *Macbeth*. You know that's why we keep on doing Shakespeare because it can be accessible and you can try new things with it.

OUZOUNIAN:

Interesting, you mentioned students. People always talk about what it's like to do the student matinees. Okay, you're a student yourself performing at a student matinee . . . what does that feel like?

BLAKE:

It's a bit scary because I felt like in a way I was being judged by my peers. And you know, some students are great and some students aren't. No, I've had things thrown at me on stage and screaming and yelling and it's frustrating. But Stratford has a program for students before student matinees and they bring three actors out to talk to the students about the play. I think it helps them appreciate it a lot more.

OUZOUNIAN:

The next year you got to play the leading role in The Diary of Anne Frank. *How did that come about?*

BLAKE:

I'd always wanted to play Anne Frank. It was almost a dream role for me. And I knew Al Waxman was directing it and so I had a meeting with him. Now, when I was in grade six, I had written a short story about Anne Frank, and I brought that to Al. We sat down and he read it and we discussed our thoughts on Anne Frank and what she meant to us and what we thought we could bring out in a play . . . and after that I found out that I had gotten the part.

OUZOUNIAN:

One of the interesting things about that production was that Al very much delved into the Jewishness of the family. Did you ever feel it was strange that you, a gentile girl, was playing in such a very Jewish production?

BLAKE:

I don't think so. I mean that's why we're actors, right? One of the first things Al said to me was, "I don't need someone Jewish to play this part." You know I played Helen Keller and I wasn't deaf or blind. That's all part of acting.

OUZOUNIAN:

What was your relationship like with Al during rehearsals?

BLAKE:

I was very close with him. We met a lot and went out for brunches and breakfasts and dinners to talk about the play. And I think we had the same feeling about how magnificent Anne Frank really was as a person and we both wanted to show that she was just a normal girl. We wanted to give the audience the feeling, especially the kids that came to see the show, that this was an average girl who could have been them, and I think we captured that. And I was very close with him and I don't think I could have done it without him. He was a brilliant man. *(Al Waxman died on January 18, 2001.)*

OUZOUNIAN:

What's it like to be seventeen years old and a member of the Stratford family as a leading actor?

BLAKE:

It's pretty neat. It's pretty cool. I mean I started to grow up at Stratford. And it's a really supportive place. Lots of people talk about it like being at summer camp because you're there with all your friends. You come back one year. You don't come back another year. I think of Stratford in some ways as my home. I mean I grew up there; there's a comfort I feel there. And just walking backstage there's the smell that I recognize every time I'm there and just the feeling of it. I feel it in my body and I love it.

OUZOUNIAN:

This is a question I've asked everybody, but it probably has more meaning for you since you're at the very start of your career—what would you wish for the Stratford Festival for its next fifty years?

BLAKE:

To keep on striving for what it's been striving for. To keep on doing Shakespeare and teaching the kids the stories and making it accessible. And I think that's what Stratford's doing now and I hope it will continue to do that.

OUZOUNIAN:

Now, just open your mind and if I say "The Stratford Festival," what do you think?

BLAKE:

I think . . . Shakespeare. I think . . . wonderful, exciting, full of possibilities. I think . . . home.

Richard Ouzounian
Photograph courtesy of CBC.

Richard Ouzounian

Richard Ouzounian joined the Festival in 1986 as an associate director and staged productions of *Pericles*, *The Three Musketeers*, and *A Midsummer Night's Dream*. He returned in 1999 as the author and director of *Dracula—A Chamber Musical*. Currently the theatre critic for the *Toronto Star*, he has also spent the past two years working on *Stratford Gold*.
I spoke to him in Toronto
in the spring of 2002.

OUZOUNIAN:
When did you first come to the Stratford Festival?

RICHARD:
As an audience member? It was August of 1967, I was seventeen years old, and I had convinced my parents to make the journey from our home in New York City to Southwestern Ontario in search of great classical theatre. Alan Bates was starring in *Richard III*, but we'd see him on our second evening. First up? Christopher Plummer and Zoe Caldwell in *Antony and Cleopatra*. It would be powerful, it would be magical. And we would be late.

My father had underestimated the last leg of our journey and I watched with mounting horror as the clock drew closer to curtain time and we were still miles away. A sign that said we were passing through a town called "Shakespeare" seemed a good omen, but I've learned over the years it still means you're about ten minutes from the theatre. We finally arrived, got our tickets, and were guided through the hushed and darkened lobby, waiting for a scene break to allow us entry.

"How much have we missed?" I asked the usher and, taking pity, she consoled me with the knowledge that it was only two short scenes. A signal came, the doors opened, and she pushed us through into the theatre. That's when I saw the blazing lights.

I don't think anyone—actor or audience alike—ever forgets that first view of the Stratford stage. Reduced to its essentials, it's nothing more than a small platform of polished wood surrounded on three sides by a steeply raked auditorium. But oh, the magic that resides in that configuration!

Tanya Moiseiwitsch and Tyrone Guthrie had gone to the sacred amphitheatres of ancient Greece for their inspiration and there was truly something holy as well as classical about the space. My immediate response was to try and focus on the smaller-than-I'd-thought-it-would-be stage where thousands of watts of white light shone in glory.

As I looked down, it was offering two giants up to me. Christopher Plummer as Antony I recognized instantly, tanned and glorious, a damaged hero with a voice that still rang out with the sharp clarity of a finely tempered blade. His partner was shorter, but every bit his match in passion—dark hair, flaming eyes, and a body that coiled and uncoiled like a serpent: that was my first introduction to Zoe Caldwell's Cleopatra.

They were quarrelling, that took no time to figure out. What was strange to my ears—raised largely on a diet of American method acting—was the boldly extroverted way they were using Shakepeare's language like weapons to hurl thunderbolts of emotion at each other. I can still hear Caldwell consumed with desire as she remembered how "eternity was in our lips and eyes" before turning on her lover with the blunt accusation that "the greatest soldier of the world/Art turn'd the greatest liar."

Plummer reached out to grab her wrist as he said, "How now, lady!" and I felt that the stage was about to explode. The stage was filled with burning passions that matched those blazing lights and I wouldn't have wanted to be anywhere else in the world. I've continued to feel that way for thirty-five years.

OUZOUNIAN:
What do you wish Stratford for its next fifty years?

RICHARD:

This above all: to thine ownself be true,
And it must follow, as the night the day,
Thou canst not then be false to any man.

OUZOUNIAN:
And when I say "The Stratford Festival," what comes to mind?

RICHARD:
Blazing lights, burning passions.